Praise for *Poor Man's Feast*

"*Poor Man's Feast* is two overlapping love stories. It is a pleasure to get to live both at Altman's joyously, irreverently laid table."
—Tamar Adler, author of *An Everlasting Meal*

"*Poor Man's Feast* is a wild ride with biting highs, withering lows, and tremendous wit and humor. But throughout, there is a great tenderness that is so consistently warm and moving that when the end came, as it was bound to, I found myself searching for even just a bit more, like picking up especially divine pastry crumbs with a moistened fingertip, before gently closing the covers. A beautiful story."
—Deborah Madison, author of *Vegetarian Cooking for Everyone*

"Who wrote the book of love? Elissa Altman did. Poignant, funny, and full of wisdom, every single page should be savored."
—Tracey Ryder, founder and CEO of Edible Communities Publications

"Named after her James Beard Award–winning blog, *Poor Man's Feast* is Altman's smart yet tender tale of her gastronomical and spiritual evolution. . . . Altman gradually attains the peace that has eluded her as Turner imparts the gentle lesson that, most of the time, more is less. Sometimes heartbreaking, often hilarious, this is one of the finest food memoirs of recent years."
—*The New York Times Book Review*

"Delightful . . . A wealth of food tales about foodies and food phobics, cooks and kitchen disasters, cooking successes and failures—all in clear, pleasing prose . . . *Poor Man's Feast* deserves a place on the shelf with the finest food writers."
—*New York Journal of Books*

"[Altman] artfully merges relationship narrative, personal history, and food memoir in this satisfying book. . . . Luminous writing brings many stories small and large to feed the heart."
—*Publishers Weekly*

"[Told] with her delicious trademark blend of humor, love, and dedication to simplicity in life and, of course, in food."
—*Portland Monthly*

*To Joan —
Thank you*

PooR MAN's fEAST

A Love Story of Comfort,
Desire, and the
Art of Simple Cooking

ELISSA ALTMAN

BERKLEY BOOKS, NEW YORK

BERKLEY

An imprint of Penguin Random House LLC
375 Hudson Street, New York, New York 10014

ISBN: 978-0-425-27835-2

PUBLISHING HISTORY
Chronicle Books hardcover edition / March 2013
Berkley trade paperback edition / August 2015

PRINTED IN THE UNITED STATES OF AMERICA

10 9 8 7 6 5 4 3 2 1

Cover design by Sarah Oberrender.
Cover photo © Laurie Rubin / Getty Images.
Interior text design by Vanessa Dina

TO MY BEAUTIFUL PARENTS,
RITA ELLIS HAMMER, WHO TAUGHT ME
ABOUT SAFETY, AND THE LATE CY ALTMAN,
WHO TAUGHT ME ABOUT FOOD.

AND TO MY DEAR SUSAN, WHO TEACHES
ME EVERY DAY ABOUT LOVE.

It grew in the black mud.
It grew under the tiger's orange paws.
Its stems thinner than candles, and as straight.
Its leaves like the feathers of egrets, but green.
The grains cresting, wanting to burst.
Oh, blood of the tiger.

I don't want you just to sit down at the table.
I don't want you just to eat, and be content.
I want you to walk out into the fields
where the water is shining, and the rice has risen.
I want you to stand there, far from the white tablecloth.
I want you to fill your hands with the mud, like a blessing.

—"RICE," BY MARY OLIVER

CONTENTS

PART II

PART III

PROLOGUE

There is poetry in food, kindness in the act of preparing it, and peace in sharing it.

There are gray areas: years ago, I'd heard about a restaurant where hundreds of samurai swords hang, point down, from the ceiling, directly over the heads of the diners while they eat.

This is not kind; this is sociopathic.

But in the act of preparing the most mundane grilled cheese—choosing the cheese, buttering the bread, warming the pan, pressing down the sandwich with the flat of your grandmother's spatula so the cheese melts and the bread tightens and crackles and smooths like solid silk—lies an inherent and basic subconscious attention to detail that exists almost nowhere else in our lives, except in the small daily rituals that we all have. You squeeze your toothpaste onto your toothbrush in exactly the same manner every single morning and every single night. When you step out of the shower, you towel dry your hair before putting your makeup on. You shave one side of your face before the other, and that's the way you've done it since you were in college. Mundane though they may be, these are the rituals that make us who we are. But they don't necessarily make us kind. The act of preparing food for ourselves, and for others, does. And the act of conviviality, of sharing it with others—Marion Cunningham called it *modern tribal fire*—is what makes us human, whether it is tarted up and tortured into vertical excess, or nothing more than butter spread on a piece of bread.

I did not grow up in a home that valued conviviality; my mother and grandmother cooked our meals—plain but hearty, filling, sometimes delicious and sometimes immolated, they were not experimental or contrived until the mid-'70s, when my mother went on a fondue binge like the rest of middle-class America. Generally, we ate in silence drowned out by the presence of a small Zenith black-and-white television that sat, like a dinner guest, at the end of our table. While eating, we would watch *Name That Tune!*, my mother calling out between bites of limp, canned asparagus, "I can name it in three notes!" while my father sipped his Scotch and I picked at the flecks of onion in my meat loaf. After I was done, I climbed down from my chair and went into my bedroom, where I turned on my own television set and watched as reality and make-believe converged. There were fake families sitting around their own fake tables, eating fake dinners: there was the Brady Bunch, with its gay father and wing-nut maid and libidinous eldest son. There was the Partridge Family, with its catatonic little sister who played the tambourine like a methadone addict, and a lead singer who looked more like a lady than his sister. There were the simpering, unsmiling Waltons, with their fake farmhouse that always looked filthy, and a commie grandfather living upstairs in the attic.

"See him," my grandmother Gaga once said to me, tapping her long "Cherries in the Snow"–shellacked fingernail on the round glass television screen after barging into my room with the last potato latke. "The man was a commie, blacklisted by McCarthy." And then she slammed the door behind her.

They were all convivial, casserole-passing people, even though they didn't actually *exist*; for me, the line between television family dinners and reality was blurred like a picture taken from a shaky camera, and when I saw in the news that Ellen Corby had had a stroke, all I could think of was *who's going to make biscuits for John-Boy now that Grandma can't move her arms?*

One night, after a silent dinner of what was marketed as chicken roll—chicken pieces that were deboned and then mechanically compressed into a loaf shape for easy slicing—I left the table where my parents were watching *Let's Make a Deal!*, went into my room, and turned on a local television station. A Southern Prayer-a-Thon had interrupted regular broadcasting, so instead of seeing *The Brady Bunch*, there was a greasy, black-haired, slick-suited man marching across a stage, sobbing like a baby, and telling me that if only I'd call and offer money, that Jesus would give me whatever I wanted. I scribbled down the number with a chewed-on number-two pencil, crept across the hallway into my parents' room, picked up the phone, and called.

A male voice answered with, "Hello! Have you taken Jesus Christ as your Lord and savior?"

I cupped my hand around the mouthpiece and whispered, "No, I haven't. I'm a Jew."

I could hear him light up like a pinball machine, all the way from Mississippi.

"Well, do you want to?" he asked, hopefully.

"Not really," I said.

"Then what can I do for you?" he asked, suddenly all business.

"You said that if I offered some money, then Jesus would give me what I want."

"That's right," he replied. "Do you have money to send us?"

"I do. About six dollars."

"And what do you want Jesus to help you with?"

"I want a big family and a big table where everyone sits down together, like the Waltons"—I thought for a minute—"but without the commie grandfather. And I want everyone to be happy."

The man cleared his throat and promised to send me an envelope for the cash.

"You have a good night and God bless," he said before he hung up.

I lusted after conviviality, and was drawn like a moth to the modern tribal fire; I yearned for the poetry that food writes. But I was also lured to the kitchen, to the standing there and the cooking and the serving and the feeding, because, I was certain, it would bring magic and happiness. Everything begins and ends for me in front of my stove, and if D-Day were to strike me down where I stood, where I stood would likely be right *there*, in my kitchen.

Ultimately, I found the poetry, and even the fire. But until I shared my kitchen with Susan, I hadn't found the peace.

PART I

CHAPTER 1

Bread and Cheese

In my family, we tend to overdo.

Like throwbacks from another time and another era, we blanket the commonplace with a heavy cloak of formality; we struggle to elevate the mundane to the extraordinary, the simple to the dazzling. Even if it isn't.

Especially.

One Sunday morning in my tiny midtown studio apartment, I brought in a bag of still-warm pumpernickel bagels, smoked salmon, and weighty containers of thick, scallion cream cheese for two college friends who were lying on an air mattress in the middle of my living room floor, sleeping off a Hendrick's Gin hangover from a party the night before. I told my Aunt Sylvia later that day that I had "hosted a brunch." It wasn't exactly a lie.

Once, Aunt Sylvia—a comely, Ava Gardner lookalike now pushing ninety-three—had waited for her fifteen-year-old granddaughter to return from a neighborhood party, unaccountably attended by a group of leather-jacketed hooligans carrying travel bongs in their knapsacks.

"Did any of the nice young gentlemen ask you to dance?" she asked her granddaughter the next morning.

"Yes, Grandma," Rebecca answered, rolling her eyes, "they did. Right after they threw up on my shoes."

In my family, *nice* is perfectly fine. But *fancy* is always much better, and what we seem, genetically, to aspire to. My cousin Eleanor once cooked Thanksgiving dinner out of *The French Laundry Cookbook*, stopping just short of Thomas Keller's Oysters and Pearls because she didn't have time to make a sabayon of pearl tapioca before the guests showed up. That same year, Susan made her Thanksgiving recipes from a cookbook that her mother assembled, chapter by chapter, in 1959, with S&H Green Stamps. It involved a green bean casserole with the little crispy fried onions on top.

During holidays, my family likes to dress up in outfits, like one might for an early-twentieth-century costume party involving hand-held masks on sticks, formal bowing, and games of chance. Instead of picking out plain, normal clothes to wear to family functions—a skirt, a favorite sweater, maybe a brooch—we generally like to assemble in well-considered, thematic get-ups that, barring an abrupt conversion to Presbyterianism, we might not otherwise ever be seen in at any other time of year, like bright-red corduroy trousers and plaid sport coats, or hacking jackets with elbow patches that imply we will be running with the hounds just as soon as sherry hour is over.

Susan's family also dresses up in outfits, which usually include velvet pants bought at a church rummage sale in 1968, and spangle-embellished slip-ons acquired during the G. Fox after-Christmas sale, right before the store went out of business in 1982. Everyone always looks very *nice*.

In my family, we aim for the swank and the rococo, as if this way of living offers some sort of inherent security and protection from the plebian, the dangerous, and the more unpredictable parts of life.

✛✛✛

On the Thanksgiving before I met Susan, my cousins and I were dressed in Scottish tweeds and tartans, cashmere and velvet, each of us straining our voices to be heard over the din and past the array of drained bottles of Sinskey Pinot Noir and Sonoma-Cutrer Russian River Chardonnay so oaky and rich that it poured like thick maple syrup on pancakes. The hyperextended, French Provincial table had been opened up using every available leaf; there were twenty of us, growing louder and more emphatic with every cut-crystal goblet of wine drunk. Being an eavesdropper at one of our dinners would have been like watching a master weaver at a treadle loom—the conversation threads dipped and bobbed and passed in and out of significance while we gesticulated for impact, the noise growing so shrill that you couldn't actually hear what was being said anymore. The rare, single malt Scotches—the Laphroaig and the Lagavulin—and the aged Armagnac and the treacle-smooth Hennessy had just been plunked down on the table with eight heavy Waterford snifters. Our Chanukah gifts were passed around to the sighs of *ooh* and *aah*, when I started to squirm and look at my watch. I wanted to get home, back to the city, back to my tiny apartment on Fifty-Seventh Street.

Leaving in haste wouldn't have caused much of an uproar, since I saw my family a lot back then, more than just at Thanksgiving (which doubled as Chanukah, which doubled as our winter birthdays celebration) and Passover (which doubled as our spring and summer birthdays celebration), but also on group vacations to Greece and Turkey, Aspen, and Captiva. In the warmer weather, there were always family golf outings and tournaments at the country club on Long Island, and Father's Day tennis matches followed by barbecues. If we'd worn white and had a country house in Hyannis and tossed a football around after eating piles of cold fried chicken prepared by a cherished family cook, you might have mistaken us for a kind of wannabe Kennedys. Still, it was hard to envision my father—a short, corpulent man with tiny legs and a small Santa belly, who'd had two coronary bypasses and both his carotid arteries roto-rootered by the time he was seventy—tackling my tall and strapping Uncle Marvin, an often dour and serious architect and former captain in the Army Corps of Engineers, whose platoon had chased the Nazis east right after the Allied landings, and who never once in his adult life was seen wearing anything less casual than a tie, a pressed olive-green business shirt, and cordovan wingtips.

But Thanksgiving is still Thanksgiving, and if I had wanted to leave on the early side that night—living in the city, I had no car and depended upon my father to drive me home from my cousin's house on Long Island—I'd have to at least explain why. And at that point, the *why*—the fact of Susan—was still very much my secret.

After hours of sitting around and talking over each other and drinking hundred-dollar Scotch, my father and his longtime companion, Shirley, dropped me off in Manhattan. Shirley was a near-fanatical vegetarian and a therapist. She typically spent every family holiday in deep conversation with one cousin or another whom she would lovingly shrink while simultaneously spearing the dark meat on my father's plate when his head was turned, and moving it to her own, where it would be forgotten. Usually, he wouldn't notice until, on the ride back into Manhattan, he'd announce that he was inexplicably hungry again. If Shirley hadn't been in the car with us, he would have made a detour to Katz's to pick up a corned beef on rye, its edges laced in wide swaths of soft, ivory fat, and eaten it while driving me home up Third Avenue, carefully wiping any trace of putative deli mustard off the brown vinyl dashboard with the Armor-All wipes he kept in the glove compartment.

"Our secret," he'd say to me, looking over from the driver's seat, the long, angry, still-pink scar from his heart surgery peeking out of the top of his shirt. "Right, honey?"

✛✛✛

That night, my father helped me upstairs and into my apartment, carrying a long, white disintegrating cardboard box emblazoned with the name "S. KLEIN," while Shirley waited outside in my father's double-parked sedan. The box, which my Aunt Sylvia had hung on to for the thirty years since the store's demise, buckled under the weight of consolidated gifts: Aunt Sylvia, who always felt that a woman could never have too many black purses, had given me an exact duplicate of the one she'd given me the year before, with a tiny mirror embedded into the top flap, making the reapplication of lipstick during my many dates a breeze. My cousin Peter, a classical pianist and a voracious reader with a penchant for esoteric books on impenetrable subjects and the unfailing belief that everyone loves them as much as he does, had given me a four-volume science-fiction mystery involving a sixteenth-century British sailor and the vessel that was named for a mysterious Egyptian princess deity/space-being bearing a striking resemblance to the sailor's first, long-dead wife. Peter's sister, Lois, the only other serious cook in the family and the host of our holiday dinners, gave me a set of cookbooks, which assumed that the reader owned a home foamer and a kitchen blowtorch. I owned both.

Three hours away, Susan was spending her first holiday back in Connecticut as a single woman, living alone in a small house in a rural area, deep in the middle of nowhere in a town of 3,500 that had only recently gotten its first stoplight. During the previous Thanksgiving, she told me in an email one night, she'd made a special Black Spanish Heritage turkey for herself, for Jennifer—her ex-girlfriend with whom she'd recently broken up after eight years—and two of their friends, in an attempt to shoehorn joy and conviviality into the sad occasion of what she knew would be their last holiday together. There was the fancy bird, which wound up being tough, stringy, and barely edible, wearing those little frilly white paper booties at the end of its drumsticks, looking like a fullback dressed in bobby socks. It sang of the holiday season in the most contrived of ways, and yielded roughly two pounds of gristly leftovers that were still sitting in her freezer as she wrote to me. There was the fancy sweet-and-sour red cabbage. There was the fancy flaming bourbon pumpkin pie and the special runny cheeses and the delicate, crumbly espresso biscuits. But *fancy* couldn't rescue them—Susan and Jennifer. There was the end of a long relationship gone awry, tarted up in the culinary excess of the season by someone who still cared enough to feed the person she was saying goodbye to, punctuating the end of their life together like a bitter grape.

+++

It had been more than a month since Susan had first responded, along with 211 other women, to my posting on a popular dating site—my online plea for a relatively normal relationship with a relatively normal person who actually *liked* food; who wasn't threatened by it, wasn't allergic to it, and was genuinely interested in it—and we still hadn't met, or even seen pictures of each other. I did know some key facts: that she was fanatical about dogs, and had a curly-coated retriever named MacGillicuddy, who attracted and then carried all manner of hiking trail dross in her thick, Persian lamb–like coat, and who, when she shook her head, launched strings of magnetic drool onto anything that was nearby. Susan also admitted to being almost freakishly attached to an ancient edition of *Larousse Gastronomique*, and lulled herself to sleep every night by reading her way, entry by entry, through the disintegrating, threadbare volume—MERE DE SOLE, MERE GOUTTE, MERGA, MERINGUE, MEROU—that she'd find, the next morning, lying open on her chest. She loved Jacqueline du Pré and Emmylou Harris and Hazel Dickens and Patti Smith equally. Raised in a devout Roman Catholic home, she had profound attractions both to fourteenth-century ecclesiastical art and Tibetan mandalas. She had been a dedicated film photographer as a graduate student at the School of Visual Arts in the late 1970s, in love with the work of Diane Arbus and André Kertész, but hadn't touched her camera in ages. She hated cilantro but adored beets and fresh rhubarb and Jean Anderson, whose *Doubleday Cookbook* she read like the Bible and refused to throw out even after she left it out in the rain one late-summer night, which resulted in black, quarter-size splotches of mold sealing the pages of the beef chapter together like meat glue. She lusted after old and vintage, and loathed new and sleek; she prized her long-dead uncle's jar of 1950s swizzle sticks that now sat on her bar and stirred the small Sapphire Gin Gibson she'd make herself on Saturday evenings when she was home. She preferred tag sales to the fake, farmhouse-chic, must-have excess of gourmet kitchen supply stores that made her wince with every catalog delivery, that demanded she own a two-hundred-dollar cast-iron jalapeño roaster. But hers wasn't the prepackaged, pseudo-cozy, vintage *affectation* that was just beginning to afflict most of flannel-shirted Brooklyn and its young residents who were turning to pickling and jamming instead of clubbing and doing Ecstasy. Susan came by it honestly, and the two dozen 1920s vintage blue Ball canning jars in which she stored her beans and grains and flours didn't come from an auction won on eBay; they had belonged to her grandmother, who had fed her family out of them through the Depression. And during the previous autumn, her mother unearthed a dusty 1920s Roseville bowl for seventy-five cents at her neighbor's garage sale, and thought for certain that she'd *been had*.

That night, after my father dropped me off and I changed out of my holiday velvet and cashmere outfit, I logged on to my computer and there was a long message waiting for me, about Susan's mother showing up at her house that night with a small wooden bookcase that she'd just paid a neighbor five dollars for, unaware that it was stamped STICKLEY on the bottom, and worth about five hundred dollars more.

"I served my mother and Auntie Et Thanksgiving dinner off tag-sale TV trays in my den tonight," she went on. "They're very nice. They have eagles on them. They were three bucks."

I hit REPLY.

"Auntie *Et*? You actually have an Auntie Et? Are you living in Kansas? Is there a *storm a-comin'*?"

"That was Auntie *EM*," she responded. "Et is short for Ethel, but she's been Et forever. There's also Aunt Phyllis, Aunt Sally, and Aunt Mary, who's married to Uncle Jim, who's a skirt chaser. He's almost ninety."

My mind wandered back to Aunt Sylvia, who people in their eighties still called Aunt Sylvia, and who I believed, until I was eighteen, woke up each and every morning with her hair teased and her makeup done by some mysterious midnight makeup entity, while she slept soundly.

But eating Thanksgiving dinner off of eagle-bedecked, three-dollar tag-sale television trays with her Yankee mother and someone named Auntie Et was not something I was accustomed to hearing about from a person with whom I was considering having a romantic alignment, even though we hadn't even set eyes on each other.

It all felt a little too small-town.

A little too *Grammy Hall Hates Jews*.

✝✝✝

Seconds after she sent her email, Susan pinged, and our relationship graduated to Instant Messenger.

"How was your dinner?" she asked.

"It was fancy," I wrote.

My cousin, I told her, had twenty for dinner and managed to make a delicious, giblet-less, dripping-less turkey gravy out of a Sauce Espagnole that she had started preparing three days before the holiday. We had gone through half a case of Sinskey Pinot Noir, at least one bottle of Armagnac, and I'd been certain that my Aunt Sylvia, in typical fashion, had tried to fix me up with a guy who was a ringer for Davy Crockett. Dessert, I added, was a pumpkin flan dusted with crushed candied violets.

"Wait, your aunt tried to fix you up? I thought you were *out* to your family."

"I am," I typed. "But she would rather I be in, so she ignores the fact that the last man I brought home ten years ago was gayer than Liberace."

"So your aunt just sprung this guy on you?"

Although this man who looked like Davy Crockett was, it turned out, mercifully meant for one of my younger cousins, my aunt's fervent desire to "marry me off" had become something of family lore. Some people had holiday traditions involving paper-turkey centerpieces, or menorahs with flickering orange lightbulbs, or white aluminum Christmas trees, or bowling ball–heavy matzo balls made from Streit's mix. But our holiday meals always coincided with the repeated appearance of someone I, after having kismet forced upon me like a too-small pump, started to call The Strange Man.

For years, wherever I was, The Strange Man was sure to follow: two of them showed up on separate occasions while I was visiting cousins in Virginia. One showed up at a *shiva* call that my aunt insisted I pay with her, despite the fact that I had absolutely no idea who the deceased was. Even on the day of her own husband's funeral, my aunt—her eyes swollen and red from crying over the loss of her beloved—mustered enough energy to inform me that a gentleman she wanted me to meet was going to be bringing his mother, one of my aunt's bridge partners, to pay a condolence call.

"They say he was arrested for spousal abuse," Aunt Sylvia whispered, leaning around her heavy walnut bedroom door while all of my cousins napped in neighboring rooms. "But I don't believe it."

+++

Susan's holiday dinner was more benign than ours, she said.

"I made my mother and Auntie Et vodka tonics, we had a small roast with gravy that I made from pan drippings, canned cranberry sauce, and some Big Italian Lady," she wrote.

"A roast *beef*?" I asked.

"A nice roast beef," she replied.

"Why not turkey?"

"Who honestly likes turkey? No one I know. But the ladies love roast beef, so that's what I made—and I sent them home with loaves of Levy's rye bread and enough meat to make sandwiches tomorrow."

Roast beef did not mean Thanksgiving to me; it meant stately English Sunday dinners and heavy, crested family silver. I remembered back to the days when I was a semester student at Caius College, Cambridge, and forty-foot tables creaked beneath the ancient dining room rafters, laden with platters of bloody, thick-sliced meat and horseradish sauce, and each place setting glittered with more utensils than the average American student knew what to do with. Years later, I would make a small Sunday dinner for an English-themed Christmas dinner party, doing absolutely nothing to my prime standing rump roast for four but massaging it with imported *sel gris* that cost as much as a Maine lobster. Three-quarters of the meat stood, looking like the roast beast in the *Grinch*, in my refrigerator until New Year's, left over and sad, until Madeleine, a Parisian friend, scoffed at me.

"Go out and get some tomatoes and onions, and make a *miroton*," she said, and I did; layered in a shallow baking dish between the vegetables, the leftover meat went from good to glorious and, in my mind, the only reason to ever make roast beef again.

"But what about tradition?" I wrote to Susan.

"Who cares about it, if we're together?"

"And the canned cranberry sauce? Like with the ridges?"

"That's right," she answered. "They love it."

"And Big Italian Lady—"

"*Yup*," she typed.

"Okay," I said. "What exactly is Big Italian Lady?"

"A gigantic bottle of Sangiovese with a Big Italian Lady in a red babushka and giant gold hoop earrings on the label. It's nine dollars."

I stared at the screen.

"Exactly how cheap *are* you?" was what I wanted to say, but I couldn't bring myself to type it. So I kept my mouth shut, and when it became clear to both of us that the other was not one of the Manson Girls and likely to show up for our first date with a shaven head and an X carved into her forehead, we decided to meet.

+++

Three months. It took that long. A woman given to deep introspection and constitutional reticence, Susan worried that I'd find her too quiet. I worried that she'd find me a loudmouth New Yorker. When we eventually decided she'd come into the city rather than have me travel with the Donner Party up to the outer reaches of Connecticut, where no one would ever think to look if I went missing, I planned to make brunch reservations at La Goulue on the Upper East Side, where fashionable New Yorkers used to go to pretend they were French, where a simple steak tartare might arrive along with a demitasse of Beluga caviar instead of French fries, and where I always wore my black suede Gucci loafers without socks.

"Always let your date choose the place," my father once instructed me before I left for college. "It'll let you off the hook if the food stinks," he said, "and it'll make him feel more like he's in control."

Of course, *him* wound up being a *her*, but I still let her pick, since she was the one who was going to be driving three hours in each direction. And on a bone-chilling, frigid Saturday afternoon, I stood waiting for her in the lobby of the Museum of the Moving Image, dressed in a fancy yellow Bogner ski jacket and Vuarnets and banana-yellow Timberland boots, like I was about to leave for Sun Valley. Susan loped in, tall and thin, wearing a slouchy, long boucle Japanese wool coat cut like a 1930s bathrobe. She pulled her steel-gray fleece headband off as she walked over to me, smiling with the greenest, warmest eyes I'd ever seen; we linked arms and walked into the theater, the only ones there, to watch an endless reel of early *I Love Lucy* episodes, one after the next after the next. It was late afternoon when we finally left; we took a cab downtown to the divey Christine's Polish Kitchen in the East Village, where we ate vast, diner-size platters of pierogi, boiled kielbasa, fried eggs, and toast, brought to us on heavyweight, chipped Buffalo china. Svetlana, our young, blonde waitress with braids tied up around her ears like Princess Leia headphones, didn't rush us, and refilled cups of lukewarm, weak coffee. She smiled and walked away when Susan touched a tiny scar on the top of my right hand, below the base of my middle finger. At less than half an inch long and the result of a freak accident when I was twelve, no one had ever noticed it before.

"Maybe they just weren't looking for the details," she said, smiling, while an electric shock buzzed inside my kneecaps.

Four hours later, I walked Susan to her car, stopping at an old-fashioned Italian market on First Avenue; it smelled armpit-strong and rank like the inside of a moldy cave, and we both picked up loaves of crusty semolina bread speckled with sesame seeds, and wedges of cheese for our separate dinners alone—plain Saracino table cheese for her, Pecorino Toscano for me.

Bread and cheese—the swipe of musky, oozy Epoisses across a roughly torn baguette end; a slice of bitterly pungent sheep's milk Roncal oozing and dripping over the edges of toasted peasant bread set under a broiler—is the most elemental, lascivious meal in the world, second only to buttered toast. I had learned this years before, in the high-food 1980s, when, too tired to cook one night after working at Dean & DeLuca, I brought home a short demi-baguette and a square of runny, soft Taleggio so stinky it made my cats howl. I climbed the stairs to my Chelsea apartment, sat down on the floor with a glass of cheap Albariño, and the cheese and bread on a scuffed cutting board, and ate dinner. My ex-girlfriend came home later that night and found me asleep on the couch, crumbs on my chest, a Cheshire Cat smile on my face, like I'd had the best sex of my life.

"Hey," she whispered, shaking me awake. "Do you need a cigarette?"

That's what bread and cheese still does for me, and in the face of trout foam and twenty-four-hour, sous-vided eggs and black-market caviar and thousand-dollar Piemontese truffles and eating steak tartare while wearing Gucci loafers, it's easy to forget.

✦✦✦

We stood on the busy sidewalk in the dusky freezing evening, staring over each other's shoulders uncomfortably. People careened past us in the gray and black blur that is winter in Manhattan.

"So can I see you again next weekend? We could cook," Susan said, squinting at something uptown.

"I think so," I replied, trying to be cool, sweating through my black cashmere turtleneck, completely unaware of the toothbrush that was lurking at the bottom of the tiny Italian leather knapsack she had slung over one arm.

She hugged me, and I let her. And then I walked back to my apartment—all the way up to Fifty-Seventh Street—and planned an elaborate menu for the following weekend, which could not arrive soon enough.

"Promise me you won't do anything fancy," she said when she got home, calling to say she'd arrived safely and was about to pour herself a small glass of Chianti and settle in on the couch with her dog, her *Larousse*, her bread, and her cheese.

"I'll try," I assured her.

SIMPLE SUNDAY ROAST BEEF

Regardless of tradition or holiday, there really is no point in going to the trouble of wrestling with a turkey if: a) you don't actually *like* turkey, and b) it's only going to be a few of you at the table. Who really wants to spend hours brining and massaging, and jamming their butter-smeared hands up an ill-tempered bird's backside only to have it still be bone-dry and planning to take up residence in the back of your freezer for a year? Susan's decision to make a simple roast beef for Thanksgiving, rubbed with nothing more than salt and pepper and then cooked to rosy perfection, was a brilliant one, and spoke to her love of all things elemental.

Serves 4, with leftovers

One 4- to 5-pound boneless sirloin roast, tied in 1-inch intervals

1 tablespoon kosher salt

1 teaspoon freshly ground black pepper

1. Place the roast on a platter, drape it loosely with aluminum foil, and let it rest until it comes to room temperature, two or three hours. Twenty minutes prior to cooking, preheat the oven to 500°F.

2. In a small bowl, combine the salt and pepper, and massage it all over the roast. Place the roast in a large cast-iron skillet or medium roasting pan, and slide it into the oven.

3. Roast undisturbed for 20 minutes; then immediately decrease the heat to 300°F, and continue to cook for 20 minutes per pound, without basting, until an instant-read thermometer inserted into the center of the meat registers 130°F.

4. Remove the roast to a cutting board, tent it loosely with foil, and let it rest for 15 minutes before carving it into thin slices. Serve on warm plates with grainy mustard and cornichons.

MIROTON

Traditionally made with leftovers from a *pot au feu*—boiled beef with vegetables—*miroton* is reason enough to bring a large piece of meat into your house. Forget about the ubiquitous sandwiches, and instead layer leftover sliced beef in a shallow casserole or skillet along with jammy, cooked-down onions, beef broth, tomato, and bread crumbs; the result is a spectacular nod to country French leftover know-how.

Serves 4

1½ tablespoons extra-virgin olive oil

2 cups sweet onions, cut into rings

1 teaspoon unbleached all-purpose flour

½ cup prepared beef broth

4 to 5 ounces thinly sliced leftover roast beef

1 medium tomato, cut into ¼-inch-thick slices

½ cup fresh bread crumbs

Kosher salt and freshly ground black pepper

1. In a large skillet set over medium heat, warm the olive oil until it begins to shimmer, and add the onions to the pan all at once. Cook slowly, stirring frequently, until they have turned a dark caramel brown, about 15 minutes.

2. Add the flour and broth to the pan, stirring well, and continue to cook until the mixture has thickened to a paste. Remove from the heat and set aside.

3. Preheat the oven to 400°F. Lightly grease a shallow ovenproof gratin dish.

continued

4. Ladle a tablespoon of the onion mixture in the gratin dish, spreading it uniformly over the bottom of the dish. Top the onions with a layer of meat, tearing the pieces if necessary to fit into the pan, and then top with a layer of tomatoes. Repeat the process as though you were building a lasagna, ending with the tomatoes.

5. Using the back of a serving spoon, press down gently but firmly on the gratin to bring some of its liquid to the surface. Sprinkle with the bread crumbs and season with salt and pepper. Bake until the gratin begins to bubble and ooze, and the top goes golden brown, about 30 minutes.

6. Serve warm, with rounds of garlic-rubbed toast and a green salad.

CHAPTER 2

Executed Chicken

When Susan and I met, I was working in SoHo as the food and entertainment editor at a doomed high-visibility dot-com, in a tall-windowed, light-splashed loft space so cramped—there were twenty of us sharing it—that one of my office mates regularly crawled under her desk in order to speak to her boyfriend in private. One day, while walking over to the Xerox machine, I tripped over her hyperextended legs, which were sticking out from beneath her chair like the striped ones belonging to the Wicked Witch of the East moments before they shriveled up like garden slugs sprinkled with salt.

The loft was directly across the street from Dean & DeLuca, where, fifteen years earlier, in the late 1980s, I had been an associate in the cookbook department. At that time, the city was in the throes of an art boom the likes of which hadn't been seen in over thirty years. It was also in the throes of a drug boom—they often travel hand in hand—and in SoHo circles, those two booms, aided by piles of cash, made for a cataclysmic social explosion of epic proportion. So while my days would be spent standing at the back of the store, leaning against an immense pillar in the shadow of the wall-mounted eight-point buck that hung above Joel Dean's skylight-lit desk, and helping earnestly befuddled Yohji Yamamoto–clad customers choose what Italian cookbook to buy—Giuliano Bugialli or Marcella Hazan or Elizabeth David—because they were *really getting into agnoletti*, I was also frequently called upon to silently trail some of our more famous drug-addled patrons, like Jean-Michel Basquiat, just to make sure he didn't lose his balance while buying bags of high-end gummy bears.

My first day on the job, I blew through the front door at nine on the dot, arriving at the store dressed from head to toe in black—black turtleneck, black leggings, tall flat black boots made of soft leather that scrunched down around my ankles—when a slight, balding man called out to me from behind the counter.

"Yoo-hooo, gorgeous. You *new*?"

"Me?" I turned around.

"Yes, *you*! Are we applying for the rocket scientist job today, honey?" he said, laughing. "Taste this and tell me what you think."

He leaned far over the counter and handed me the end of a baguette dripping with bright-orange marinara sauce that had been bubbling away in a twenty-quart stockpot over a small single propane burner set up on the fifteen-foot work island behind the counter.

"Oh, my god!" I gasped, my mouth full. The sauce was explosively flavorful and sweet and outclassed anything I'd ever slaved over for hours in my own kitchen.

"Does it need anything? Salt?" the man asked.

"Nothing," I swooned, "nothing at all—it's incredible!"

"Four ingredients," he barked, holding up four fingers of his right hand. "I'll show you how. My name is Eric." He wiped his hand on his apron and reached across the counter. "You need to get downstairs before The Boys show up or they'll kill us both."

The Boys—Giorgio DeLuca, Joel Dean, and Jack Ceglic (Jack was Joel's longtime partner, and creator of the gorgeous white-on-white Dean & DeLuca minimalist aesthetic, who could be seen regularly sashaying around the store with a Pekingese on each arm)—were constantly in and out, arranging and rearranging shelves, buying taxidermied grouse in mid-flight to use as Christmas displays, and testing staff members' off-the-cuff knowledge of obscure cooking processes, lest a customer ever, on the off chance, ask them about it. In the back of the store stood an eight-foot-by-four-foot metal Metro shelving table upon which sat approximately forty cream-colored Hall ceramic crocks containing every conceivable cooking implement invented since the late 1800s: there were larding needles and tiny, perforated metal caper spoons so you could lift the pungent nuggets out of their brine and not remove any of the precious liquid; there were French can openers and lemon zesters, wooden citrus reamers and white-handled oyster knives, wire egg separators and single-blade mezzalunas, melon ballers and clam shuckers, French bread *lames*, black cast-iron flame tamers, escargot tongs, stainless truffle shavers, mesh China caps, Swiss garlic presses, Italian salt mills, nonswivel peelers meant specifically for thick-skinned root vegetables, and chestnut knives.

At three o'clock on my first day of work, one of The Boys came straight to the back of the store, eyed me from head to toe through tiny round wire Oliver Peoples glasses, said "nice boots," and then grabbed a larding needle and waved it around like Leonard Bernstein conducting the Vienna Philharmonic.

"Quick!" he shouted, like a Marine drill sergeant. "What's this?"

"Umm," I stuttered.

"Larding needle. Quick! How do you use it?"

"Well," I considered, thoughtfully, "I think you probably put the fat in *here*, and insert—"

"Not fast enough," he barked, cutting me off. "What's *this*?" he asked, pulling a wire egg separator out of a crock on the other side of the table.

"A round whisk," I answered confidently.

"Wrong!" he roared, shaking his head. "We're going to do this again tomorrow—and I want you to learn what every single tool does, and exactly how it works—it has to be on the tip of your tongue," he instructed, snapping his fingers, just inches from the tip of my nose. And then he marched away.

That first morning, Eric-the-sauce-maker directed me downstairs to punch the time clock, tie on my apron, and carry back upstairs the stacks of books that had arrived in a shipment the day before. At ten, the doors swung open for business, and I took my place, leaning against the enormous pillar in the very back of the store, and nervously waited for customers. Five minutes later, David Lynch, Kyle MacLachlan, and Isabella Rossellini—she, wearing pearl-gray sweatpants and sweatshirt and pushing a red-cheeked, doe-eyed baby in a striped Italian stroller—came in and did their grocery shopping. These were the days of *Blue Velvet* and *Twin Peaks*, and regardless of how jaded my colleagues at the store had become, serving everyone from Joel Grey to John Kennedy Jr., when this triptych ambled into the store, you could hear silent gasps. As they passed the meat counter, Michael, the cute charcuterie guy who was a *Blue Velvet* fanatic, held a round plastic deli container over his nose like an oxygen mask and snorted loudly, like Dorothy Vallens and Frank Booth in the lurid, suburban underbelly of Lumberton.

"They're in all the time," Eric whispered to me. "Watch what they buy—it's fascinating."

Dean & DeLuca, to some people, was just another grocery store stuck in the shoulder-padded, cocaine-addled abyss that was the moneyed, AIDS-riddled mass of contradictions called 1980s SoHo. Walk up and down Prince Street, Spring Street, Broome, West Broadway, Grand—each street was lined with galleries packed with leggy Italian, black-clad models dying for a glimpse of Mary Boone and Leo Castelli, Cindy Sherman and Eric Fischl, and a chance to land in the pages of Ingrid Sischy's *Interview* magazine. Each street was lined with glaring white, minimalist restaurants decorated with a single three-foot display of flowers and twigs. Each street was decorated with art illegally painted on city property in the middle of the night, showcasing a frustrated, apoplectic Reagan under the words *Silence=Death*. In the SoHo of the *go-go* 1980s, there was money everywhere, and there was food, and art, and drugs. And, giving not a fat rat's ass about what was in someone's bank account, or up their noses, or in their stomachs, there was AIDs that, five years after I left my job at the store, had killed more than half the male employees, including Eric, who was collateral damage: after finding a mottled purple splotch the size of a dime on his neck while he was shaving one brilliant spring morning in his Hudson Street bathroom—it was Kaposi's sarcoma—he hanged himself.

But step inside Dean & DeLuca on any sunny day in 1988, and everything was good, and luminous, and clean. We sold tomatoes for ten dollars a pound; prenatally tiny Brussels sprouts for eight dollars a pound; fresh morels for thirty-nine dollars a pound; fiddlehead ferns that no one had any idea what the hell to do with for thirty dollars a pound; plus two-hundred-dollar electric copper polenta makers that our import director, Carlo, had brought to us from a buying trip to Parma; immense jars of voluptuous San Remo oil-packed sun-dried tomatoes (the culinary plague of the 1980s first introduced to the United States from Italy by Dean & DeLuca) for sixty dollars; loaves of sourdough and pain de mie for eight dollars; English mustard for fifteen dollars; Piemontese truffles for a hundred dollars an ounce; and candied violets for fifteen dollars a quarter-pound, which we kept stocked specifically for a customer who would come in once a week with her Norwich terrier, Richard, tucked under her arm, buy a bag, and feed them to the matted dog while he sat perched on Joel Dean's desk underneath the dazed, marble-eyed head of the buck, peering down from above at the bizarre world beneath him.

Locals like Lynch, MacLachlan, and Rossellini would walk up and down the two long aisles opposite the refrigerated case filled with cheeses and charcuterie from all over Italy and France, and shop a few times a week, like we were their neighborhood mega-mart. That first night, I went home, back to Julie, my then-girlfriend, and our white brick-walled Chelsea apartment toting a small white D&D shopping bag containing a smoked chicken breast, a pound of Martelli penne, a peppered pyramid of Coach Farms goat cheese, a handful of cippoline, and the smallest jar of sun-dried tomatoes I could afford on an eighteen-thousand-a-year salary; with my store discount, it came to nearly forty bucks.

"What the hell are you going to make with *that*?" Julie asked, stretching her hamstrings after a fourteen-hour day running around with the rest of the residents at St. Vincent's. I was always coming home to find my aerobics-freak girlfriend, who took Jane Fonda's workout video a little too seriously, stretched out in the middle of the living room floor, still wearing her stethoscope and white coat, and contorting herself into completely unnatural and inhuman positions.

"Pasta," I replied. "With goat cheese, onions, sliced smoked chicken, and sun-dried tomatoes."

I decanted the oil from the tomatoes into a plastic squeeze bottle I'd recently picked up at a beauty supply store, dumped the cooked pasta into a small mixing bowl and inverted it gingerly onto a white charger the way I'd seen them do at the Sign of the Dove. Julie sat down at our tiny table, and I placed it in front of her, drizzling perfect jagged squiggles of oil across the mound of dry, gloppy, ultimately vile penne, and poured some cheap Muscadet into two heavy, blue-lipped Mexican glass goblets. Despite her recent decision to become a vegetarian—*Moosewood Cookbook* and *Laurel's Kitchen* were always sitting, unopened, on the dining room table—Julie ate it, smoked chicken skin and all, declared it spectacular, and took the rest of it to the hospital the next day to have for lunch. She was a devout vegetarian, she explained, *but not a judgmental one.*

After immersing myself in the world of food all day, I rode the subway home up Seventh Avenue, my nose buried in cookbook after cookbook; and every evening after work, I cooked and experimented with the often peculiar combination of ingredients I'd drag home from the store. Sometimes I was successful and sometimes I wasn't, but I was always so addicted to the actual process and act of cooking no matter how late it was, that eventually, I took the train uptown, climbed the stairs to Peter Kump's Cooking School in the East Nineties, and enrolled for evening classes.

✛✛✛

During the time I worked at the store, I came home almost every evening with shopping bags full of what I deemed to be sophisticated and rare ingredients: bresaola, anolini, fraise des bois, Liederkranz, raspberry vinegar, and very seriously precious, obnoxiously petite vegetables that I regularly incinerated under the broiler, or boiled to death until they were sad and flaccid, like an underwhelmed penis. If it was a late night and I was closing out the registers, I'd get home at nine, which gave me more than enough time to torture unassuming ingredients into vertical sculptures bearing little resemblance to their original ingredients. With my store discount, I bought tin-lined copper pans from Villedieu and molds and rings and dowels—the kinds of kitchen tools that most restaurants have stacked up by the dozens—and rendered ordinary ingredients unnaturally tall and shaped and gloriously overwrought, like they were stuffed into girdles that were cinched too tight: an innocent scallion was pared down to a thin strand so that it would more freely wave while stuck, long and frisky, into a lumpish hockey puck of carnaroli rice squiggled and polka-dotted with Eric's virginal, four-ingredient marinara sauce. A semi-boned quail, pan-roasted, packed to the gills with preserved, canned black truffle shavings, drizzled with wine and set ablaze on our tiny apartment stove would be perched up on the spot where its ass used to be, its gaping neck cavity the perfect orifice for heavily steamed fiddlehead ferns, which would curl up and out of the tiny headless beast, like an Elizabethan collar on a recently executed chicken.

Even now, almost twenty-five years after I left my job there, walking into the store induces a sort of culinary panic that shocks me into the same submission that you can recognize in the faces of every customer, including those coming from local kitchens and dressed in chef's whites, checked pants, and clogs. No one ever goes in there to buy steak and potatoes without also coming home with a box of lobster and white truffle ravioli. Or a goddamned larding needle. A ball of smoked mozzarella. A crate of still-warm-from-the-Ojai-sun pixie tangerines. An olive-wood caper spoon. A small, round container of piment d'Espelette. The sheer possibility of it all, if one is culinarily inclined, is immense, and so working directly across the street from the store fifteen years after I left, and being involved in a new relationship with a beautiful woman who read *Larousse* in bed, was a boon. And I went a tiny bit crazy.

✛✛✛

I called Susan from my office overlooking Broadway and Prince Street; it was barely ten on a frozen, frigid morning and Dean & DeLuca was already a mob scene, with a throng of holiday shopping–crazed, jittery espresso drinkers clogging up the coffee bar at the front of the store. I remembered back to the day when they'd installed that behemoth, which a few weeks later, sprayed hot milk foam all over my face and apron much to the glee of a pack of black-clad Milanese art dealers who were standing at the counter, sucking down their morning cappuccinos.

"What train will you make?" Susan asked. I was leaving work early that day, I told her, and taking Amtrak to Hartford, where she'd pick me up at the station, conveniently located in the absolute worst part of the city, which was under gangland siege on a regular basis.

"I'll do a little shopping at lunchtime," I offered, kicking the small overnight bag under my desk.

"Okay," she said. "But I do have plenty of food here, you know."

I couldn't imagine what; living alone in the middle of nowhere for a year, Susan probably ate cereal for dinner four nights a week while I was home on Fifty-Seventh Street, sprinkling my roasted songbirds with grains of paradise.

"I promise," I sighed. "I won't go crazy. I swear."

The store was crowded with the usual holiday shoppers; I rolled my eyes at the store's ubiquitous taxidermy display of woodcock and grouse and floated up and down the aisles and across the store from one side to the other, selecting various items and putting them in my basket. Susan professed an almost religious devotion to good toast and tea in the morning, so I found a jar of rare, raw Hawaiian honey, some English gooseberry jam, and a loaf of the dark date-nut bread she loved. She lusted after strong, washed-rind cheeses, the more pungent the better, so I picked up a round of oozy Epoisses that had been sitting out, unrefrigerated for a day or so, stinky as a rotting durian. By the time I navigated the zombie-like crowds and made it to the front of the store, there was a box of six, small, disgustingly adorable petit fours in my basket, along with a foot-long garlic saucisson sec, and a six-dollar baguette from the Policastro Bakery, just like the one that Eric had dipped into the bubbling marinara sauce fifteen years earlier. The aroma of the Epoisses and the sausage together overtook the petit fours, and by the time my train pulled into the Hartford station that night, no one was sitting next to, or anywhere near, me.

As the train screeched to a halt almost three hours later in Hartford, I looked out through the dirty train window at the ancient brick station, which was laden with fake Balsam garlands and plastic Christmas trees in every corner. Susan stepped out of the waiting area and hugged me warmly when I climbed down the steps. I handed her my shopping bag and she peered in, eyes closed, inhaling deeply.

"For you," I said, smiling.

"Bread and cheese?" she asked, smiling at me with her gorgeous green eyes.

We slipped and slid across Asylum Street to the icy parking lot, and the black Hyundai that she had clearly spent hours having detailed before my arrival; there was no sign of the drooling dog she told me about, no doggie eyeball goobers with the sticking power of Gorilla Glue attached to the dashboard. Susan's car was pristine, and here I was, inside it, sitting next to her, on my way to her tiny house in the middle of nowhere, for a weekend of lascivious behavior interspersed with noshing on the bizarre mosaic of incongruous foods I'd schlepped from the city and that, with the exception of the Epoisses, would mostly go untouched for the next three days.

ERIC'S MARINARA

Golden orange, tangy, and perfect for use in everything from a basic bowl of spaghetti to a drizzle on a grilled vegetable sandwich pressed between two cast-iron pans, Eric's marinara remains the *sine qua non* of not-quite-red Italian sauce in my book. His secret was a Foley food mill—a hand-crank tool through which tomatoes are processed, sans seeds, directly into the pot. While his original version included only four ingredients—canned tomatoes, carrots, onions, and celery—I've added garlic and basil over the years to give it more earthiness. Sprinkle in a bit of red pepper flakes to give it additional heat, or a touch of red wine vinegar to give it more sweetness and depth.

Makes about 8 cups

2 tablespoons extra-virgin olive oil

1 large yellow onion, chopped

2 large carrots, chopped

1 large celery stalk with leafy tops, chopped

2 garlic cloves, chopped

Two 28-ounce cans whole San Marzano tomatoes

2 tablespoons minced fresh basil

1. In a large saucepan or soup pot set over medium-low heat, warm the olive oil until it begins to shimmer. Add the onion, carrots, and celery and cook until softened, without letting the onions take on any color, about 12 minutes, stirring frequently. Add the garlic, give it a stir, and continue to cook until it's translucent, about 5 minutes more.

continued

2. Set a Foley food mill over the pot, pour in one of the cans of tomatoes (with juice), and process the tomatoes directly into the vegetables. Wipe the skin and seeds out of the food mill and discard them, and repeat with the second can. Give the tomatoes a stir, partially cover the pot, increase the heat to medium, and simmer for 60 minutes, stirring frequently. If the sauce seems too thick, add up to 1 tablespoon of water at a time to thin it out. Stir in the basil during the last 5 minutes of cooking.

3. For smoother sauce, purée it directly in its pot by using a hand-held immersion blender. Let cool, and decant into freezer bags or canning jars. It will keep for up to 6 months in the freezer and up to 1 week in the refrigerator.

CHAPTER 3

Tall Food

I've always had a small addiction to hand tools.

My father's battered dark green navy metal footlocker, which sat in our hallway closet in Forest Hills for the duration of my childhood, held all manner of wrenches and screwdrivers, hammers and files, nuts and bolts. Often on rainy days, I would haul the thing out, open it up, and run my hands through its contents, like I'd just unearthed buried pirate treasure. It was the bigger, noisy things, like drills and reciprocating saws, that terrorized me, and once, when I was four and had nothing to do, I entertained myself by getting my own right thumb stuck in my father's vise, which I had proudly clamped to the side of the dining room table. Fascinated, I turned the little handle that made it close around and around, until it squeezed my dainty digit and stopped the blood flow, and I shrieked in pain.

Even now, I own twenty-five odd knives of varying styles and sizes, ranging from a *hochmesser*—a heavy cleaver—that could easily sever the head of a small dinosaur to a triumvirate of nasty French carbon-steel paring knives that lash out and rust in anger if you so much as glance at them from across a crowded room. All of my knives attach to a magnetic strip that hangs along an eight-foot wall across the kitchen from my stove, making them look like I share my home with a carnival knife-thrower who can't leave his work at the office.

My mother, a fur model who neither understood nor condoned my desire to attend cooking school, nevertheless bought me my first set of knives—the usual eight-inch chef's, a six-inch flexible boning, and a three-inch paring—from a knife and scissor salesman who had a tiny shop across the street from her showroom on Thirtieth Street. It was bizarre, standing there at the cash register with this woman who hated every single moment I spent at the stove, but whose idea of support could always be reduced to a little retail therapy.

"I just don't understand why they have to be so *sharp*," she said, shaking her head, while the salesman just stared.

Eventually, other tools worked their way into my small apartment: there was the traditional French salamander—a small, heavy metal disc at the end of long handle that you heat in an open flame and gently set on the sugar-dusted top of a crème brûlée (or the filthy shoulder of a captured pirate about to be tortured, depending upon what channel you're watching). There were various cake pans and muffin rings, even though I don't ever bake cakes or muffins. All of these tools—the cake pans, the muffin rings, the salamander—were stuffed into the drawer of a four-foot-long butcher-block cart on wheels, which I'd bought to give me more kitchen counter space.

And then there were the timbale molds. Eight of them, which I bought one evening at Dean & DeLuca with my employee discount, right before the store closed for the night. Psychologists would classify it as an impulse buy, although I had given it some advance thought and rationalized the purchase—even on my pathetic salary.

My goal was simple: I wanted to make tall food—*very* fancy, *very* tall food that would impress my dinner guests—and leave them astonished and surprised and gazing in awe at my hidden talent—"Who knew?"— and ooh-ing and aah-ing and saying things like "Gosh, we had no *idea* you could do this." Set down upon a rice-stuffed timbale mold, even something as elemental as a piece of roast chicken could be elevated out of the mundane into the architectural and breathtaking. Assuming everyone could figure out how to eat it without a degree in deconstructive architecture, or before it got cold. Or the seasons changed.

Growing up in Forest Hills in the '70s and '80s, so close to Manhattan, dining out—unless I was out with my father and we were eating strictly classical French cuisine—always meant dinner and a show, because dinner *was* the show: the food was often tall and over-wrought and, like the clothes of the time, excessive and showy, and bordering on the garish in its desire to stun. It was always vertical and provided the diner with a kind of extreme experience that resulted in one being so wowed, or exhausted, by the various flights of fancy sitting on the plate that by the time the meal was over, you couldn't actually remember what you had eaten. It didn't matter where you ate: Was it a mousseline dotted with pomegranate purée? Or a Napoleon of chicken galantine *en gelée* dribbled with unnaturally green persillade? Lion's Rock, Sign of the Dove, The Quilted Giraffe, Mr. Chow, Jams, Windows on the World, The Four Seasons, Chanterelle, Vienna '79, Simon's, Maxwell's Plum, and the well-upholstered sinkhole that was Tavern on the Green—the tallness of their food screamed culinary whimsy, but it also resulted in ordinary home cooks racing to their apartment kitchens and contorting everyday, hapless ingredients into completely unnatural and unfortunate situations, even if they couldn't toast a piece of bread without burning it.

Studying French technique at cooking school in the late 1980s, I was learning how to make mother sauces and vinaigrettes and blanquette de veau. I had no desire to learn how to make leaping dolphins with spun sugar, or a three-dimensional Eiffel Tower out of ganache. I just wanted my food to stand at attention, tall and high, excessive and extraordinarily impressive, so I took the easy route: if I was going to learn how to prepare and properly serve the imposing, fashionable food of the time, I was going to have to own timbale molds.

So I brought them home, unpacked them, went into the bedroom to change, and when I emerged in a sweatshirt and jeans, Julie was standing in the kitchen, sipping wine out of one of them.

"Can you *not*, please," I pleaded, taking it away from her lips and pouring the wine into a glass.

"Why?" she asked, totally confused.

"They're molds. To make tall food."

"I thought they were drinking cups."

"No!"

"They look like thimbles on steroids." She turned one over and squinted at the markings on its bottom.

"Why eight?" she asked, mystified.

"Because if we have a dinner party for eight, I'll need to make eight timbales, right?"

She looked at me blankly.

"Don't worry," I said. "They nest like Dixie cups. You won't even know they're here."

"But we never have dinner parties for eight," she replied weakly. "We can't have more than four people here."

She was right, but I knew that someday I would need to make eight timbales, and when that happened, I would be prepared. Years later, when I registered for Apilco service for twelve and my cousin Lois bought me eight settings because she made the executive decision that I'd never have more guests than that for dinner unless I was planning on opening up a restaurant, I went out and bought the other four sets. Because I wanted to be prepared.

By the time Julie and I broke up and I moved in to a studio apartment with my hundreds of cookbooks and my French copper pots and my heavyweight baking sheets and my eight timbale molds, I was set for anything. But my Chelsea walk-up was where it all began—this crazy love affair with single-purpose kitchen tools that produced a specific, desired culinary effect by perverting ingredients into completely abnormal states: The molds that produced a tall timbale of rice upon which you might set down a thick slab of quickly seared foie gras, into which you might poke a single, perfect, delicate, long, flowering garlic chive that, if the wind blew gently from the right direction, might wave in the breeze. That goddamned, eighteen-inch larding needle designed by Torquemada that you used to infuse with fat a sirloin of venison from a deer that was bagged and butchered that day. The pitter made specifically for cherries—never olives—designed so that it would in no way bruise the fruit, and so that you could stuff its now pit- and-blemish-free middle with 80 percent cacao chocolate ganache, as a little surprise for your thrilled and applauding dinner guests.

But timbales especially—those squat fireplugs of tastiness and vertical culinary illusion and completely inauthentic chic—were so innately filled with promise and possibility and height. They harkened back to my first dinner at Chanterelle, when it was one smallish, flower-bedecked dining room on Grand Street, when the poached oyster mille-feuille in anchovy cream arrived on a glistening white charger, and I tried to re-create it at home using canned oysters stuffed into one of my new timbale molds. And lunch in a neo-modern bistro on the Left Bank, where a torchon of foie gras was sliced and set down upon a timbale of lightly truffled wild mushroom salad, which I tried to re-create at home with a cold slab of prepackaged foie gras mousse balancing on a hockey puckish timbale of braised, shrink-wrapped, grocery-store button mushrooms, because I couldn't afford the wild variety. It was that black-tie party that Julie's residency director had thrown in his white-washed, brick-walled loft down on Broome Street, and the timbale of lobster, caviar, and dill, topped with the fleshy point of the lobster claw, which made it look like a shark's fin, and awed me breathless to the point of tears; I tried to re-create it by boiling a small Maine lobster, extracting the meat from the shell, purée-ing it with egg white and then forcing the mousse into a timbale and sprinkling the result with squeeze-tube salmon roe. My dinner guests, who spent most of the night trying to keep the cats off their laps, were stunned. Mostly in a good way.

Tall food broke through the demilitarized zone between the plate and the diner, like an actor kicking down the fourth wall; it's what took a dish from humdrum to engaging and interactive, because it required the diner to figure out how to eat it. And from the minute I started cooking, that's what I wanted to give my dinner guests, even in my fifth-story walk-up: I wanted to engage them, and to give them food that was show-stopping and impressive. Sometimes it worked, and sometimes they thought I was insane; sometimes everything wobbled and eventually toppled over as I carried the plates to my dining room table from the kitchen. Sometimes, the cats ate very well, licking up the residual timbale out of the cracks in my wood parquet floor, where it had fallen and splattered, landing with all the grace of a balloon filled with horse manure.

+++

"So let me get this straight," Susan said to me on the phone one night before we met, when I told her the timbale story. "You make tall food *all the time*?"

"I wouldn't say that," I told her. "But I do like to make nice meals. Even if it's just me."

"Even if it's just you. *Then* what?"

"It could be anything: if it's really late and I'm starved, an open-face fried quail egg sandwich drizzled with white truffle oil and maybe some baby arugula."

"Why not chicken eggs, like the rest of us?" she asked, laughing.

"Cholesterol, naturally."

"*Naturally*," she snorted. I could hear her rolling her eyes, one hundred miles away.

"I'm not *sure* about this," she went on. "How about if you have all the time in the world, and it's just you?"

"Well, last week, I made poussin wrapped in pancetta on a timbale of wine-braised lentils du Puy."

"For yourself?"

"Why not?"

"Was it sitting upright, like a chicken on a beer can?"

"No—it was just perched on top of it, like a bird on a wire."

"But why does it always have to be tall? It just seems so—I don't know—*indulgent*?"

"So what do you do when it's you, just you? Make peanut butter and jelly?"

"Well," she answered, "sometimes I'll make a poached egg on white toast. And sometimes—it's kind of extravagant," she added, sheepishly, "I make a sort of peach and veal stew."

"A *what*?" I nearly choked on my wine.

"A peach and veal stew—it's actually very good, especially during winter."

"You actually buy veal with the purpose of cooking it with peach?"

"I do, but only if it's stew meat, and only if it's on sale."

"And where do you get the peach from during the winter?" I asked, mystified.

"Oh," she said. "I don't use actual *peach*, silly—"

"I'm afraid to ask."

"I use canned peach nectar. It makes a perfect braise."

Months later, after my train got stuck one Friday night and I arrived in Hartford two hours late, and a late-spring snow was falling and we were both exhausted, Susan had dinner waiting for me: a bowl of her veal and peach stew on steamed rice, flecked with parsley, red pepper flakes, and a handful of minced chives. I dubbed it Veau à la Pêche.

I was tired, cold, infuriated from the trip, and hungry enough to eat my own arm; as we sat at her counter with MacGillicuddy snoring on the couch in the living room and the snow piling up outside, I inhaled two meaty, sweet, tender, spicy, deliciously bizarre bowls full, washed down with a large glass of peppery Syrah.

CHAPTER 4

Sing Along with Mitch

Susan grew up an adopted, only child in a jolly family, packed with people who liked to party and have a good time, anywhere, for any reason. A good Catholic girl who went to parochial school for years and then to Marymount in the early '70s, she took such illuminating classes as "God, Man, and Art," and her teachers were nicknamed things like "Sister Bonwit Teller."

She spent her holidays as a child being dressed up by her mother, Helen, in frilly Christmas outfits and then taken to see Santa at G. Fox in Hartford, which, at that time, was still a busy, safe city filled primarily with insurance companies. I imagine her at four years old, jet-black hair and green, yearning eyes, the map of Ireland on her young, freckled face. She's reserved even then, determined to fly way under the radar for fear of causing her nervous mother upset and fuss; Susan is quiet and shy sitting on the lap of that year's particularly fabulous Santa, all dressed up in a red wool coat with black velvet trim that her parents bought for her at Myrtle Mills, the place in town where her mother worked when the doctors told her that a job would refocus her attention away from what, in the 1950s, they called *nerves*. Susan whispers softly to this enormous, bearded man what she's hoping he will bring her for Christmas, and then goes with her parents to a party at her Auntie Et's house on Main Street in Unionville.

There is noise, and snacks like celery sticks stuffed with pimiento cheese, crab dip, clam dip, onion dip, shrimp dip, spray cheese, and sliced Cracker Barrel extra-sharp Cheddar for those who want something fancy. There are drinks—triple-shot Rusty Nails and old-fashioneds and vodka tonics—maybe too many, for the adults, who crank up Mitch Miller's *Holiday Sing Along with Mitch* album on the new, faux-walnut Motorola Console Hi-Fi phonograph, until a scratchy LP playing "Have a Holly, Jolly Christmas" over and over rattles the front window overlooking Main Street, and the sing-along begins to turn into a slur-along. Auntie Et, a big, loving, thick-waisted, boisterous woman dressed from head to toe in colored rhinestones, her champagne-tinted helmet hair shellacked into an updo, has just returned from a European cruise with a girlfriend; she left her husband, Jack, a former state trooper and bodyguard for Senator Abe Ribicoff, at home, and needles him relentlessly with tales of being vigorously pursued by the recently divorced Arthur Miller, who was also on the cruise, traveling solo. No one in this family ever does this sort of thing, this traveling alone; it just isn't done. Of all the sisters and brothers—and at one time, there were eleven of them—only Mary, the quiet one, traveled the world with her husband. The rest have never even left New England. It was considered mysterious—almost aggressive—to have outlying interests that take you away from home and the tight clutch of family.

But no matter what Et does—even that time that she lost three-year-old Susan in the parking lot of a department store—and no matter what anyone says to or about her, Susan loves her in that deep, visceral, almost cellular way that children love a grandparent or an auntie who can do absolutely no wrong. Susan loves everything about her, from her hilariously boorish manners to the cheese-on-a-Ritz-with-a-dollop-of-ketchup hors d'oeuvre she loves to serve to the fact that her husband the trooper "got" her license for her, and forgot to teach her to drive. Et is the fun one, the wild one, the one without the nerves that afflict most of the aunts and uncles in this family, at least four of whom will have breakdowns before they turn fifty.

On Christmas Eve, after church, after Susan finally settles down in her bed and struggles to go to sleep like every other wish-filled, hopeful Christian child in the world, her father, George, places her gifts under the tree. There are decorations everywhere in the house: miniature, illuminated trees fashioned from wire hangers, plugged into every outlet both upstairs and downstairs; a family of small, stuffed velvet reindeer milling around on the center of the dining room table, heads cocked inquisitively; and electric candles in every window. George, an enormously tall and imposing man with kind eyes who loves his little girl to the ends of the earth, has made sure that the simple sugar cookies that she's baked with her mother and left out for Santa have a few small nibbles taken out of them, just so that she knows he was really here.

The next day, after the toys and the gifts, there is more family, and a gigantic ham and round coils of boiled, garlicky smoked kielbasa, bought from Rosol's Meatpackers over in New Britain. There are baskets of warm Parker House rolls, vast covered Pyrex casseroles heavy with mashed potatoes soaked with salted butter and milk, and frozen string beans cooked with mushroom soup and baked with a breadcrumb topping that Susan picks off when no one is looking. After the family eats, George, Susan, Helen, and Helen's mother, who lives with them, travel the ten miles up to Winsted, where they do the same thing all over again for dinner with more family. There are homemade angel wings—fried dough sprinkled with confectioners' sugar—and more ham and kielbasa. After the dishes are done and the kitchen is clean, sandwiches are made from the leftovers just a few hours after dinner itself is over.

+++

"It all sounds so charming," I tell her, plopping my feet on her lap. I'm stretched out on Susan's old, worn, goose-down sofa, which, having had its legs sawed off impetuously by her ex, Jennifer, when she couldn't get the couch through her tiny apartment doorway, is abnormally low to the ground, making it an easy climb up for MacGillicuddy, who fights me for space. We're sitting in Susan's tiny living room on a snowy Saturday morning, housebound except when we put on ski pants—the kind that make a svelte lady look like the Michelin Man—and oversized parkas and take the dog out for an exhausting hike through the woods. We've been together only a short time at this point; every Friday since that first date in Manhattan, I travel up to Hartford on Amtrak, leaving my office at five and arriving in Connecticut after nine. We have a perfunctory dinner of strange, exotic cheese that I've brought from Dean & DeLuca—we're still in the frenetic, earliest stages of romance, and a week apart is a very long time—and the rest of the weekend is spent doing the things that two adults who are wildly attracted to each other, do, wherever they can possibly do it.

"It *was*," Susan says, rubbing my feet, and smiling sadly. "Christmas was always loud and raucous, and you never knew when someone was going to take their teeth out even before the eggnog started to flow. But there were decorations everywhere, and to see that Santa had nibbled one of the cookies I left for him was totally thrilling."

And as she tells me this, and shows me family Christmas pictures—her mother in a white fox stole sheared close to the skin to resemble mink; her Aunt Mary with her overly sprayed hair piled high upon her head, doing the limbo with a five-year-old Susan in someone's paneled basement inches from a short, artificial Christmas tree—I realize that she's likely never experienced an urban child's Christmas, much less a Jewish urban child's. She never traveled into the city to see the immense tree at Luchow's, and to listen to the oompah band play Christmas carols, or to watch the lighting of the Rockefeller Center Christmas tree with her parents and grandmother the way I have, to see the enormous spectacle at dusk, glowing like a beacon. She's never stood on line for hours to see the Dickensian windows at Lord & Taylor—a display of blissfully happy families of beautiful, velvet-wearing children, with barking dogs, and a goose as big as a sow on the table—and she's never watched the Yule Log on television the way I have, with my mother's mother, Gaga, who insists that we watch it together, as it burns lustily in someone else's fireplace out there in TV land, first in black-and-white, and a few years later, in color.

CHRISTMAS CLAM DIP

Try though they might, absolutely no one in Susan's family remembers the derivation of this clam dip recipe without which Christmas at her house simply does not exist. Thick, rich, creamy, smoky (if you choose to include my addition—pimentón, sweet smoked Spanish paprika), and undeniably Yankee frugal, the dip does best with an overnight rest in the refrigerator. Let it come to room temperature before serving with plain, salted potato chips or Club crackers.

Makes 2½ cups

One 8-ounce package cream cheese, at room temperature

One 8-ounce container sour cream

One 10-ounce can whole baby clams, drained

2 garlic cloves, minced

⅛ teaspoon cayenne pepper

Pinch of sweet pimentón (optional)

Salt

Crackers or potato chips, for accompaniment

1. In a medium bowl, whisk the cream cheese and sour cream together until smooth and lump-free.

2. Fold in the clams, garlic, cayenne, and pimentón (if using) and stir to thoroughly combine. Taste for salt, and correct, if necessary. Cover and refrigerate overnight. Return to room temperature prior to serving, with crackers or potato chips.

CHAPTER 5

Brunch with Mrs. Eisenberg

My first official cooking job took place the week before Christmas in 1988, at a time when I was still working at Dean & DeLuca during the day, going to cooking school at night, and believing, with every fiber of my being, that the combination was going to one day result in my commanding my own professional kitchen.

It was a no-brainer—the desire to be the lead in the balletic dance that is the act of running a kitchen, of taking charge, of moving from stove to pass, from station to station with graceful economy of purpose. In the glimmering, silver, stainless-and French copper–lined professional kitchens that lived in the recesses of my imagination, there was no shouting, no sweating, no fires, no cuts, no burns; there were no line cooks getting blow jobs in the walk-in, no pastry chefs snorting lines of coke in the bathroom. The professional kitchen of my mind was ordered, safe, and clean. Like heaven.

"But will you have to wear an apron?" my mother asked, a pained expression spreading across her face when I told her I was going to go to cooking school.

"Yes, Mother," I told her, "just like Jeffrey Dahmer."

She winced at my smartass response, knowing full well that I would never be the physician that my family prays every child born to our name will become. But it was too late. I had just seen Anne Rosenzweig doing a holiday cooking demonstration at Bloomingdale's, and I was hooked. Teeny tiny Anne stood high on a riser, and in a hot sauté pan set atop a small propane burner, carefully seared a gorgeous expanse of tuna belly rolled in crushed peppercorns. When she was finished, she sliced the belly thickly, its ruby-red center glowing like a garnet stoplight. Fastidious, white-coated assistants distributed plates to the audience, each one with two slices of tuna belly artfully arranged in a slightly askew, tall stack. Everyone tasted the fish to strains of *delicious and incredible*, while Anne stood there on her riser, tall as a giant, unsmiling, confident as a neurosurgeon.

That would be me. I was sure of it.

+++

Julie supplemented her meager medical fellowship stipend by working part-time as a private exercise instructor for a small group of tightly wound Sutton Place ladies—the Mortimer's-for-lunch/art patron crowd.

She of the headlight-size Cartier diamonds, linebacker shoulder pads, and heavily lacquered Kenneth Salon helmet hairdo sprayed to the point where she was a walking fire hazard, Eleanor Eisenberg lived with her oil magnate husband, Ernst, in a Roy Lichtenstein–draped, I. M. Pei–designed Sutton Place town house so cavernous and minimally decorated, it echoed. Each room contained no more than two pieces of furniture, one of them being a Wassily chair, the other, a custom-made, white Eames spindle that could get picked up and moved around as needed.

Eleanor had taken an immediate liking to bubbly Julie who, a few times a week and like a human Pilates machine, rode the small glass elevator up to Eleanor's private aerie on the top floor and stretched, pulled, massaged, coaxed, and generally cajoled her five-foot-ten, preternaturally thin employer into impossible positions guaranteed to keep her long and lithe, which is how Eleanor intended to stay.

So when Eleanor, who knew that I was attending cooking school at night while working at Dean & DeLuca during the day, decided to give me what she was sure would be my first big break in the catering business, I didn't have a lot to worry about: the food was to be *minimal*. "Like my décor," she said, when she called our apartment one night to talk to me about the party, which would be a Bar Mitzvah luncheon for her grandson to which everyone in the art world, from Eric Fischl to Julian Schnabel, would conceivably be in attendance.

"What are you thinking?" I asked her that night, perched on our beige futon couch in my flannel sock-monkey pajamas, a yellow legal pad in my lap.

"No, my dear," she sighed, "thinking is *your* job." I heard her take a long, slow drag off her cigarette. She was waiting.

I thought *1980s*. I thought *Bar Mitzvah*. I thought *smoked fish*.

"Oh heavens—*no!*" Eleanor gasped dramatically, like I'd just told her that I'd seen her corporate CEO son shimmying down Christopher Street with a fruit basket on his head, dressed as Carmen Miranda. "How about some of that lovely raspberry dipping sauce I had recently at a party catered by those two nice girls from the West Side?"

"The Silver Palate? You mean raspberry mayonnaise?"

"Yes, darling," she agreed. "—*exactly*. And some imported white asparagus would be lovely."

"Caviar?" I asked.

"Of course—and blini. You can make them here. And the caviar has to be osetra. Beluga has become so trendy. It's absolutely *everywhere*."

"Spot prawns if I can find them?"

"Perfect!" she squealed. "But can you wrap them in some nice Ibérico ham?"

"I can, Mrs. Eisenberg. But didn't you mention this was a Bar Mitzvah luncheon?"

I had attended plenty of Jewish weddings and Bar Mitzvahs where Talmudically prohibited shrimp and cold lobster were served—one could somehow always manage to look the other way—but a line was always drawn like an electric fence at the appearance of ham.

"It is, my dear. We're just trying not to make it"—she whispered into the receiver—"too *Jewish*. You do understand, of course."

I stared at the phone.

"Charles will come and get you with the car at eight forty-five. The party starts at ten, right after the service is over. I want the blini to be *warm*, the arrangements to be tall, and everything to be fancy."

And then she hung up.

+++

The morning of the luncheon, I awoke at six, turned on the oven, and began prepping the prawns that had been buried overnight in the depths of my counter-height refrigerator, along with the Ibérico, the caviar, and the unsliced side of smoked salmon that Ernst decided he wanted at the last minute. There were tiny black breads to be cookie-cuttered into unnatural shapes, white asparagus to be shaved, steamed, and drizzled with a warm shallot velouté. There was Belgian endive to be cleaned and arranged high on a platter, overlapping like a tower of dominoes, and surrounded by still-warm gougères slit in half and overstuffed with micro-watercress and barely discernible swipes of fresh, thick quark. I gently poached the spot prawns in a lemon-infused butter bath, chilled them down, wrapped each one in a paper-thin slice of Ibérico, and emulsified the eggs and the oil while Julie drizzled in driplets of the required raspberry vinegar for the mayonnaise. Quail eggs, which had replaced the blini when Mrs. Eisenberg decided that no one really needed the extra bread, were boiled, gently peeled, and sliced in half, their precious little yolks gingerly popped out like tiny eyeballs, restuffed with the Osetra, and then sprinkled with the crumbled, hard-cooked yellow yolks.

My buzzer rang precisely at eight forty-five, and as Julie answered it and instructed Charles to double park and climb the five flights of stairs to reach me and my assorted platters, I was just drawing my rapier-like salmon slicer—flexible as a saber and on loan from the smoked fish department at the store—through the bunched-up apron in my left hand. The doorbell rang, I looked down, and there was blood: I'd sliced my left palm straight through to the bone. By the time Charles and I arrived at Eleanor's extremely white town house and set everything up in her extremely white parlor, I was pale, woozy, and struggling to keep my towel-wrapped hand out of sight and not dripping on any food, priceless artwork, artists, the white-washed pickled maple floor, or the Bar Mitzvah boy, who seemed to be more interested in what was under the larger of his grandmother's three white Christmas trees than in whether he'd successfully recited his haftorah that morning at Temple Emmanuel. Eleanor cooed over everything, declared the lunch a success, handed me a thousand dollars in cash, and Charles drove me home to my walk-up thirty blocks south. It was the fastest money I'd ever made, not including the cost of the stitches.

At some point in the 1980s, food professionals all over New York, Los Angeles, San Francisco, and everywhere in between seemed to make the connection between how stoned or rich or both their patrons were at the time of service, and how conceptual or outrageously minimal or sculptural they could be with the food. A dollop of dry, cottony out-of-season, bland, unexceptional tomato innards served on ceramic Asian soup spoons crisscrossed like swords at a Marine wedding might be considered high edible art if a party-goer was toasted enough, or the server pompous enough. Tuna tartare, dotted on the end of an upright, miniature cucumber like the metal clicker on a Bic pen was, in wealthy circles, considered the height of culinary genius. Foie gras "lollipops" rolled in black truffle shavings and served on ice—devolving into the ubiquitous and trite lamb chop lollipops after the market crashed—showed up at every black-tie cocktail party and museum opening above Fourteenth Street for years. And catering managers all over New York took to roaming Central Park, Felco rose-pruning shears hidden in their back pockets, in search of barren forsythia branches and fallen leaves from which they would smugly fashion "natural" centerpieces and for which their clients would pay hundreds of dollars. In the '80s, with money and drugs and high food everywhere, anything was possible and plausible, right down to the 175-dollar-a-pound Ibérico ham from an acorn-fed Spanish pig named Hector that Eleanor wanted wrapped around the asparagus at her grandson's Bar Mitzvah luncheon. Everyone wanted their food to be towering, fancy, and overwrought, as though sheer height validated their importance, their sophistication, their sense of savoir faire, and their place, safe and secure within the outrageous social structure of the time.

And I was no different.

POACHED ASPARAGUS WITH PROSCIUTTO AND DUCK EGGS

The days of raspberry aioli–dribbled white asparagus are thankfully long behind us, but the appeal of wrapping fresh stalks of asparagus in ham remains, with good reason: On the one hand, the salt of the ham beautifully offsets the sweet earthiness of the vegetable and really needs no dipping accompaniment (especially not a pink one). On the other, sliced into two-inch pieces, the wrapped asparagus makes for easy cocktail-friendly finger food that can be dressed up by substituting white asparagus for green, or topping them with a few scrapings of top-quality Parmigiano-Reggiano or even a small amount of black caviar. My catering days behind me, I now prefer this dish for dinner, topped with a fried duck egg and served with a hunk of fresh Italian bread, which I use to sop up whatever egg remains.

Serves 2

½ **pound freshly picked, mature (thick) asparagus**

4 ounces prosciutto di Parma or San Daniele, or Ibérico ham

2 tablespoons top-quality extra-virgin olive oil, plus more for drizzling

2 duck eggs

Freshly ground black pepper (optional)

1. Have a bowl of ice water nearby. Using a paring knife, trim off the woody stems of the asparagus, and place the stalks in a large skillet. Cover them just barely with water, and bring to a boil over high heat. Cook for 3 minutes, cover, and remove from the heat. Let the asparagus stand for 3 minutes in the pan, and then plunge the stalks into the ice water. Remove, and pat the asparagus dry with a clean kitchen towel.

2. Roll up each asparagus spear in a slice of ham, starting an inch below its feathery top. Set aside.

3. In a medium skillet, heat the 2 tablespoons olive oil over medium heat until rippling. Carefully crack each duck egg into the oil, and cook until the very edges of the whites begin to go brown and crispy and the yolk is just cooked, about 4 minutes.

4. Top the asparagus with the fried eggs, drizzle with more olive oil, and season with black pepper, if desired. Serve immediately.

CHAPTER 6

Mornay

Set back from a narrow, winding country road twenty-five miles west of Hartford, and tucked behind an unfinished picket fence, Susan's house was tiny, and perfect for one person and a dog, living alone. It had been owned for years by a bottle-red woman called Cherisse, the town eccentric, who was known in the area for collecting her golden retriever's errant fur and knitting great, gigantic balls of the golden, dander-laden fluff into warm, blond sweaters for her children. When Susan moved in the summer before we met, her mother and one of her aunts—well into their eighties—showed up one day with an Oldsmobile trunk full of ancient garden tools, went out into the perfectly flat, three-quarter-acre backyard, and dug up the remnants of Cherisse's overgrown and straggly garden, which included a healthy and vigorous patch of ganja.

During the bitterly cold New England winter and in the earliest days of our romance, Susan and I spent the majority of our time inside, in this petite half-Cape, the first floor of which consisted of one small, main room cut in half by a heavily-shellacked, cantilevered dining counter on the other side of which was the kitchen. My tiny apartment kitchen, seven-foot-square with a twenty-four-inch stove, made me hungry for room to have at least two burners going at the same time, and so I fell in love with Susan's cooking space. At a time when every home design magazine in America was showing kitchens that looked as frigid as morgues, with granite countertops and high-gloss Italian cabinets, Susan's was scuffed and lived in, grazed and nicked by life. There was virtually no counter space, but what was there was warm and honey-stained, and fashioned from rough-hewn wood, as were the few cabinets. The enormous, vintage Kohler white triple-basin farmhouse sink sat in the middle of the wall facing a generic electric stove, beneath the kind of old-style, wall-mounted plumbing fixtures that swing away in case you needed to bathe an infant or fill a canning pot. There was no dishwasher and no room for a dining room table, but one of the kitchen walls was a slider out to the elevated deck, which overlooked the vast, snow-blanketed backyard where, until Susan mistook them for weeds and overwintered dill and dug them up, a vast field of asparagus had thrived for decades.

One late evening, when we finally emerged after a whole week apart, Susan and I sat side by side at the counter, sipping a cheap Sangiovese so tannic that it made my teeth hurt. I eyed the small pine bookshelf above the sink: there was a tag-sale-tattered, hardcover copy of *Mastering the Art of French Cooking;* a kitschy, modern paean to 1950s suburban grilling called *Patio Daddy-O*; Maida Heatter's *New Book of Great Desserts*; a jacketless, book-club edition of Jean Anderson's *The Doubleday Cookbook*; *The Breakfast Book*, by Marion Cunningham, stuffed to overflowing with yellowing recipes clipped from ancient newspapers, and lovingly inscribed by Susan's ex, Jennifer, an artist who, once Susan confided that she'd met someone, had begun calling the house every Saturday night at eight o'clock sharp to *check in on us kids.* And there was a dog-eared, tiny paperback, top-stained edition of *The French Chef Cookbook*, by Julia Child, which I pulled down off the shelf and flipped through.

Susan had answered my posting because, she said, she was hoping to eventually get to the point in her life where love was something that made her feel good again, and not queasy, or at least not scared; her life with Jennifer had imploded under the weight of financial exhaustion and the sort of flailing, angry attacks on her self-confidence that always seem to bubble to the surface during the last, desperate days of a relationship. So Susan, a poster child for the kind of Yankee reserve that might be mistaken for diffidence, took solace and refuge in the deep, Zen-like serenity that cooking for oneself can, for some people, engender, as it does for me. Susan made food for herself that comforted and consoled, like Marion Cunningham's ethereal, yeasted waffles, and Maida Heatter's chocolate cookies. While I was home on East Fifty-Seventh Street, performing delicate surgery on a quail so I wouldn't choke on its needle-like bones, Susan, a mass of contradiction, was up in Connecticut, reading *Larousse* every night from cover to cover, while making macaroni and cheese with the odds and ends of Cheddar and Saint André, Velveeta and Wensleydale that sometimes went together and sometimes didn't, but that always solaced. Together and apart, in different states. We lived alone and took comfort in our kitchens.

But, for Susan, there was also Julia, and the M.F.K. Fisher that she read in the bathroom, and the stacked copies of *Saveur* that dated back to the magazine's first issue in 1994. Her sets of *Gourmet* were bound together in old navy-blue leatherette loose-leaf binders emblazoned on their spines with the magazine's name in fancy gilt script, and sat in her design studio, not far from a small, tattered upholstered chair. It was there where she'd take short afternoon breaks from designing books for various publishing houses in Manhattan; she'd make herself a pot of tea, take down a year or so of *Gourmet*, and read the work of Joseph Wechsberg pining for the sacher torte at Demels, or a then-unknown Annie Proulx's first published short story about garlic. With the exception of the *Larousse*, which she kept on her bedside table, everywhere I turned in Susan's tiny house were books about the goodness of simple food and life, as opposed to process and precision. And Julia Child, she said, was the first person in her life who made the almost carnal pleasures of the table more than just okay, but *acceptable*; growing up in a home where food was plentiful but considered fuel, Susan was enamored of it, and of her.

"Careful with that," Susan said, taking the paperback out of my hands. "It's my childhood cookbook."

"Your childhood cookbook was *The French Chef*?"

Susan nodded, and gingerly opened the book to page 309 and the stained recipe for sole mornay, where the spine had cracked thirty years earlier.

"One afternoon when I was fifteen, I was watching Julia on television after school," she explained. "I made my mind up to cook dinner for my parents, so they bought me the book. Sole mornay—this recipe," she added, tapping the page with her finger, "is what I decided on. It was the first time I'd ever cooked."

She closed the book wistfully, reached up, and put it back on the shelf. I was aghast.

As a child, the closest I'd ever come to cooking for my family was during the 1973 Christmas Eve ice storm, for my father's fiftieth birthday surprise party. With the roads iced over, the caterer couldn't make it down the street. I decided that our guests—mostly his office mates from the Manhattan advertising agency where he'd been creative director for over twenty years—had to do more than just drink the bucket loads of Johnny Walker they were downing while listening to Yma Sumac's bird calls on my father's teak Garrard high-fi. So I fished out every package of Italian and kosher salami that I could find buried in the recesses of my mother's harvest-gold refrigerator, asked her for the biggest platter she had, and proceeded to make what amounted to a three-foot-wide, interfaith meat mandala in the middle of which sat a small, yellow melamine bowl of deli mustard. This was my first unofficial catering gig, and it ended like so many of them did years later—with one of the drunken guests wearing a fez and playing the bongo drums.

A week later, my father rewarded my efforts by subversively squirreling me away for a four-course lunch together in Manhattan while my mother was off having her hair done.

"They're showing *The Red Balloon* at MoMA," he lied to her, when we dropped her off at Vidal Sassoon, where she'd just started to go after seeing Mia Farrow in *Rosemary's Baby*. But as soon as she disappeared through the revolving door, we drove uptown to First Avenue and Seventy-Third Street to the Praha Restaurant, where we ate massive plates of weighty Czech food—sweet-and-sour braised red cabbage; pan-fried spaetzle, and chicken stew with caraway seeds. For dessert, the white-jacketed waiter brought us apricot palacsinta—a paper-thin, sugar and hazelnut–dusted crêpe wrapped around warm apricot preserves mellowed with liqueur. We ended the meal with a small glass of explosively powerful slivovitz, which my father allowed me to taste, and which left me hacking and snorting like a midget-size fire-breathing dragon. Two hours later, we were back at the salon to pick up my mother.

My mother never knew about our hidden culinary outings; but she did make it clear, when she bought me one-size-too-small clothes, or hid my father's Mallomars, that she wanted neither a fat child nor a fat husband, and so my father carefully scanned my sweater for any stray crumbs that might give away our whereabouts.

"Cy," she said, climbing into our dark green Imperial, "did you remember to give her a snack? Fruit is always a nice idea."

+++

"But did you even know what sole mornay *was*?" I asked Susan, incredulous.

"I read the recipe—it just involved fillet of fish, which I knew my parents loved, and cheese, which I loved. So I put the two together, included Julia, and sole mornay seemed like the perfect choice."

By the time I was the age Susan was when she made the dish for her parents, I had already eaten more restaurant-prepared mornays than any child should. The very first time was in Los Angeles, at the Bantam Cock on La Cienega Boulevard while on a three-week summer jaunt with my parents. I was seven, pouty, and constitutionally annoyed, dressed in a frilly white-lace number with a big pink bow and white patent leather Mary Janes, and chronically exhausted because my mother—who was dressed in a similar white-lace jumpsuit that matched her bone-toned lipstick—thought that we should dine late, rather than get an early table like the rest of the tourists. The odds of seeing Hollywood's stars were greater if you weren't eating at six and going to bed at eight, so every night, at every restaurant, we sat down to dinner after eight, which was after eleven New York time. That night, three waiters brought our plates over, and on cue, lifted their silver covers, *et voila*, there was a very white fish, on a very white plate, covered in a very white, very gummy cheese sauce.

I stared at it and stuck out my tongue.

"It's *very* fancy," my father said under his breath, looking at me over the tops of his black plastic aviators, while my mother rolled her pike quenelle around on her plate, trying not to eat it.

"I don't want it," I replied—crossing my arms and yawning.

"Just try it, just once. You know *Aunt Sylvia's Rule*." He lowered his voice in a way that made me nervous.

My father's sister, a metaphysically pressed, ironed, and spit-shined woman, had a rule that we all adhered to: no matter what you were eating, or where you were, you had to try everything, just once. Of course, she'd conveniently forgotten that decree years later when we all took a trip to Turkey together and were faced with eating luke-warm red mullet that had sat, baking in the hot Mediterranean sun for hours, before our arrival at the restaurant. She wouldn't go near it.

That night, sitting in the semicircular, Naugahyde banquette at the Bantam Cock, staring down at the plate of pasty white sole mornay in front of me, I whimpered hard enough that my parents finally relented, called over the captain, and sent out for my favorite dish—onion rings—which arrived, courtesy of our neighbor at the next table, in a white corsage box with a note that said, "May you have all the onion rings your heart desires. Just *please* stop crying."

+++

"Did you ever make mornay again?"

"Never," Susan said. "There was nothing fancy in my house growing up. My father's idea of a perfect meal was a porterhouse slathered in butter, potatoes slathered in more butter, followed by cream puffs filled with chocolate ice cream, all washed down with a few cocktails. My mother was a dutiful 1950s housewife, and so whatever he loved is what my mother made, and what we ate."

"Every *night*?"

"Pretty much," Susan admitted, pouring us more wine.

I thought back to our dinners in Forest Hills—to the plain lamb chops that my mother would drizzle with Wesson oil and immolate in the broiler. Every. Single. Time. I remembered the large slabs of quivering beef liver that terrorized me, that my grandmother would unwrap while I shuddered nearby, the victim of a slew of old wives tales about liver making Jewish children strong. I thought back to the over-broiled, hockey-puckish hamburgers that my mother cooked until you could snap them in half like charcoal brickettes. True— every once in a while, mostly during the summer, my mother would try something new, like grapefruit dusted with sugar and broiled, a single maraschino cherry sitting in that little depression in its center. There were boneless, skinless chicken breasts rubbed with mild, bland curry powder and broiled until they could bounce. And fillet of sole dusted with paprika and broiled until it fell apart en route to the plate. My mother was very big on broiling.

But in Susan's childhood home, whatever her father loved to eat, he got. His wife was a blissful ignoramus treading water in the land of hypercholesterolemia and her husband's fast-clogging Widow Maker, and totally unaware of the fact that all those boiled, butter-drenched lobsters; all those simple, salt-crusted steaks coated in fat; all the baskets of double-fried French fries and the baked potatoes erupting like a sour cream–stuffed Vesuvius; all those edible, fat-laden manifestations of postwar American middle-class affluence—they all had to go somewhere.

On a beautiful Saturday afternoon in May 1973, just as the horses were lining up to run the Kentucky Derby, George Turner and his wife carried their brand-new, nine-foot flowered sofa in from the garage, where the delivery men had left it, into the family room, and minutes later, he was dead.

Susan was nineteen.

CHAPTER 7

Mother Sauces

I was a cheap date.

I didn't drink, and I didn't eat very much.

I didn't like sweets—not even ice cream—so I never ordered dessert, and I only rarely reached across the table with my fork to nibble on my father's.

Whatever he wanted me to try, I tried. Whenever he lowered his voice, I lowered mine. Whenever he implored me to ask the waiter about a dish I didn't understand, I asked, without shame. And if a waiter ever dared laugh at me—at the fact that I was a seven-year-old, trying to successfully pronounce coquilles St. Jacques or *le foie gras chaud aux pêches*—he would push himself away from the table and have a quiet chat with the captain, and the waiter would suddenly appear at the table again, apologetic and flushed with embarrassment.

Together, we spent secretive, languorous lunches at Le Grenouille and La Côte Basque and Le Perigord, and, until it closed in 1971, Le Pavillon, meals that were paid for on maxed-out credit cards and a household budget that was stretched tight as a rubber band. My father, who seditiously introduced me to haute cuisine right under the nose of my excruciatingly thin, gorgeous, weight-obsessed mother, was a natural teacher, and I worshipped him—even with his sometimes violent and unpredictable temper that would manifest itself in a crystal ashtray hurled across the living room, or a front door slammed so hard that the bell would ring spontaneously, or a very private, stinging slap across the face so hard and sudden that I'd find myself crumpled on my bedroom floor in a heap just for giggling at the wrong thing at the wrong time, or if he thought I'd laughed at him. But when we were alone together and dining in the softened lighting of Manhattan's finest restaurants, my father's focus was on two things: food and me.

It was not at all Nabokovian: my father worshipped food in all its guises and shapes, and promises of pleasure and safety. Growing up in Brooklyn, the only son of an Orthodox Jewish cantor who doled out regular corporal punishment for everything from talking during the family's four-hour, entirely-in-Hebrew Passover seder to mild bad-boy behavior at school, my father took refuge under the legs of his mother's baby grand piano, while she, a former concert pianist, practiced muted Debussy and Chopin études and mazurkas in the late Coney Island afternoons of the early 1930s. He lay there listening, on the thick, mustard-colored carpeting, his eyes closed in delicious ecstasy, noshing on the after-school snacks she made just for him: spiced Liptauer cheese on warm challah; white toast, its crusts removed with surgical precision, laden with creamy lemon curd; imported Norwegian sardines blended with farmer cheese; crispy-fried potato latkes with edges that crumbled like ancient yellowing lace, spread with English apple butter. Food was safety, and peace. And through my Romanian-born anglo-maniacal grandmother's sad attempts at surrounding herself with what she thought were the trappings of a fancy life—she filled her pantry with Tiptree Damson Plum and Little Scarlet Preserves, Droste's Chocolates, English mustards, and Heinz squeeze-bottle salad cream because she thought they wreaked of the British upper crust—my father learned that food could also be transformative. Wherever she shopped, from the height of the Depression on into my childhood, she bought the most expensive foods and clothes she could find in her immediate Brooklyn neighborhood, turning up her nose at anything she deemed beneath her standards. She believed, with every fiber of her being, that what she ate and what she wore, would define her and that her place in society—in a two-bedroom apartment less than a mile from the Coney Island parachute drop that she shared with her children and her cantor husband who spent his days writing the social page column for the Yiddish newspaper, *The Day*—was, in fact, a mistake that could be corrected.

"*Bilig*"—cheap—she'd say under her breath in Yiddish, scoffing at the Entenmann's cakes and cookies my mother would offer her for dessert after our family get-togethers. She'd turn on her stacked Ferragamo heels, close her eyes, tip up her chin, and toddle away.

+++

When my parents fought, I watched and listened closely, which didn't stop me from getting frequently roped in to the conflagrations like collateral damage. My tall, rail-thin, mother—constantly on any number of radical crash diets to keep her imaginary weight gain to a minimum—was terrified of food, and the memory of the weight she'd carried as a child, years before she became a popular television and cabaret singer in the late 1950s and then, a model. She found my father's devotion to and need for food repulsive. They despised each other's families: my father's mother hated my mother for being a fancy, skinny, gorgeous New Yorker and for redirecting her little boy's attention away from her. My mother's mother hated my father for being the child of a woman who put on airs, who'd wasted money on frivolity, like the clothes and foods that she was sure would elevate her out of her place in the world. And there, amid the chatter and the rage, and what the Buddhists call Monkey Mind—that unsettledness that comes with disappointment and the constant search for happiness—my father took solace in the hushed, elegant French dining rooms of the city. As sack-suited Presbyterian businessmen in fine gold wire-rim glasses and gold watches on grosgrain bands and English Lobb wingtips drank their lunches, and cads escorted ladies they claimed were their nieces, and as fathers taught their young daughters about the mother sauces—lessons they'd learned, perhaps, during the War, only thirty years earlier—order was commanded from the chaos of the kitchen and of life, and one could eat gloriously and gracefully, peacefully.

+++

When my mother left us together on late Saturday mornings while she spent a few hours at the beauty salon—and years later, when she went back to working as a Saturday afternoon fur-showroom model in the mid-1970s—my father and I always waited at least a half hour to make sure she wasn't coming back for anything, then got into the car, drove the seven miles into midtown Manhattan, and dined together subversively, under the radar, out of sight.

"Make sure to give her a snack around noon," my mother would say to my father as she'd leave the apartment, to which he would nod silently without looking up, and finish doing the *Times* crossword puzzle. An hour later, he and I would be sitting together, having that *snack* at Le Perigord or Lutèce. There, in the hushed glow of some of the finest dining rooms in the world, alone with my father, I ate my first escargot de Bourgogne and my first mille-feuille, my first foie gras and my first partridge; I learned how to use a *couteau à poisson*—a traditional French fish knife—and by the time I was nine, I knew the proper placement of a water goblet versus a sherry glass, and that when the table was cleared, it happened only after both diners were finished, and only from the left.

But my father was an egalitarian man. He was just as happy to wave goodbye to my mother as she grabbed her Vuitton tote and headed out for a touch-up and trim at Vidal Sassoon, load me into the Imperial and drive us to deepest Brooklyn, where we'd sit ourselves down at Brennan & Carr, next to firemen and cops on break, and order a trio of jus-drenched roast beef sandwiches that left my face and hands dripping with beefy goodness. Or we'd head to Randazzo's Clam Bar in the farthest reaches of Sheepshead Bay for platters of enormous baked clams, redolent of oregano and garlic and melted butter. If my mother's appointment was early and there was no time to sneak into Manhattan or Brooklyn and back before she returned, we'd end up at Ben's Best on Queens Boulevard, where my father introduced me to their specials platter: two immense, kosher beef franks with the girth of the transatlantic cable, nestled in a snood of sweetened baked beans. His taste in food ran the gamut from the sublime to the plebian. He could rattle off the mother sauces—béchamel, velouté, espagnole, hollandaise, tomato—without hesitation; he could eat an entire jar of *griebenes*—crispy rendered chicken skin and onions that is known in some circles as "Jewish crack" for its sheer addictiveness—while visiting his mother for lunch, and then have the *quenelle de brochet Lyonaisse* at Le Grenouille for dinner. He would take the dog out for a walk early on weekend mornings and come home with a can of Spam, which the dog assumed was for him, fry it up in thin rectangular slices, top it with a soft-boiled egg and a squeeze of the cheap black caviar that came in a tube, like toothpaste, and set the whole thing down on a pillowy, butter-laden croissant from Dumas on East Sixtieth Street. He'd sit me down at the breakfast counter, and hand me a knife and fork while my mother watched, orange melamine cup of Sanka in hand, convinced that I would be scarred for life.

But whenever he and I went out alone, and before we walked back through our front door, my father, who carried a pocket-size lint brush under his car seat, made sure to remove any telltale crumbs from the black velvet Scotch House blazer I'd always wear if we were going fancy, or the red knit poncho I'd put on if we weren't.

"Did you remember the snack?" my mother would ask him late in the afternoon, when we all met up again in the apartment.

"What do *you* think?" he'd snort, turning on the television and pouring himself a small Dewar's.

✝✝✝

Years later, after the divorce—after the magazine he launched failed, after the Summer of Sam, the blackout, the gas shortage, the garbage strike—when I was old enough to spend part of each August working for him in the small, industrial advertising agency he was running, my father was still given to culinary extremes, although lack of where-withal made our four-star binges far less frequent and our roughing it far rougher. No longer able to afford regular, multicourse affairs in French dining rooms covered in ruby dupioni-silk wallpaper, our dates found us lunching together at the dimly lit Irish dive across the street from his office on Second Avenue and Forty-Second Street, where we'd eat the special corned beef and cabbage entrée that had been floating for hours in a lukewarm chafing dish covered with a thin rime of grease. One afternoon, he took me to the Belmore Cafeteria—a dive made famous by *Taxi Driver*—where my stiff brown preppie Weejuns stuck to the linoleum floor, and the clatter of dishes was so loud that you had to shout to be heard. We sat among cabbies and bicycle messengers eating cheap plates of white toast and eggs and limp, half-cooked, fat-striped bacon. A gray-haired, wild-eyed woman in a moth-eaten, stained orange cardigan sat next to me, spooning seeping scoops of melting vanilla ice cream into her mouth painted like Caesar Romero's Joker in the *Batman* of my childhood, wide with fuchsia lipstick, her chin resting on her chest. When the woman saw me staring at her, unable to look away, she grabbed her water glass, reached over to our table and slammed it down violently between my father and me. The water exploded out of the glass, as if detonated by a small bomb, soaking our table, our plates of rubbery eggs and toast, our laps. And then she left.

My father looked around quickly, hot with embarrassment, while I pulled a wad of napkins out of the black metal dispenser and handed them to him.

"I'm so sorry," he said, his face red.

"It's okay, Dad," I told him, but he just shook his head *no*, over and over again.

What he never understood was that high food or low, Le Pavillon or the truck stop he had once taken me to on Long Island on the way home from visiting Aunt Sylvia, the *where* just didn't matter to me. I loved him, wherever we ate, and wherever we went. And because of him, I ate it all: the escargots and the Spam, the quenelles and the baked clams, the foie gras and the franks, the baked beans and the all-butter croissants from Dumas. And the *griebenes* that his mother spooned out of an old mayonnaise jar covered with wax paper held in place with a thick red rubber band that she kept in her Brooklyn kitchen sideboard so close to Coney Island, alongside a dizzying array of the fancy English foods that she was certain would propel her like a Lunar Launcher into another social class.

"Do me a favor," he whispered that day at the cafeteria. "Don't tell your mother about this."

"I won't," I promised him that afternoon. "I never do."

CHICKEN SKIN GRIEBENES

Traditionally made with the skin and fat procured from one's Friday night Shabbos soup chicken, *griebenes* are what you get when you render the fat and the skin together along with chopped onion. While the fat cooks away, it crisps the skin and onion to a papery caramel brown crunch so miraculous in its chicken-y goodness that it has been known to lure ancients from their death beds, and bring grown men to their knees. Packed with every stripe of cholesterol under the sun—bad, good, enough triglycerides to kill an army—it is a cardiac nightmare not unlike pork rinds and is so delicious that my father, while living in Canada, once bought a chicken in order to make it, and then threw away the chicken.

Makes about 2 cups

Skin from 1 large soup chicken (5 to 6 pounds)

1 medium onion, coarsely chopped

Salt and freshly ground black pepper

1. Slice the skin into narrow strips, and place it, along with the onion, in a large cast-iron skillet over medium heat. Cook slowly, stirring frequently, until the fat has been rendered away from the skin and the skin begins to crisp, about 30 minutes. If it looks like the skin is beginning to burn or the fat is starting to blacken, reduce the heat to medium-low.

2. Once all the fat has been rendered from the skin, increase the heat to medium-high and continue to cook until the onion and skin have turned a dark mahogany, about 20 minutes. Season with salt and pepper, and toss well.

3. Line a shallow bowl with paper towels. Using a slotted spoon, remove the griebenes to the prepared bowl to drain.

4. Store in a tightly-sealed glass jar under refrigeration for up to a week (they won't last that long).

CHAPTER 8

Calling

Susan's phone rang constantly, starting at eight A.M., from the time we came downstairs for breakfast every morning to the time we went to bed. Typically, it rang at two-hour intervals for the rest of the day, stopped between five and seven at night, than rang once more, at eight. Susan picked up all of them.

After a whole lovesick week apart, so early on in our relationship, we rightfully should have been sitting in our robes, cooing at each other, drinking our tea and coffee like lovebirds trapped in a Vaseline-lensed International Coffee commercial. But just as we sat down, the phone would ring, and Susan's mother would be on the other end, wanting to talk about her Christmas plans, even though the holiday was two weeks away. If she couldn't reach us—if we didn't, or couldn't answer, or were simply out of the house for longer than two hours—she would call Susan's next-door neighbor to check on us.

"Laurie," she'd ask sweetly, "could you be a dear and go outside, and make sure that Susan's car is in her driveway?" And unless Laurie put down the phone and did it that very instant, which, because Laurie's house was behind Susan's, entailed her having to put her coat, hat, gloves, and boots on, Susan's mother would keep calling her.

Some people plan months in advance for holiday celebrations. My cousin Lois, who possesses the organizational skills of Field Marshall Montgomery, once wrote out a ten-page, longhand letter containing detailed, day-by-day instructions for Peter and Ellen, who would be making Passover dinner that year. Every day, it was something else, like *make the matzo balls and freeze them*, or *roast the game hens and freeze them*, or *make the charoset and freeze it*, or *roast a shank bone and freeze it*. The idea being, of course, that when the big day rolled around, everything would be ready and all Peter and Ellen would have to do was defrost the food, warm it, and dinner would be on the table without fuss. But some people's brains simply aren't wired that way, and Peter and Ellen are two of those people. When the family arrived at their house, they were just starting to read the instructions on the matzo ball box and pulling the plastic wrap off the birds. It's not a comment on skill or talent or latent aggression; it's just the way Peter and Ellen—who often prefer the happy, frenetic bustle of a busy kitchen trying to crank dinner out with tons of family members milling around underfoot—are. And it's why I love them.

"Of *course* I'll make the clam dip," Susan would say when her mother called, tucking the phone under chin, picking up her mug, and walking into the guest room while I pretended to be interested in the local newspaper.

Clam dip? I just climbed out of bed with someone whose family eats clam dip on the most important holiday of the year? No tartan taffeta? No foie gras? What about goose?

"Fine," I heard her say. "A ham. I'll get a ham."

Silence.

And then, "Yes, mashed potatoes, and glazed carrots."

More silence.

"Mom, I don't really care if Nancy thinks that her skin will turn orange if she eats carrots."

Silence.

"Oh, for god's *sake*, Mom!"

And then the conversation was over and Susan was back at the counter right next to me, reading the paper from cover to cover, sports section first—until two hours later, when her mother would call back to say that a filet of beef was really a much better idea since ham could sometimes be tough and Et was having problems with her new bridge since it had been pulled out once already after attaching itself to a frozen Heath bar. Two hours after that, she'd call back again to ask if Susan needed help with her Christmas decorations, and if not, then when, exactly, was she planning on putting them up.

She'd driven by the other morning and seen nothing.

"It doesn't exactly look like Christmas at your place yet, does it?" she remarked to Susan, during call number three.

"She drove by to *check* on you?" I asked when she got off the phone. Susan sighed.

"Does she do this often?" I considered the expanse of our activities since we met, and the thought of an eighty-one-year-old woman skulking around the premises made me a little uneasy. Even if she *was* there to help.

"More than I'd like," Susan admitted. "We should just be relieved that she hasn't barged in on us."

"Wait a minute. Your mother would actually just let herself in, *unannounced*?"

"She would," Susan said. "If she couldn't get me on the phone for more than two hours, she'd just let herself right in."

And some months later, she did just that. On a late Sunday morning while we were sitting at the counter in our robes, me mindlessly running my hand up and down Susan's back while reading the paper and sipping my coffee, the slider out to the deck creaked open, and in walked Helen Turner, in her 1958 Persian lamb coat with the three-quarter sleeves, gripping her purse, and pursing her lips.

"You didn't answer the phone," she cried, her bottom lip quivering, "so I thought you were *dead*."

"Why didn't you leave a message?" Susan asked, spinning around on her counter stool while I sat there, stock still.

"Because I couldn't understand what the man wanted me to do!"

"What *man*?"

"The phone man. You know, silly, the *man* who says, 'Please leave a message.' I couldn't figure out if he wanted me to talk before the beep, or during the beep, or after the beep. And I couldn't wait because I knew you were dead—kidnapped. In a ditch, somewhere."

"No, Mom," Susan groaned, taking a sip of her Lapsang souchong. "Not dead. Just having breakfast. Want some tea?"

But when Helen called to talk to Susan about Christmas, she wasn't exactly calling about *Christmas*. Susan is a procrastinator of Olympic proportion—she once took down her holiday lights in April—and when her mother wanted to know whether or not her adult, forty-something child had accomplished a task that she knew, full well, hadn't been done, it wasn't a question. It was code for *You never invite me to the house anymore. And I would like to know whyever not.*

Neither Susan nor I had mentioned the fact of each other to our parents. We weren't kids, and neither of us felt the need to. I wasn't ready to share the news that I had met someone who exhibited all the qualities I'd been looking for for nearly a decade: Susan loved food and the act of cooking for others almost as much as I did. She had been a charter subscriber to *Saveur*, and had piles of the magazine sitting virtually everywhere, from the bathroom to the guest room to the den. She could talk in vivid detail about an early article on Old Stoves—the Italian men and women who cook homestyle food in San Francisco's North Beach—and remembered that Peggy Knickerbocker had written it. She read *The Gastronomical Me* in the bathroom, and she wept, in the early days of her breakup with Jennifer, over Jane Kenyon's poetry while drinking her morning tea, alone. She was besotted with old, badly battered cookware to the point that she hadn't bought so much as a new skillet in years. She was tall and thin and looked, in a certain light, like Jean Seberg, with a thick, short crop of prematurely steel-gray hair that had turned silvery black while she was in her twenties. And she had the greenest eyes I'd ever seen.

On Susan's side, she wasn't quite ready to share the news that she had met a Jewish New Yorker who came with a complete set of carbon-steel Sabatier knives, six French copper pudding molds, a profound affection for vertical food, and a small collection of leopard-print pumps from Barneys.

It wasn't so much that I was a New Yorker, or Jewish, although Susan did assure me that her mother and pile of Polish aunts did not come without their prejudices. It was just that I was a foreigner, an out-of-towner, which translated, simply, to *not a member of the family.*

A few years after we got together, during a late-spring afternoon on the deck, rife with pollen and bottomless vodka tonics served in tall Tom Collins glasses, Auntie Et—who waited until no one else was around to hear—said to me out of the blue, "The problem with *you* is that we all thought you were going to take our Susan away from us."

The statement, which I still sometimes struggle to parse, made me reel a little bit, and when Et said it to me, I could feel the hair on the back of my neck go straight up. Clearly, she had been thinking about this for a while, this *problem with me.*

"But that wasn't exactly *my* problem," I responded politely, sipping my drink.

Et flushed a deep crimson and looked out toward the backyard, where Susan and her mother were bent over in the garden, pulling weeds.

"I know it," she mumbled under her breath. This was her stock response, meaning *change the subject, since I'm not going to win this.* She never brought up *my problem* ever again.

✢✢✢

Susan and I felt proprietary about each other, and our relationship. We wanted to hang on to that sharp little sliver of time when things are very new, when we spent our days in and out of bed, sitting in the living room between stacks of cookbooks and ancient food magazines, pondering stories and the recipes we wanted to try, talking about cooking projects that we had begun in earnest and then walked away from because we either got bored or the projects failed. She had a small brioche fixation before we met, and spent weeks perfecting a recipe; I had devoted the entire autumn before we met to experimenting with homemade duck confit for the cassoulet that I would eat by myself, every night, for two weeks until my arteries began to clog like a stuffed drain. I committed to my brain every one of the light freckles that dotted her nose, and the childlike way in which she held her knife and fork, and how she beat an egg and buttered her toast to perfection, dragging a small pâté knife from an ancient silver service that Et had passed along to her all the way to the edges of the crust so that every yeasty crater and crevasse would be filled with melting butter. I memorized the way she barked her laughter, so that when we spent our long weeks apart—me in New York, she in rural Connecticut—I could close my eyes and hear her voice. It was just the two of us, and we didn't want to share it with anyone.

But on a rainy, cold Saturday evening before Christmas, we were sitting on the couch with the dog between us, sipping rye Manhattans out of her father's favorite etched old-fashioned glasses, and nibbling on a wedge of Maytag Blue I'd brought up from the city when she suddenly turned to me.

"I have to drop something off tomorrow at my mother's. Will you come with me?"

"Of course," I agreed, although I knew that that Sunday was going to throw our tightly patterned weekend off kilter. Since the first time I'd come up to her house, our Sundays had remained the same: we got up late, made coffee and tea, read the paper in silence, went on a hike in the snow with the dog, drove into town to go to Skee's—a grubby boxcar diner whose short-order cook made remarkable griddle-roasted potatoes, onions, and eggs—got back into bed for a few hours, and then went back to the train station in Hartford, where we said goodbye. Every week. Rinse and repeat.

And now, I was meeting her mother.

SKEE'S MASH

Deep in the middle of Torrington, Connecticut—a gritty, former industrial town a few miles from Susan's house, whose thriving infrastructure died when Eisenhower took office—sat a tiny boxcar diner comprising six stools and one wooden booth. It was owned by a dirt-under-his-fingernails-type man named Skee who stood at the griddle every weekend morning and produced all manner of breakfast wonders—feather-light pancakes, gorgeous mozzarella-filled omelettes. He was known in Susan's house for producing something we called "mash" rather than "hash," for the manner in which it was pulverized to a crispy, griddled, unrecognizable pancake of love. It was composed of leftover bits he had kicking around—sweet peppers, potatoes, bacon, ham, corned beef—tossed together and crunched under a grill press. Topped with a couple of poached eggs, there was no better way to greet a snowy weekend.

Serves 2

1 tablespoon grapeseed oil or safflower oil

½ cup chopped onion

¼ cup diced jalapeño chile

¾ cup peeled and diced waxy potatoes

½ cup diced green bell peppers

½ cup crumbled, cooked bacon (or cubed ham or chopped corned beef)

Salt and freshly ground black pepper

2 poached eggs (see page 113)

continued

1. In a large cast-iron skillet set over medium heat, warm the oil until it shimmers, and add the onion. Cook for 5 minutes, stirring constantly, and add the chile. Continue to cook until both have softened, 5 to 7 minutes.

2. Add the potatoes to the pan, tossing well, and cook until they begin to brown, about 8 minutes; use a sharp spatula to scoop up and turn any potatoes that stick. Add the bell pepper and bacon, and continue cooking until the vegetables are completely soft, pressing and turning the mixture with your spatula so that it browns and crisps and begins to resemble a pancake. Season with salt and pepper.

3. Using the spatula, slice the pancake in half, slide one half on each of two small breakfast plates, and top each with a poached egg.

4. Serve immediately.

CHAPTER 9

The Family Baby

She had been the beauty, the one with the chiseled features and the thick blonde hair, and the cheekbones to die for. In her engagement picture, which hung on Susan's hallway wall, she wore a string of pearls and a broad-collared, nubby Donegal tweed jacket, her hair pulled tightly back off her face, her glimmering, cool blue eyes looking away from the camera. It is wartime, and her fiancé, Joseph, is a Marine, fighting in France. The youngest child of eleven, she will be the last one to marry, but that won't be for a while. Joseph, she finds out soon enough, has met a woman in Paris, and like many other men who went to fight overseas, his plans have changed.

I imagine Helen weeping in disbelief when she gets the letter from him, and holding the rough, calloused working hands of her mother, Valentina, a subsistence farmer. Valentina knew her own heartache when her husband died young, after a short lifetime inhaling metal shards as a grinder working at the local axe factory, leaving Valentina, in 1921, alone with eleven children. Susan's mother never trusted anyone or anything ever again after Joseph. And she had breakdown after breakdown.

"It wasn't Joseph, though," Susan tells me, taking my hand. "Not really."

"What happened?" We're walking the dog along the Farmington River bike path on a freezing Saturday afternoon, before driving the mile or so over to Helen's house to drop off the family recipe box Helen's been searching for. Susan discovered the box in her crawl space, amid piles of ancient, yellowing, musty issues of *Good Housekeeping* that haven't been opened for years.

"She and Auntie Et and Uncle Jack got stuck in the Holland Tunnel one day in the late 1940s. There was an explosion—a fire—and my mother jumped out and ran toward the exit. A week later, she was hospitalized for the first time."

I am quiet, and I look straight ahead as we walk, pulling my jacket collar up around my neck. This is murky territory for a new relationship, and I can tell that Susan is uncomfortable.

"You should know—because she can be completely unpredictable."

"Great," I replied. "So exactly what am I in for?"

+++

Helen greeted us at the door of her pristine, white Colonial, dressed in black velvet trousers, fake-amethyst-encrusted purple wool flats, and a lime-green sweater so heavy with spangles that she looked like she was wearing chain mail. At eighty-two, her white-silver hair was cut in a neat pageboy with not one strand out of place except for a tiny, inch-long, rubber-banded ponytail that gathered a few stray locks together near her forehead, like a small whale spout. It made it hard to look at anything else, in the way it's hard to smile back at someone with a pierced tongue.

I smiled and introduced myself while she stared at me and chewed on her lower lip. I held my hand out, but she backed up into the living room and floated away, like a ghost.

"Will you take a drink?" she asked, turning around in the living room and looking me up and down, unsmiling.

"It appears I'd better," I said.

She walked over to the bar and mixed me a tumbler-size vodka tonic, with two and a half shots poured by her shaking, permanently clenched right hand. She thrust it at me, and walked away.

"Come into the kitchen," she instructed Susan. I plunked myself down into a bright yellow, velvet barrel chair, MacGillicuddy at my feet. I could smell the pungent, gassy combination of cooking cabbage and percolating coffee coming from the next room. I sipped my drink and looked around the darkened room at the piano in the corner, covered with family photos and an assortment of tabletop Christmas trees fashioned from tortured wire hangers wrapped in multicolored tinsel, like a child's bicycle handlebars; a tall, voluptuously healthy spider plant sat on a stand in front of a south-facing window, and much of the furniture—two turquoise club chairs and a matching sofa—was tattered and worn. The artwork, primarily of the black-velvet spaniels-playing-poker variety, spoke of a disconnected whimsy, like it was bought by a happier Helen at another time. The place was eerily quiet and immaculate, like every single day of this woman's life since her husband died of a massive heart attack in the adjoining den had been spent cleaning, cleaning, and cleaning again. There were no lights on that didn't need to be on. There was no music, and no stereo in sight. This was the home of a woman who was used to being uncomfortable, and without pleasure, for a long, long time.

"Elissa, can you come in here please?" Helen called from the kitchen. "I have a question to ask you."

"Sure thing," I said lightly. "Can I help you with something?"

I like older people, and generally, they like me. Even the tight-ass, persnickety ones tend to loosen up the minute I ask for a family recipe, or swoon over their turtle-and-jellyfish soup. I was positive that I'd have Helen singing like a canary about her meat loaf in no time flat.

The three of us stood in a huddle in front of the kitchen sink, under the shocking glare of a ceiling light so bright that I started to feel like Dustin Hoffman in *Marathon Man*. Helen had a pen and a small red spiral notebook in her hand.

"I understand that Susan is going to be staying at your house in Manhattan one night this week. Is this correct?"

Susan seemed very far away, like her hearing had suddenly failed, or she had just somehow, mysteriously, forgotten how to speak English.

"What?" I asked, unaccustomed to being grilled like this. At least not since I was thirteen.

"Jeepers. It's not like I am hard to understand, am I?" Helen barked, chewing on her lower lip and feeling for her whale spout with her shaking, clenched fist. "*Is. Susan. Staying. With. You. One. Night. This. Week*. She said she was."

My mouth went dry. I was stunned, in the way I used to be when the mother of one of my school friends reprimanded me, right before I put my hands on my hips and said, "You're not the boss of me."

"She is," I responded, matter-of-factly. "Is there a problem with that?" I looked over her hunched, chain-mailed shoulder to the harvest-gold refrigerator behind her, and to the blond, blue-eyed rendering of a Ted Neely–esque Jesus hanging on its door, held in place with a plastic magnet fashioned in the shape of a daisy.

Helen chuckled dangerously, unsmiling. She gazed out the kitchen window at the partially snow-covered gnome sitting at the edge of the garden. All that was showing was the point at the top of his hat.

"Yes. There's a problem," she said coldly, turning back to face me. "I don't have your phone number."

I stepped back, surprised, like I'd been hit with a bullet. I looked at Susan, who was having an out-of-body experience and hovering around the planet Krypton.

Look, lady, I imagined myself saying. *I'm from Queens, so don't fuck with me. I don't know who the hell you think you're talking to, but you can reach your daughter—your adult daughter, who hasn't lived at home since Gerald Ford was vice president—on her cell phone. I will give you my number when and if I deem it necessary. And right now, it's not.*

"You DO have a phone number. Don't you?"

"I do," I replied quietly. And I gave it to her.

"Good," Helen said, clicking her Bic ballpoint shut, stuffing the pen into the spiral binding, and setting the notebook down in front of the toaster.

"*Now*," she continued, "we can eat. Susan says you eat pork even though you're a Jew. Why is that? Most Jews I know never eat pork, unless it's in Chinese food, which has always confused me. Susan's friend Donny—we went to his Bar Mitzvah in 1968 and good GOD that was a long affair and I kept saying to my husband *when on earth do you think he's going to stop nattering on like a space alien and say something we actually understand*—he never ate pork unless he went to a Chinese restaurant and then his mother said it was okay. Remember that, honey? I want you both to sit down and have a nice bowl of my stuffed cabbage. I made it this morning."

She turned her back on me to take the lid off the pot while I stood there, teetering back and forth on the balls of my feet, like a Weeble who had just been hit by the nasty truck driven ninety miles an hour by Eva Braun.

"Sit," Susan mouthed to me, pulling out the Hitchcock chairs at her mother's round kitchen table, under the gaze of an almost life-size kitchen crucifix. We sat down to a late lunch of sweet-and-sour *galumpki*—Polish cabbage rolls filled with ground pork and beef and braised in a pungent tomato sauce studded with raisins. They were fall-apart tender, and we silently mopped up the sauce with slices of untoasted, spongy white potato bread, its crust as wide and brown as masking tape. When I asked for a second helping, Helen picked up my yellow-flowered Corelle-ware bowl and took it back to the pot. She seemed pleased, and curtly cocked her head to the side in acknowledgment, like a parrot.

"I'm *so* happy you like them," she cooed. "I know they're not fancy, but—Susan tells me you know about food."

I just smiled.

GALUMPKI (A.K.A. STUFFED CABBAGE)

It was the icebreaker—the way into the heart of an older woman who didn't quite know what to make of her daughter's Jewish New Yorker "friend," namely, me. I was and am an experienced stuffed cabbage maker and eater, but the bowl of *galumpki* that Helen Turner set down before me that fateful winter afternoon paved the way for a relationship that, while not always beautiful, has always proven to be delicious. This dish, which can be easily made with ground beef, chicken, pork, or a combination of any of those meats, is worth the time it takes to prepare them; they're delicious served immediately but even better after an overnight in the fridge, or a month in the freezer.

Serves 6

1 medium onion, diced

½ teaspoon sweet paprika

1 pound ground pork

1 pound ground beef

2 tablespoons long-grain rice

1 tablespoon freshly squeezed lemon juice

1 large head green cabbage

½ cup red wine vinegar

½ cup sugar

One 28-ounce can crushed San Marzano tomatoes

1 cup golden raisins

Salt and freshly ground black pepper

Thick-sliced crusty bread or steamed rice, for accompaniment

1. Fill a large stockpot with water, cover, and bring it to a boil over high heat.

2. Place the onion in a large saucepan and cover with water by 2 inches. Sprinkle in the paprika and bring to a very low simmer over low heat, uncovered.

3. In a large bowl, combine the pork, beef, rice, and lemon juice and blend well; set aside.

4. When the water in the stockpot has come to a boil, add the entire head of cabbage, cover, and boil for 10 minutes until the outer leaves are pliable. Remove, let cool on a platter, and pull the leaves off, flattening them as you go (take care not to tear them).

5. Add the vinegar, sugar, and half of the tomatoes to the pot with the onion, stir, and bring to a simmer over medium-low heat.

6. Place ¼ cup of the meat mixture in the middle of each cabbage leaf and roll them up, tucking in the ends as you go. Repeat until all of the meat mixture is used.

7. Using a large serving spoon, carefully settle the stuffed cabbages into the simmering onion mixture, seam-side down. Pour the tomatoes over the cabbage rolls and add the raisins. Increase the heat to medium-high, bring to a boil, cover, and cook for 10 minutes. Decrease the heat to a simmer and continue to cook over medium-low heat for 2 hours. Taste and season with salt and pepper.

8. Serve the *galumpki* in shallow soup bowls with thick slices of crusty bread, or on a bed of steamed rice.

CHAPTER 10

Arnaud

"Every lady should carry a hanky in her purse," Gaga, my mother's mother, once told me when I was four. I was on my way to a family event at the time—a Bar Mitzvah or a wedding—when she presented me with a tiny white-and-pink ruffled bag that matched my dress, and looked like a miniscule version of those round, French wire salad spinners, only made out of the kind of crinkly crinoline polyester fabric that every parent prays nobody backs into with a lit cigarette.

My grandmother knelt down, opened up the purse as it dangled off my tiny arm, and placed a nickel and a neatly ironed and folded handkerchief embroidered with the letter E, in pink, flowery script in it.

"Just in case," she said. "You never know when you'll need some mad money, or to dab something."

Four-year-olds do not generally need mad money, or to dab something. But the phrase "every lady should have" stuck in my mind like glue, and for years after, and even now, I've used it to rationalize purchases, and even some relationships. Every lady should have a black Armani suit for fancy cocktail parties and the funerals of rich people. Every lady should have one seriously good pair of black pumps, even if she wears heels only once a year and at great risk of breaking a hip. Every lady should own and know how to use an eyelash curler. Every lady should have a great colorist. Every lady should get used to the idea of a bikini wax.

And every lady should have an overpriced, libidinous French butcher named Arnaud, who came to New York straight from Toulouse.

+++

After Julie and I broke up and I moved uptown from Chelsea to Fifty-Seventh Street, it took me a while to find Arnaud. There are virtually no grocery stores in that particular stretch of Manhattan—it's mostly office buildings and restaurants, and, around the corner, the Fifty-Eighth Street entrance to Bloomingdale's. So after a few months of dragging myself to the Upper West Side for weekly shopping trips to Fairway and Zabar's, where I would cab home carrying overstuffed bags filled with mesh pouches of lentils du Puy, oozing rounds of odorous Explorateur, semi-boned quail, and prime filet mignons individually wrapped so that I could freeze them safely, I went out looking for food shops in my own neighborhood. One glorious spring Saturday afternoon when I was neither giving nor going to a dinner party that night, I strolled over to First Avenue and headed south, past the bodegas and the wine shops and the Ray's Pizza places—each one claiming to be the *real* Ray's. I meandered along until I came to one block that had, on the east side of the street, a fishmonger, and on the west side, a tiny butcher shop no larger than fifteen feet deep, and maybe nine feet wide. I peered through the window, and there he was behind the counter: Arnaud.

Looking like a taller, younger version of Mr. Magoo, Arnaud, who couldn't have been more than forty-five, wore perfectly round French horn-rimmed glasses smudged with meat juice; the white apron that was tied around his tiny, protruding French belly was splattered with fat and sinew and dried blood, the bottom of his Levi's were shredded and dragging on the ground over his black, scuffed clogs, and his thick butcher's hands gave way to a set of short stubby fingers that looked like flesh-toned thimbles. Still wearing his thinning, silvery russet hair in an English schoolboy style that made it casually and seductively fall in his face every time he bent his head down toward the meat he was cutting, Arnaud, I would learn, attracted every culinarily minded woman and man in midtown Manhattan. Gay, straight, old, young—it made no difference; the only thing that Arnaud required of his customers was an unabashed love of and dedication to very high-end meat, and to pleasure. An open wallet and an American Express Platinum Card helped.

That first day, when he noticed me staring at him through his front window and beckoned me to come in, I'd had no plans to cook dinner that night. But I was hooked, sucked in by a French culinary vacuum that would not let me leave until I introduced myself and impressed him like a moronic tourist trying to order in French, by buying something *different* and uniquely un-American. Something that would show him that I was a serious cook and not like other knuckle-dragging Neanderthals who shopped at ordinary grocery stores. It would be something he approved of. Assuming he knew what it was.

I was cool.

"Do you have *culotte d'agneau*?" I asked.

"Of course I do," he responded matter-of-factly, a slow smile creeping across his face. "How many?"

With the exception of long-cooked leg, I rarely made lamb in my kitchen at home because I'd wind up setting off every smoke alarm in every apartment on the sixth floor of my building and it would take my neighbor at the end of the hall hours to get her two Papillons to stop screeching at the top of their lungs.

"Just one, please."

"One? So, this must be a hot date that you are having?" he mused, the corner of his mouth curling up in Gallic mockery.

I blushed, shook my head *no*, and looked down.

"Ah, so this is *my test*, then," he said, waving his finger at me across the counter and then pushing his glasses back up on his nose. He reached into the case and pulled out a garnet red, baby leg of lamb, turned on his band saw, and cut me one thick, round slice from the top of the shank, its femur intact, a thin, bright white round of fat circling its edges. He put it on a sheet of butcher paper, came out from behind the counter, and showed it to me.

"Will this do?" he asked.

It was gorgeous, and the most perfect specimen of this traditional French cut I'd ever seen in New York.

"It will," I said, pulling my wallet out of my bag. "How much do I owe you?"

"No," Arnaud replied, smiling, and looking me square in the eye. I could feel my face growing hot. "Too fast. First, tell me exactly what you're going to do with it."

My knees turned to gelatin.

"You're kidding, right?"

Arnaud's face went stern.

"Madame," he barked, "if I am going to cut a piece of meat for you that is *this* good, I would like to know how it is going to meet the end of its life."

"But it already has!"

"No, madame," he said. "It has *not*. People come in here, buy excellent cuts from me, and then take them home and make what you call—cube steak—by pounding the *ell* out of them with a metal mallet. So, I would like to know: what exactly are you going to do with *eet*?"

I was on the spot.

"I thought I would sear it in some olive oil, and then maybe braise it quickly in red wine with some chanterelles I bought yesterday at Fairway."

For thirty dollars a pound, big boy, so I'm not frightened of you, I thought.

"You rich New Yorkers are all so *reedeeculous*," he said, shaking his head.

"I'm so *not* rich," I said defensively, actually starting to choke on my words. I felt like I was going to cry. I was taking this personally, the way I used to take it personally when Parisians gave me wrong directions on the Metro. I may not have been starving, but I was certainly not rich.

"You take a perfectly *deeleecious* piece of meat—an *expensive* piece of meat—and you all overdo. You all go overboard." He was actually shouting at me.

"It's like a woman with too much perfume. More is not better, you know—it's just more. It *steenks*."

"Okay, *okay*," I implored. "So what do you suggest I do?"

"Let it come to room temperature, slowly. Drizzle it with olive oil on both sides and some nice sea salt—"

I stopped him, holding my hand up and shaking my head.

"I am *not* salting meat before it comes to room temperature. I'll wind up with shoe leather," I said, expressing my voluminous knowledge of meat cookery, obtained from exactly one semester at cooking school that taught me never, ever to salt meat ahead of time, lest its juices be leached out all over the cutting board before it ever hit the pan.

"You're going to argue with me? You do it my way this time. If you don't like it, I'll give you your money back, okay?" he bellowed, gesticulating madly. We were standing nose to nose.

"*Okay*—okay," I said. "Just *stop yelling at me!*"

"You sprinkle it with some herbes de Provence and some nice sea salt while it's resting—that will get the juices flowing. Then open up your windows, turn on a fan, and place it in a very hot, very dry cast-iron pan for a few minutes on one side, and a minute or so on the other. Take it out and let it rest for ten minutes or so. Maybe more."

"It'll be cold."

"No, it won't. It will be warm, not hot. And it will be happy."

"And so will you, I suppose," I said, rolling my eyes.

"*Oui*, madame." *Oui* came out like a soft woof from a dying dog.

And then he charged me twenty-eight bucks. For one slice of the hip end of a leg of lamb.

It was the best, juiciest, sweetest, most succulent *culotte d'agneau* I'd ever eaten.

✢✢✢

Over the years, Arnaud and I developed the sort of relationship that every food person dreams about, making me feel like I lived in a small French village instead of an American city of nine million. He instinctively knew what I would like and what I wouldn't. Even if I walked into his shop in a sour mood, I walked out feeling at peace. If I was mystified about what to serve at a dinner party where some of my guests ate meat and some of them didn't, he warned me never to apologize; just to prepare at least one thing that everyone could eat. One day when I showed up at the store with a horrible cold, my hair unwashed, and wearing a rumpled college sweatshirt, he pulled me into the back near his walk-in, asked his assistant to take over the counter service, heated up some red wine in a saucepan on a hotplate, and made me drink it out of his grubby coffee mug. I felt like a human being again when I walked out, filet in hand. Drunk and poor, but human.

I loved this man like I had not loved a man in years. He was French, and dripping with Gallic self-assurance. We had a wildly sensuous, heart-pounding, knee-weakening, totally nonsexual relationship that revolved solely around food, and he loved to play a game with me: I'd ask for a specific cut, and he'd guess what I was going to do with it. Like the veal breast with the pocket (stuffed with dried fruit, sewn back together with a carpet needle, and braised in Banyuls). Or the leg of lamb with the shank bone in place, but the pelvic bones removed (roasted slowly, for seven hours, and served with pommes Anna). Or the boned-out duck (a ballotine). Or the half pork loin opened up like a jelly roll, its skin intact (porchetta, its skin scored with a carpet knife that I'd purchased the same day as the carpet needle). Or the two lobes of foie gras and the prime filet mignons—tournedos Rossini. It took a while for us to realize that whenever we did this, there were always other customers in his shop, or his phone was ringing. But when we talked about food, Arnaud developed tunnel vision, the way men do when they're having sex.

"So what have you cooked for her?" Arnaud asked inquisitively, one Wednesday evening when I dropped by after work for a poussin. We hadn't seen much of each other since Susan and I were spending our weekends together; instead I was limiting my purchases to week-night cuts that would cook quickly, like this tiny bird that I'd split up the backbone, rub with fifty-dollar-an-ounce fennel pollen and sea salt, and shove under the broiler until its skin crackled and puffed away from the meat, turning papery-crisp and golden. I'd eat it at room temperature with my fingers, over some wilted baby arugula, with a squeeze of lemon.

"We've been having a lot of cheese," I replied, grinning idiotically, the heat rising from my face as I handed him my credit card.

"So am I saving a brace of pheasant for you for Christmas again?" he asked, changing the subject.

"I don't think so, Arnaud; I'm not sure I'll be in town this year—at least I'm hoping not."

"You could bring them with you." He grinned sheepishly, reaching into the case and pulling out a magnificent game bird, its skin pearl white, its flesh the color of a light pink rose.

He put the pheasant back into the case when I shook my head *no*.

"So you haven't actually *cooked* for her?" He stepped back from the counter and over to the ancient butcher block that he'd turned into a stand for his register, and he stared at me gravely, through his per-fectly round, meat juiced–smudged horn rims.

"I haven't, Arnaud."

"What are you *worried* about?" he asked solemnly. I just looked down at my feet, like a child.

The only sound was the oddly comforting, vibrating scream of the band saw in the back room, and his assistant breaking down a side of beef.

I realized that we had spent so many weekends nibbling on strange cheese and walking the dog, and listening to music, and talking, and sleeping, and not sleeping, and driving to and from the train station in Hartford, that, really, I hadn't cooked a single proper meal for her. We might have had toast and tea in the morning, but other than that, we were noshing and picking like scavengers, never actually cooking and sitting down to dinner. It had been a few weeks, and I hadn't even been to her local grocery store yet. And deep down, I *was* worried that I'd be a disappointment. I could just see it on her face and imagined the scene:

Serious cook, my ass, she'd think, as the Harwinton volunteer firemen extinguished the immolated duck I'd superciliously tried to roast in her little Magic Chef stove, small globules of exploded, incinerated duck fat schmaltz stuck to the sides of the oven.

"Come back on Friday at lunch," Arnaud said. "I'll cut some *braci-ole* for you to bring up there. Stuff it and braise it for hours while you do other things. It will cook itself; I promise you. Okay? No worries. She'll love it."

"Okay," I said. "Thank you, Arnaud. See you then."

He came out from behind the counter and gave me a gentle bear hug as another female customer came in and pretended to stare into the meat case.

"Just friends." I smiled at her, taking my poussin and leaving.

FENNEL-ROASTED POUSSIN

Quick-cooking, succulent, and perfect for a single girl living in a small apartment with a small kitchen, poussins are baby chickens that are no more than twenty-eight days old. (In the United States, it's easier to find Rock Cornish hens, which are twice as old and twice as cheap.) Give them a gentle pat-down with a bit of fragrant, earthy fennel pollen (a gentle pat-down is all you'll be able to afford, unless you're rich as Croesus; fennel pollen—the pollen extracted from the plant that grows wild all over Tuscany—costs a small fortune), a drop of good olive oil, a bit of salt, and some lemon and you'll have a luscious, light dinner in almost no time. If you have access to a live-fire grill, take advantage of it and cook the birds, skin-side down, over indirect heat.

Serves 1

1 butterflied poussin (backbone snipped out with shears, breast flattened)

1 tablespoon extra-virgin olive oil

½ teaspoon wild fennel pollen

½ teaspoon kosher salt

Pinch of red pepper flakes

Wedge of lemon

Fresh arugula, for accompaniment

1. Preheat the broiler to medium-high.

2. Place the poussin on a plastic cutting board, and rub all over with the olive oil, carefully getting under the skin without tearing it if possible. Massage the bird on both sides with the fennel pollen and salt, and scrunch the red pepper flakes over the breast between your fingers.

3. Place the bird in a cast-iron pan or in your oven's broiling pan, and broil approximately 6 inches below the heating element, breast-side up, until golden brown and blistered, about 8 minutes. (Check the bird every few minutes to make sure it's not burning.)

4. Turn the bird over and continue to cook until an instant-read thermometer inserted into the thigh reads 160°F, another 5 minutes.

5. Remove to a plate, tent loosely with aluminum foil, and let rest for 8 minutes before drizzling it with lemon juice.

6. Serve it warm atop a pile of fresh arugula.

CHAPTER 11

Cast-Iron Stomach

Nobody ever went in through the front door at Auntie Et's house.

An original 1919 Sears Roebuck bungalow with a deep porch and built-in, leaded glass–fronted cabinets lining every wall of the house, it faced Main Street in Unionville, Connecticut, standing equidistant from St. Mary's Church and Ahern's Funeral Parlor.

"They won't have far to go when they carry me out," Et would say, laughing until she coughed so hard that her face would go cherry red against her snow-white hair, which she wore blunt cut and almost to her shoulders, even in her nineties. She'd cough and she'd cough, and then she'd choke, and then she'd have to take her teeth out, and it never really mattered much where she was, or who she was with. Laugh, cough, choke, and out they'd come, right into her purse.

The back entrance to Et's house, which involved a precarious climb up three spectacularly steep, wobbly wooden steps, dumped you right into her linoleum-tiled kitchen, with its tiny table big enough for two, its disintegrating palm cross from Easter 1978 taped to the wall, its free-standing fridge covered with pictures and ages-old, yellowing Christmas cards from friends and neighbors, and a slightly grimy white range, upon which stood, in perpetuity, an ancient aluminum soup pot, dinged with age, and filled with a watery stew that she had made days before and left unrefrigerated. Because, in Susan's family, everyone believed—firmly, the way you'd believe in the laws of gravity, or the sun rising and setting every day, or the sky being blue—that if food is cooked, it's cooked, and therefore, it's safe. Refrigerator or no refrigerator.

So when we woke up on Saturday morning, took the dog out, and came back to find that Et had called and left a message saying that Susan was expected at her house for an early holiday supper because she'd *made chicken stew last week* and she knew how very much Susan *loved her chicken stew,* we stood together, side by side in Susan's office, staring at the answering machine.

"Is she serious? She made this stuff last week?" I asked Susan, expecting her to say *don't worry, I'll call her back and beg off.*

"She's serious—I totally forgot."

"Wait—we're actually *going*? But I brought up *braciole* from Arnaud," I said, pouting.

"I know, I know, but if we don't go, I'll never hear the end of it."

"But I have to leave at four tomorrow to get back to the city," I said, pouting harder, and reminding her that I had a business trip to Los Angeles with a flight scheduled for the crack of dawn on Monday morning out of La Guardia. "We'll have to have it for lunch, which means I'll have to start cooking it early in the morning—it's the first meal I'm making for you. I wanted it to be perfect."

"I *know,*" she said, raising her voice slightly. "Look, I'm sorry, but we really need to do this."

"But she just invited *you,*" I said.

"She loves my friends; it won't be a problem."

"Your friends? Am I your *friend*?"

My voice was quivering a little.

"You know what I mean," she answered.

"I think you need to call and ask her if it's okay for me to come with you." And then I left her alone in her office to make the call.

I sat at the kitchen counter with my head in my hands, trying to hear over the din of NPR, which we always listened to over breakfast.

She's from New York.

No, we're not bringing Jennifer.

Because I don't really see her anymore, that's why.

Two o'clock. Okay.

And that was that.

A few hours later, I was walking up the wobbly back steps and into Auntie Et's kitchen, my knickers in a twist over the fact that Susan couldn't bring herself to say "I have plans; can we do it tomorrow evening?" And instead I was going to be eating a chicken stew that quite possibly could kill me while the *braciole* that my darling Arnaud had so painstakingly cut for us the day before sat languishing in Susan's fridge, along with the organic shallots, the hard-to-find Pecorino di Pienza, parsley, three kinds of fresh wild mushrooms, and imported San Marzano tomatoes. I was furious.

✝✝✝

Ethel Zekas—Auntie Et—was a woman with the shoulders of Dick Butkus, a soft heart, a tendency to mercilessly and relentlessly tease anyone she could, at least twenty pairs of chartreuse rhinestone earrings, a self-proclaimed and not inaccurate resemblance to Walter Cronkite, and the undying belief in the power of suggestion in the extreme: if you walked into her house through the back door, you would have to walk through the kitchen, and if you had to walk through the kitchen, you had to sit down and have a bowl of her stew. It didn't matter if you weren't hungry, or a vegetarian, or on a hunger strike, or just frightened by the dark milky coffee color of the stuff, regardless of what it contained. If the pot was on, the suggestion was that you were going to sit your ass down and eat whatever it was she was going to feed you. If the pot wasn't on, it meant she had broiled hamburgers earlier in the day—like maybe at six in the morning, on a whim—in one of her jet-black, so-old-they-were-stick-proof Griswold cast-iron pans. Et had a nesting set of them given to her as a wedding gift in 1931, and Susan coveted them the way you're not supposed to covet thy neighbor's wife. She'd swoon whenever she saw them, along with the ancient, foot-long potato grater that her grandmother had used to make potato pancakes for the better part of a century. In Et's kitchen were all manner of bedraggled wooden spoons, a flexible spatula that was made when Grover Cleveland was in office, and a spice chopper that she'd picked up at a tag sale that predated World War II. That afternoon, I found Susan quietly bent down on one knee in front of Et's grimy stove, the bottom drawer—where she kept a rag-tag pile of mismatched aluminum skillets and chicken fryers and saucepans, and the nested Griswolds—pulled open, caressing the gleaming ebony cast iron like it was a small, whimpering puppy.

Et looked me up and down when Susan introduced us. At ninety-one, she was now perpetually bent over at the waist after a fall down her own back stairs one night at three A.M. taking out the garbage in an ice storm, and she moved through her house by hanging on to the backs of every chair she could reach, like she was doing the hand-over-hand monkey bars in an old-fashioned Army obstacle course. Finally, she fell into a big yellow silk barrel chair circa 1930s in the corner of her living room and instructed me to take a seat and a few of the Ritz crackers she'd put out before we got there.

"Susan will make us the drinks," she said, motioning for Susan to go into the kitchen. Up Susan got, and left us alone.

"So, you're from New York?" she asked through squinted eyes.

"Yes," I said, "I am."

Mmmm, she hummed, looking me up and down again. I checked my boots to make sure there wasn't anything attached to them.

"So do you know Jennifer?" she asked.

"Jennifer *who*?" I answered, pleasantly, trying to avoid the subject.

"You know, Susan's special friend, *Jennifer.* I like her very much. *Such* a pretty girl. I like her. She's so nice." She clacked her teeth together.

I could feel my face turn red; my ears gave off enough warmth to melt snow.

"I don't really know Jennifer," I told her, looking around at Et's collection of Hummel figurines. "We haven't met."

"Oh, *such* a nice girl. They used to live in a house together, in Pennsylvania. Pretty girl—I'm storing her things in my garage."

"What?"

"Some of her things that she has no room for in New York. They're here—she keeps calling to say she's going to come up and get them, but she never does. It'd be so *nice* to see her again. She can stay for as long as she wants. She's so pretty," Et said, stretching one swollen long leg out across her ottoman.

Susan came into the living room and handed me a tall Tom Collins glass with the family drink of choice: a double-shot vodka tonic with a twist of lime. I sucked it down like it was ice-cold Gatorade and I'd just run the Boston Marathon.

"Could you slow it down a little?" Susan whispered through her teeth, leaning down over me.

"Could you make me another drink please?" I asked, and handed her back the empty glass. She got up and went into the kitchen. I excused myself and followed her in.

"Jennifer is *storing* her stuff here?" I whispered.

"She has no room in her new apartment."

"Why didn't you *tell* me? I had to find out from your aunt?"

"I don't see what the big deal is."

"Your aunt seems to think she's coming back. At least that's what she's hoping for. She thinks she's very pretty and nice."

This was it; our first fight.

"For god's sake. She *is* very pretty. I don't know why you're getting so upset."

"I don't know why you just didn't tell me," I gasped, my stomach turning over.

But really, she didn't need to tell me. I knew every single Saturday night we were together, when the phone rang at eight o'clock on the nose, and it was Jennifer just calling *to check in* while Susan and I were sitting on the couch, alone, nibbling on the cheese I'd brought up from New York, sipping some wine, thinking about going upstairs and getting into bed, and clinging to each other at last after an entire week apart. I knew all about Jennifer, the way you know about a dog peeing on every fire hydrant in town, just so everyone else knows it's his.

In the short time that Susan and I were together, Jennifer had managed to track me down—work email address and all—and was determined to spend time together either alone with me, after work, while Susan was home in Connecticut, or with the two of us. Nearly every day, she'd call my extension around noon, wanting to go out for drinks, or to see a show, or to have lunch. I came up with every excuse I could think of: I was having an extended work meeting. Or my teeth drilled. Or a boil lanced.

"I think she just wants all of us to be friends," Susan said laconically, when I'd mentioned that I was getting phone calls from her at the office. "She's just doing that Buddhist thing."

"Buddhist *my ass*," I answered. "She's a Buddhist the way my *bubbe* was a Buddhist, right before she was mowed down by the Nazis."

It was happening almost every day: "It's *Jennifer Beth*!" she'd squeal like a cheerleader when I'd answer my office phone, and my stomach would lurch to my knees.

"Jennifer *who*?"

"Me, silly—Jennifer *Beth*—" she'd respond, having recently begun to hyphenate her first and middle names to better distinguish herself in what she referred to, hilariously in its haughty incorrectness, as her *professional milieu*.

"I've got this *super*-complicated mole recipe I've been working on— thirty-two ingredients!—and there's this *gnarly*"—she said "super" and "gnarly" the way a sand-coated teenage surfer might after he's just wiped out in the pipe waves in Malibu—"spice that I just don't know where to find. Could you be a dear and help me out?"

Gnarly spice? Be a dear? This chick wanted me to *be a dear?* The last time someone had asked me to *be a dear* was the blue-haired office lady wearing Truman-era *pince-nez* in my grade school in 1969.

"Well," I sputtered, adding, "I really can't—I'm at *work*." I tucked the phone under my chin and sent Susan an email simultaneously: SHE'S EMAILING ME ABOUT A RECIPE. HELP!

Susan responded in seconds: SHE DOESN'T COOK.

I had visions of Glenn Close and the bunny scene in *Fatal Attraction*.

That night, while Arnaud's gorgeous *braciole* sat shivering in Susan's refrigerator a few towns away from Et's, where we'd eaten her tannish-brown chicken stew, and I'd prayed to every god I could think of to quickly strike me down where I stood and not let me linger through the painful, ultimately fatal bout of salmonella I was certain I would be stricken with, we returned to Susan's house. The phone rang, as it always did, at eight o'clock on the dot.

Susan got up to get it, but I grabbed her hand.

"Please—don't," I begged. "*Please—*"

"But it's *ringing*," she whined.

"I know. But it can wait."

"What if it's an emergency?"

"They'll call back."

"It could be my mother—she might have fallen."

I was exasperated.

"Okay," I gave in, dropping her hand. "Go check caller ID."

Moments later, she came back and sat down next to me on the couch.

I'm sorry, she whispered, resting her head on my shoulder.

She never took Jennifer's call on a Saturday night again.

That night, while sitting in the living room listening to Jacqueline du Pré play *Carnival of the Animals* and sipping some wine that I prayed would still my post-chicken-stew stomach, I noticed an ancient G. Fox shopping bag sitting on the counter.

"Auntie Et sent us home with a Christmas present," Susan explained. "Go look."

Inside was a magnum of Marcus James Malbec—cheap, and sweet enough to pour on pancakes—and the nested set of Auntie Et's jet-black Griswold cast-iron pans that Susan had coveted since she first realized what they were: heavy, durable, solid, decidedly non-fancy, and meant to last forever, unlike my French copper that I had to pay specialists to re-tin several times a year. Hers was cookware that only a Yankee would dream about.

Attached to it was a repurposed Christmas card, its previous note thickly obscured with badly applied Wite-Out. In its place was scrawled, in blue Magic Marker:

> *I know you love these.*
> *Merry Christmas!*
> *Love, Walter*

CHAPTER 12

In Susan's Kitchen

In the way that some people believe you can always tell the nationality of a tourist by looking at their shoes or their underwear, I've always thought you could do the same by digging around in someone's kitchen. You can tell who they are, existentially speaking, just by opening cabinet doors, poking around their refrigerator, and pulling open a few utensil drawers.

I tested this theory years ago, long after my parents' divorce, on a visit to my mother's house: she was in the bedroom, on the phone, and I was alone in her kitchen, just looking around at her slightly peeling 1980s silver-and-white wallpaper, opening the odd food cabinet to see what, if anything, she was eating—six small cans of tuna packed in water, a one-thousand-packet box of Sweet 'n' Low—when I opened her lower cabinet doors. There was an electric knife in one of those cracked black cardboard boxes with red felt lining. I opened the box, and there was the white-and-gold plastic electric knife handle—still lightly coated with the gunk of an ancient holiday rib roast—but no actual knife. There was the fondue pot top to my mother's brown-and-white Dansk fondue set, and a box of fondue forks containing just one, lone, slightly bent one, but the base—the contraption on which the fondue pot sits—was missing.

"Your *father* must have taken them," she said, ruefully, when I asked. But it didn't make any sense: Why would my father want the bottom of the fondue set but not the top? Why would he take the knife part of the electric knife, but not the handle?

"Just for spite," she added with an angry gimlet eye.

"Come on, Mom," I said. "You're being silly."

"Then they just disappeared. Who knows what happens to these things?"

In my mother's world, inanimate objects are always developing minds of their own. When they get good and tired of being neglected and ignored, they simply say *goodbye, good riddance* and off they go, stomping away in the middle of the night like a knife and fork dancing across the screen of a 1950s drive-in movie: a single fondue fork and the top part of the electric carving knife, marching out the door in a conga line. She had even managed to lose an entire set of flatware that I once bought for her when she somehow, inexplicably, was running low. If you aren't a party-thrower, and you don't have dinner guests over on a regular basis, how do you lose flatware? But for my mother, it makes sense: she doesn't cook—she is fearful of food and every morsel that passes her lips sends her careening backward in time to the days before she lost all the weight and became a television singer, back to when she was a fat child—so the idea of caring for, of coddling cookware like it was a baby or a prized pair of Chanel pumps was utterly, ridiculously crazy.

+++

But crazy is relative. And so on the other hand, I was equally insane about what lived in my kitchen, and I doted on its contents the way you would a small, brokenhearted child: In my house, no knife ever sat in the sink. No pot filled with baked-on mess ever traveled through my tiny, eighteen-inch-wide dishwasher. No cast-iron pan ever saw a rinse of soapy water or a damp sponge, or even soap.

"This is *disgusting*," my best friend Abigail once said when she came over for brunch, picking up the Lodge cast-iron pan I'd bought specifically for making a honey-glazed, blue-corn corn bread I'd once eaten at an uptown, neo-Southern restaurant. She ran her finger along its surface and a made a face.

"It's just age," I said. "And the fact that you're never supposed to wash it."

"And I just ate something cooked in this thing? How the hell are you supposed to clean it?"

"With salt," I answered.

"Salt? Just *salt*?" She was aghast.

"Yes," I said. "It's the way it's been done for centuries. The coarser the better. Like maybe a nice flakey Maldon sea salt from England."

"So you scrub your pans with imported English sea salt. Tell me that's not completely nuts."

"It's not," I told her, waving a copy of Edna Lewis's *The Taste of Country Cooking* in her face. If it was good enough for Edna, it was good enough for me.

"Honey," Abigail snorted, "you may have noticed: you're not exactly a six-foot-tall black woman who likes to do things the way her great-grandma did back when she was a slave. Go out and buy yourself some dish soap."

In truth, the idea of using salt to scrub a pan thickly caked with baked-on food was something that I had always found secretly terrifying, especially after my first bout of food poisoning ended with a doctor friend coming to my house to hook me up to an IV for a few hours while we watched daytime television together in between my unhooking myself and racing for the bathroom. Scrubbing cast iron with salt was one of those mildly upsetting, romantic constructs, like threading adorable, tiny birds on a skewer and roasting them whole in a wood fire, like Richard Olney used to do in his tiny, sweet, sundrenched house in Provence. It was like a ride through culinary fantasy land until you stopped and thought about it for a minute.

When I better examined Auntie Et's nested set of jet-black, clean-as-a-whistle Griswold pans sitting on the counter, I couldn't imagine for the life of me how they'd gotten that way, or if they were just so old that the stuck-on food had disintegrated and fallen off over the years, like the now-empty can of rubbed sage from 1953 that Susan's mother still kept in her spice rack over her sink, having evaporated into light-green dust sometime during the Tet Offensive.

"Et must use a *lot* of salt on these babies," I said to Susan later that day, holding one of the smaller pans up to the light and running my finger along its surface.

"Are you kidding?" she barked. "Her secret is *far* more subversive."

"What is it?" I whispered, leaning in close.

"Soap and water. And a good, long soak in the sink," Susan said, matter of factly. "Salt is just so—I don't know—*twee*."

✝✝✝

Earlier that morning, when the alarm went off at eight, I threw the covers back and raced down the stairs with MacGillicuddy following me, sounding like a stampeding herd of cattle in the otherwise still house.

"What are you doing?" Susan groaned from upstairs.

"I'm making dinner," I yelled back.

"Now?"

"Yes—*now*. It'll go in at eleven and be ready at three, you can take me to the station at 4:30, and I'll be back on the train home to New York by six. So, *now*—"

At eight on this mid-December Sunday morning, with my still-new love interest drowsing away upstairs, her slobbering dog following me around the kitchen hoping I'd drop something, and the *braciole* that Arnaud had cut for me on Friday, it was now or never. I wasn't going to freeze meat as gorgeous as this, so I got up to make supper, roughly an hour after the white, wintry sun had come up.

Susan's refrigerator, a mammoth black side-by-side Kenmore, so immense that the moving men had to slide it through the living room and over the counter on blankets—like an obese Pasha perched on a flying carpet—had a reputation for swallowing up anything you happened to be looking for at the very moment you needed it. I opened it, and cheese—soft, hard, harder, some white, some yellow, some blue—fell out at my feet, draped in varying degrees in plastic wrap. A small, blue-striped yellow ware bowl from the 1930s containing beige, cardboard-colored ground turkey and covered with foil sat precariously close to the edge of one of the sliding glass shelves. I searched and looked, lifting up packages of deli meat and containers of yogurt like a child does on a scavenger hunt. But no *braciole*.

"Where's the meat?" I yelled up the stairs.

"What?" Susan was still half asleep.

"The beef—*THE BEEF, DAMMIT*—from Arnaud," I shouted, anxiously, like I was having a dinner party in a few hours to which Russian royalty might be in attendance.

"It's there," Susan pleaded. I heard her get up, her feet hitting the floor above me. "I didn't touch it!"

"I don't see it!"

"Look behind the shaker," she shouted.

I stomped back to the fridge, removed the cocktail shaker still half-filled with the watered-down remnants of the bourbon Manhattan that we'd sucked down before running to Et's house for the chicken slop, and there, nestled between a loaf of Pepperidge Farm white bread and a Tupperware container of leftover macaroni and cheese, was my outrageously expensive beef.

I rummaged around the kitchen cabinets for a small platter and came up with one—part of a whole set of blue-and-white Anne Hathaway's Cottage service for twelve—that would allow the two pieces of *braciole* to come to room temperature comfortably and slowly without daring to touch each other, which, if they did, would result in unacceptable, uneven, oxidized spotting. I covered them with foil and set them aside, out of reach of the dog, and went back to the fridge to search for the handful of wild mushrooms—golden chanterelles, hen of the woods, and brown spongy morels—that I'd dropped fifteen bucks for at Dean & DeLuca. By the time Susan trudged down the stairs, I was sitting at the counter, gingerly rubbing and patting the dirt off of them with the dry piece of raw white silk that I'd neatly folded up, wrapped in a white handkerchief, and tucked into my coat pocket before leaving my apartment on Friday. Soft, delicate, and with the tiniest amount of nap, raw silk is the perfect tool for cleaning mushrooms without bruising them.

"Good morning, honey," Susan said, giving me a sleepy peck on the cheek.

"Good morning," I said with an edge, looking at her out of the corner of my eye.

"Can I ask what is it that you're doing?" She filled up the teakettle at the sink, and glared at my little patch of silk.

"What does it *look* like I'm doing?"

"Dusting? Drying the tears of a weeping morel that misses its mother?"

"Very funny," I replied, putting the last of the mushrooms on Susan's small tag-sale wooden chopping board that was in the shape of an apple. "I need a knife—do you have anything sharper than this?" I held up a five-inch chef's knife with a plastic handle that I'd found in a drawer near the sink; a full quarter-inch of its tip was missing, sheared clean off, like it had been circumcised.

"They're all in here," she said, opening up a narrow drawer near the stove. I poked around and pulled out a paring knife that had a thin crack in its plastic handle. There was a long, heavy chef's knife, and both of them had seen better days and were about as sharp as limp celery.

"Do I need to bring my knife roll up next week?" I asked.

"What's wrong with *these*?" she said, holding up the paring knife.

"What year are they from?"

"My mother gave them to me. Or they might have belonged to one of the aunts; I can't remember."

I snorted. I prized my knives, which I never, ever let rest in the sink, or ever see the rough vulgarity of a dishwasher.

Susan shook her head, exasperated.

"I don't understand what the difference is—if it's a good knife, it's a good knife."

"But don't you think you should take better care of them? I mean, look at this one." I held it up, and nodded at the missing tip. Susan swooned and took it out of my hands.

"I love that knife. I think I found it at a tag sale, at the bottom of a box. I felt badly for it—it just needed a little love."

"You sound like Linus at the end of *A Charlie Brown Christmas*, when he gets down on his knees and wraps the tree in his blanket."

I was involved with a woman who had rescued a stray knife from a tag-sale FREE box because it needed a little love. My knives came from Bridge Kitchenware in the East Fifties, back in the day when the infamous owner, Fred Bridge, was considered the Soup Nazi of professional cookware. If you wanted to buy a bird's-beak paring knife from him and you weren't planning on using it to carve roses out of baby radishes like Jacques Pépin, he wouldn't sell it to you. My knife roll contained an eight-inch chef's knife, a six-inch carbon-steel Sabatier that rusted in mild springtime humidity, four paring knives, a Japanese cleaver, a nine-inch slicer, and a seven-inch filleting knife. And all of them were kept in pristine condition: the moment I saw a ding in one of them, I hurried it to a specialty sharpener on the Lower East Side, like an hysterical mother who rushes her baby to the emergency room after a sniffle.

"Tell me what you need chopped," Susan said, sipping on a

steaming royal-blue mug of odorous Lapsang souchong, a tea so simultaneously sweet and pungent and smoky that it made the dog throw up.

I looked at her.

"Come on—I'm really *good* at chopping—I'm a designer, remember?"

I reached into the vegetable drawer in the fridge and extracted a large onion, two celery stalks, and two carrots.

"Can you chop me a mirepoix?"

I was so fucking haughty about it, and she didn't even bat an eyelash.

"No problem," she said, putting her mug down. She took a scuffed plastic cutting board from behind the faucet and set it down on top of a lightly dampened paper towel, to keep it from moving around. I just stared at her, my arms folded.

"You gonna ask me what a mirepoix is?" I said.

"You gonna keep talking?" she replied, looking at me over her reading glasses.

And with that, she began to chop everything using that sad, tip-less tag-sale knife. When she was done, she dumped the carrots, celery, and onion into three Anne Hathaway's Cottage soup bowls, pushed them toward me, picked up the newspaper and her tea, went into the living room, and sat down on the couch. The vegetables were perfect eighth-inch cubes and lovely. I remembered the day we met, when she touched the tiny scar on my right hand.

Details.

Two hours later, while the *braciole*—paper-thin slices of Arnaud's prime beef rolled around black truffle–scented wild mushroom dux-elles, parsley, and Pecorino di Pienza, and then browned in olive oil and butter—sat braising in red wine and San Marzano tomatoes in Susan's only high-sided sauté pan, Susan began to rummage around in the fridge.

"I'm hungry," she said, gazing into it like she was expecting a human voice to spring forth from its depths.

"I'll cook," I announced, putting the newspaper down, certain that she would somehow manage to change the oven temperature and turn the *braciole* into shoe leather.

"Sit," she said, pointing at the oven. "You're making dinner, remember?"

"Okay. So, what will we have? Grilled cheese? God knows we have enough pecorino to feed a small village in Tuscany."

I moved to the other side of the counter so I could keep an eye on things.

She pulled a small, dented RevereWare saucepan out from the drawer under the oven, filled it with water and a few tablespoons of Heinz vinegar—the sort that my grandmother used to mix with water to clean the windows—and brought it to a simmer. She placed the smallest of the Griswold pans over a burner, heated it dry over medium heat, and set down four overlapping slices of Canadian bacon in it, like an edible Venn diagram.

"Stop!" I shouted, leaping up. "You're not using oil? You're going to destroy that pan!"

"You need to not talk so much," she said without looking up, carefully breaking four eggs into four small ceramic pudding ramekins. She put four slices of plain white bread into the toaster, stirred the simmering water to create a vortex, and one by one, using a slotted spoon, gingerly lowered each egg into the water, simultaneously reaching over and pressing the lever down on the toaster. The Alessi timer—the one shaped like a lady in a dress, that she'd brought back from a work trip to Italy the year before along with holy water from Lourdes and a Pope John Paul bottle opener—was set to three minutes. When it pinged, so did the toaster.

Susan set down on two lovely, hand-painted Italian breakfast plates golden slices of toast topped with Canadian bacon and four magnificent, firm, buxom white orbs, the most perfect, perfectly poached eggs I had ever seen. I sliced gently into one, and its great gush of deep yellow yolk slowly flooded the plate and the meat and the bread. She pushed a small ceramic bowl of coarse salt and freshly ground black pepper in my direction. I took a pinch between my thumb and fore-finger, rubbed them carefully together, and released a slow shower of tiny flakes over the eggs.

When people over the years have asked me, "When did you know you were falling in love with Susan," the answer is an easy one: just the simple, thoughtful action of having coarse salt in a small bowl instead of iodized dreck in a shaker was enough to make my heart careen from one side of my chest to the other. The tactile, ancient process of taking a pinch of salt from a tiny bowl between human finger-tips, and rubbing it, sprinkling it, thoughtfully, on food, connects the diner with what is on the plate with a sense of immediacy. There is no need for a grain of rice to keep the salt dry in the humidity and the shaker clear.

Bowl of salt. Fingers. Food.

Susan began slicing up both pieces of her toast, bacon, and eggs into miniscule squares, like the mother of a small child would do for her baby who has just learned to use utensils, and I laughed out loud.

"What's wrong with it?" she asked. "It lets me read the paper and eat without having to use both hands."

Details.

When we were done—it was early in the afternoon on a frigid Sunday—Susan got up and put the tiny cast-iron Griswold in the sink, filled it with soapy water, and let it rest.

"Salt," she said, "is for eating. Not for scrubbing."

✢✢✢

The *braciole*, which filled the house with the earthy essence of tomato and truffle and wild mushrooms, cooked in a very slow oven for the rest of the day, and when it was time for me to leave for the city, was not quite finished. I left it to Susan's hands, to slice into perfect rou-lades, which I was sure she could do expertly, since her mirepoix was so goddamned precise.

"Promise me you'll toss the sauce with the fresh tagliatelle I brought," I said, as we drove to the train station in Hartford.

"I promise," she agreed, glancing over at me.

"And that you'll let the meat rest for ten minutes before slicing it exactly an inch thick."

"Oh for god's *sake*, I *promise* already."

But it didn't matter: without my being there, I was sure that the first meal I'd ever made for Susan was going to be an abject failure, and I wasn't even going to be around to ask forgiveness. Or to make excuses.

"How was it?" I asked that night when I called to say I was home. It was after nine.

"Good," Susan said, "but maybe a little tough. So I chopped up the meat and stuffing and tossed it all together with the pasta. And it was so much better."

POACHED EGGS WITH CANADIAN BACON ON TOAST

In every new relationship, one dish emerges that becomes synonymous with love, safety, and goodness. Silly me, I thought it would be my *braciole,* but no; it was Susan's miraculously cooked, splendidly perfect poached eggs. Soft, runny—but not too runny—they scream comfort and howl happiness. And today, years later, when I'm either feeling frisky or like I want to crawl under a blanket and suck my thumb, it's Susan's poached eggs that I crave. Forget the fancy poaching devices and tools that I used to sell at Dean & DeLuca: all you'll need is a wooden spoon, a small saucepan, and a timer. Note to self: the fresher the eggs, the less the whites will hold together, so if your friendly neighborhood urban chicken-farming hipster rushes over with a few newly laid ones for you, give them a few days before you make this.

Serves 2

2 not-so-fresh eggs

1 tablespoon distilled white vinegar

2 slices Canadian bacon

2 slices bread of your choice (white is best, raisin is not)

Coarse salt and freshly ground black pepper

1. Carefully crack each egg into a small ramekin and set aside. In a small saucepan filled three-quarters of the way with water, add the white vinegar and bring it to a simmer over medium heat. While it's simmering, place the Canadian bacon slices in a medium, dry cast-iron pan over medium-low heat; cook on one side for 4 minutes and flip.

continued

2. When the water comes to a rolling simmer, gingerly slide the eggs into the pan, and with the dowel end of a wooden spoon, flip the white over onto the yolk two or three times. Slap a cover onto the pan, remove it from the heat, and set your timer for exactly 3 minutes.

3. Meanwhile, cook the bacon on the other side for 2 minutes, and simultaneously toast your bread. When the bread is done, the bacon will be done. As soon as the timer goes off, and using a slotted spoon, carefully remove each egg to a ramekin.

4. Top each piece of toast with a slice of bacon, and top each with a poached egg. Serve with a bowl of coarse salt and freshly ground black pepper.

CHAPTER 13

The Tree

I never had a Christmas tree as a child—my father wouldn't allow it—but we were a family completely and totally obsessed with Christmas, like a small cavalcade of Irving Berlins.

It started with Gaga, my mother's mother, and her Baby Jesus fixation; every year, she would pick me up on Shabbos, my last Friday of school before the holiday break, and take me by subway to St. Patrick's Cathedral to see a life-size, peeling, glassy-eyed statue of somebody else's savior. We'd wait for an hour or so on a long snaking line behind every gentile child in the city of New York, and then, when we caught a glimpse of Him in his manger behind the altar, Gaga—who possessed not one discernibly tender bone in her body—would suddenly get all misty.

"Look," she'd whimper, "there he is—it's a *miracle!*" Miracle came out slowly and with guttural sing-song vibrato—*m-iiir-aaa-ccc-lll-e*—and then she'd wipe a tiny tear from the corner of her eye before it cascaded down her heavily powdered cheek.

Gaga, my father used to say, was a preternaturally angry woman, prone to temper tantrums and rages that could flare up at a moment's notice. It was Gaga's anger, he said, so gorgeous and deep, that helped take down the Hindenburg that fateful day in 1937; it flew over Brooklyn on its way to Lakehurst, New Jersey, and as it rumbled and floated over Williamsburg, Gaga and her neighbor Mrs. Epstein stood outside on the street, waving their fists at it and cursing in Yiddish. Twenty minutes later, it exploded.

"With your grandmother," my father would say, "you just never know."

Our annual excursion to see the Baby Jesus somehow calmed her. After St. Patrick's, we'd leave the city and head home on the subway, stopping at McCrory's on the way for a pre-Shabbos snack of grilled cheese and bacon, griddled and oozing perfect orange, processed-food rivulets, the surface of the white bread rendered smooth and tight and firm, and flawlessly crisp in only the way that a lunch-counter grilled cheese can, and ought, to be.

✛✛✛

We weren't permitted our own tree, but every Christmas, like clock-work, my father would haul me, Gaga, and my mother down to Luchow's on Fourteenth Street to dine in the shadow of their immense Christmas pine, so enormously tall that its top spire lightly brushed the twenty-foot-high ceiling. The noise level in the restaurant was so loud that voices of diners and the sounds of eating and waiters taking orders and silverware clanging to the floor and the L train running underneath the building joined together to create a dull hum, a flat deafening rumble like a didgeridoo that made the floor shake and the light fixtures rattle. An oompah band—four Brylcreemed, obese, sweaty men in green woolen shorts and knee socks, black vinyl loaf-ers, beige short-sleeved business shirts, and lederhosen—strolled the dining room, playing German music in the faces of the unsmiling holiday diners trying to hear themselves above the tuba.

Our waiter, an older, pasty-faced man in a short black tuxedo jacket that was high in the armpits and tight in the sleeves, making him look like a wind-up, cymbal-playing monkey, carried an immense aluminum tray containing our food on his shoulder. Slithering around the band and through the crowded dining room, he set down in front of my father a thinly pounded, deep-fried Wiener Schnitzel, topped with a perfectly fried egg crisscrossed with anchovies. Small plates of sweet-and-sour red cabbage and boiled potatoes came after it, followed by a shallow soup bowl filled with pickled herring in dill sauce.

Every Christmas, I stared at the meat, which my father mistook for interest in having a taste.

"It's Wiener Schnitzel à la Holstein," he would say brightly. "Holstein. . . *H-o-l-s-t-e-i-n*," he'd repeat, in a heavy, mock Bavarian accent. "I want you to taste some."

"I'll have some if you scrape the egg off."

"But that's the best part," he'd say, slicing a wide piece of meat off the golden cutlet and putting it on my plate alongside my baked chicken. And every Christmas, just as I was about to take a bite, my father would spoon a slippery sliver of egg white and jiggly, slightly runny yolk on top of the fried meat, and add a bit of anchovy.

I wanted none of it. Not the egg. Not the meat and the egg together. And definitely not the meat, the egg, and the fish.

"Matter of fact," he'd say, between bites, "the schnitzel is an afterthought. It's all about the egg, and the anchovy." A bit of yolk would stain his chin, as he took great, dangerously large bites. I'd distract myself by whirling around in my seat, and watching the tuba player in the oompah band behind me.

"Cy," my mother would say, pushing the dilled salad around on her plate, "she said *no egg*."

"She needs to try everything just once," my father would say.

Gaga, sitting across from me at the invariably too-large round table, clacked her dentures repeatedly between bites of fatty roast goose, which always indicated her displeasure with him.

"Elissala," she'd say, standing up and taking my hand, her black leather purse dangling off her wrist, "come. Let's go look at the tree."

She turned her back on my father and mother as we walked across the vast dining room, leaving both of our meals barely eaten.

✛✛✛

Even though we didn't have a tree, the measure of holiday joy wherever we went was always gauged by the size of *other* people's trees. Growing up so close to Manhattan, I was taken for the first ten years of my life to witness the lighting of the Rockefeller Center Christmas Tree in early December, and then on the same night, farther down Fifth Avenue to Lord & Taylor, to see their Christmas windows. Inevitably Dickensian in theme, they contained small, perfectly rendered robotic characters, their wooden hair painted blond, the man in a Victorian waistcoat, the lady in a bustle, and the children dressed like small versions of their parents. A tiny, mechanical dog—usually scruffy, also blond—would wag in time to the piped-in German Christmas carols before stiffly stealing a present from under the elaborately decorated, candle-bedecked Christmas tree that always appeared, magically, to be aflame. Every thirty seconds, the dog's jaws would open, and he would say "woof-woof."

My desire to also be joy-filled and celebrate Christmas became even more furious and unquenchable when it coincided with Chanukah, because there were gifts and shopping involved. One year, my parents take me to Macy's to buy presents for my cousins, stopping to put me on the lap of the store Santa, who asks me if I'd been a good girl this year, and what I'd like for Christmas.

"A tree," I tell him, and he *ho-ho-hos* broadly, waving to my beaming mother and my father who is shooting with his new Polaroid, and Santa says "Get the little lady a tree for Pete's sake! It's Christmas!"

But I know that once we get back into the car, my father will remind me for the fiftieth time that year that we're Jews, and Jews don't have Christmas trees.

"We always had a Chanukah bush," my mother says to him

helpfully, untying the brown velvet cord on her round, astronaut helmet–like silver fox hat.

"You're not helping, Rita," my father answers, popping a Titrilac into his mouth. She looks out the passenger window as we drive home, stop and go, navigating the crowded city and the hideous holiday traffic, while my father leans on the horn.

Each year I hoped that somehow, my father would *find the joy* that everyone in all the television Christmas specials seemed to have in their eyes. That he'd wake up one morning like Scrooge after a night of visitations by ghosts who would drag him, kicking and screaming into the world of holiday cheer, of roasts and trifles, of ignited Christmas plum puddings and rum punches. That I'd come home from a day of playing outside with friends, and there, in the corner of the living room, alongside my father's Danish modern teak desk and his prized Hirshfelds and the Ben Shahn prints and the Roman Vishniac books, standing in front of the enormous picture window, right next to the orange-bulbed electric menorah, would be a gigantic green fir tree, covered with flashing white lights and tinsel and silver balls. One night near Christmas, we got home from Macy's and I ran straight up to my room and rummaged through my sock drawer, extracting a single, long, red knee sock, stretched out at the top and worn at the heel. I Scotch taped it to my bedroom door in hope and defiance.

Then I sat quietly on my bed, waiting for my father to notice. It didn't take long. When he saw it, he furiously ripped it off the door and threw it at me, overhand, like a baseball, bellowing, "We're Jews, goddamnit. Don't you *understand* me?"

And I'd shake my head *yes, I do*, my throat tightening. *I do understand.*

✝✝✝

Susan wanted to go out and buy a tree, and suddenly, I felt the small, sharp sting of guilt-ridden wish fulfillment.

"Where are we going?" I asked, lacing up my Timberlands.

"To the conservancy," she said.

"We can buy trees at the conservancy?"

"Yes," she said. "But we have to cut our own."

"With an axe?" I asked. "Like Paul Bunyan?"

"Have you *never* cut a tree down?"

"Where would I cut a tree down? In Central Park?"

"A *saw*, not an *axe*," she snorted.

"Do we have to bring our *own* saw?"

"We can, but they'll give us one."

"Do we get hot cocoa or rum or something?"

"No," she said, "but let's make dinner when we get home. It'll be early."

And there, a few miles away from Susan's house, in a snow-blanketed field dotted with trees of every style and breed and size and shape, a buck-toothed man in a red plaid Woolrich hunting coat gave us—actually, gave Susan, as somehow I must not have struck him as the sawing type—a yellow-handled, dull-toothed saw speckled with rust, and off we went, walking down paths, trudging through the snow, huffing and puffing, ours noses running and our eyes watering.

"I like *those*—they look furry." I pointed to the Fraser firs. "I hear they're the Rolls-Royces of Christmas trees."

"And you know this *how*?" Susan asked, walking around one that seemed to be the right size.

My best friend from college, who lived in Lake Forest, Illinois, and knew about these things, had once told me, when I was out visiting her for Christmas one year.

"I hear they never lose their needles."

"Do you like this one?" she asked, looking it up and down.

"Too small," I said.

So we kept trudging along until we found one that was just right: it was tall and broad, and I was in love with it.

"I think it might be too big, though—don't you?" Susan wondered pragmatically.

"I think it's perfect, really. There's never *been* such a Christmas tree!"

Susan stared at me. "You sound like Mrs. Cratchit."

"What do you want me to do?" I asked, getting down on my hands and knees in the snow.

"Stand up and hold my earmuffs."

"But can't I saw it?" I was pouting, the way I did all those years before, when I told Santa that I wanted a tree even though we were Jews.

"Sure," she said, and handed me the saw. I lay down in the snow, shimmied myself under the tree's lowest branches, placed the saw on the trunk until the teeth caught, and did what they do in cartoons involving lumberjacks. It wouldn't move.

"Don't laugh," I said. Susan was holding her chest and barking silent guffaws.

"Here—let me. You hold the trunk."

So I did while Susan sawed, and in five minutes, the poor tree was lying on its side in the snow, like a felled rhino at the end of an elephant gun.

"Yay!" I exclaimed. "Our tree! Now what?"

"We have to drag it back to the car," Susan said, turning it around so she was pulling it by the trunk.

"Can't we pay someone else to do that?"

"Let's go—you take one side, I'll take the other."

+++

Once we pulled it into the house, propped it up into Susan's cast-iron tree stand, and cut off its full-length hairnet, the tree's magnificent limbs stretched out wide and far, taking up more than half the space in the living room, and forcing the dog to go in reverse whenever she tried to walk through the room. But it was our tree, and it was my first.

"I think this deserves a nice dinner," I said. "Is there a gourmet shop in town?" After a month of visits to this northern, rural Connecticut town, I had never gone food shopping there, and had no idea what I'd be faced with if I had a sudden craving for, say, duck, or quail, or if I ran out of saffron while throwing together a paella Valenciana.

"Just Value Mart—the supermarket a few miles away." Susan walked over to the stove and filled up the teakettle. "We don't really need anything fancy—and I'm not feeling so good, suddenly."

Her face was flushed and her eyes were watery; she had one of those colds that seems to come on in minutes, and within the hour, she was stretched out on the sofa in her pajamas with the dog, coughing her head off and sounding like a foghorn.

"I'll make us something nice," I said, taking her car keys. "I promise. Just rest."

Susan's market was a shocking display of contrasts: an enormous meat case—not as good as Arnaud's but surprisingly respectable—faced off against a fish counter filled with previously frozen sea creatures that had seen better days, months if not years before. The vegetables were a morass of browning turnips and enormous, waxy rutabagas and shrink-wrapped fruit from half a world away.

I carried my basket up and down each aisle, hoping for inspiration; I stopped at the meat counter and encountered something called a spoon roast—top sirloin butt and the cut of meat that delicatessens use for sliced roast beef—but it didn't seem like the comfort food I was looking for. There were no organic chickens—just enormous, school-bus yellow, corn-fed birds who'd clearly spent their short, sad, beakless lives on factory farms—so I decided against chicken.

But there, nestled in with the humongous legs of lamb and Australian rib racks were two meaty, red lamb shanks—a cut I'd never seen or prepared before. I knew Susan had an antique blue mason jar filled with stone-ground cornmeal sitting in her pantry. We had plenty of Parmigiano-Reggiano. Done, I thought: red wine–braised lamb shanks on a bed of Parmigiano-infused polenta. I grabbed the meat, put it in my basket, and scurried to the cash register.

"That's five dollars and seventy-five cents, please," the woman behind the register said, ringing me up.

I had been so excited about finding the shanks that I hadn't even bothered looking at the price; they were a little more than two and a half dollars each.

"Is there something wrong with them?" I was alarmed. I wasn't going to be buying cut-rate meat for my sick girlfriend.

"Nobody knows what the heck to do with them," she said. "That's all."

+++

Susan was in a deep, Nyquil-induced sleep on the couch with the dog, our naked Christmas tree towering over her, when I trundled into the house with my grocery bag. I dropped my coat in the entryway, headed straight for the kitchen, and unpacked the meat. I silently rolled the lamb shanks in a little seasoned flour, browned them in Susan's one deep skillet until they crackled and popped and turned a deep, golden caramel. I removed them from the pan to one of the many Anne Hathaway's Cottage plates that filled every dish cabinet, and cooked a mirepoix in the fat until the vegetables were soft and tender, releasing their sweet goodness into the pan. The shanks went back into the pot on top of the vegetables along with sprigs of rosemary, and a few whole peeled garlic cloves when I realized I hadn't stopped for red wine to cook with.

But the large bottle of Marcus James Malbec that Auntie Et had given us the week before stood there in Susan's wine cabinet, beckoning me. So I unscrewed it, and poured the entire contents of the bottle over the meat. The whole thing braised in a very slow oven for hours while Susan slept, and I read.

"What *is* that?" She yawned, as it was getting dark. She stretched like a baby under the gold wool Hudson's Bay blanket I'd dragged downstairs from the bedroom and draped over her.

"I found lamb shanks at the store."

"Oh my *god*!"

"Oh my god *what*?"

"You can't tell?"

"Tell what?"

"Let the dog out in the yard and then come back in," she said, and I slid the front slider open and watched MacGillicuddy—a cloud of black curls and drool—race out into the snow.

When I stepped back inside, I was hit by a cloud of meaty, winey richness enveloping every inch of the house. The sauce—nothing more than a bottle of cheap Marcus James Malbec heated to a constant simmer—had thickened, its pronounced residual sugars concentrating like Manischewitz and coating the now falling-off-the-bone meat in a burgundy velvet blanket.

Susan sat down at the counter, where I'd set the table with her good silverware. There, in the middle of each Anne Hathaway's Cottage plate, I vertically propped up a tender shank, bone hole to the sky, surrounded it with a small puddle of polenta cooked with a little Parmigiano, sprinkled it with some dried parsley for color, and drizzled it with sauce from a height of about two feet.

"How am I supposed to eat this?" Susan asked, staring down at the plate.

"With your knife and fork," I said.

"Does everything always have to be tall, honey?" She smiled and rolled her eyes, took her fork, and pushed the shank bone over into the polenta, like our tree falling over into the snow a few hours earlier.

That freezing winter night, we sat side by side at the counter, in front of steaming plates of tender lamb shank redolent of wine and rosemary and garlic. We managed to eat just one shank between us; it was so rich and so filling that we shared it, pulling the meat off the other one and adding it back into the sauce to have with wide, ribbony pappardelle the next day, without any possible chance for fuss, height, or fanfare.

BRAISED LAMB SHANKS IN RED WINE

Inexpensive, meaty, and packed with flavor, lamb shanks are—or at least were, grocery stores have caught on—wildly inexpensive, but worth their weight in gold for their ability to be dressed up or down, and for providing voluminously delicious leftovers that are perfect for tossing with pasta of every variety. Patience is key in making this dish; getting a long, slow sear on the meat will result not only in a reduction of fat as the meat cooks, but additional layers of flavor sealed into the meat and unable to breach its crispy exterior.

Serves 2

2 large lamb shanks, about 1½ pounds

Salt and freshly ground black pepper

Unbleached all-purpose flour, for dredging

2 tablespoons extra-virgin olive oil

1 large carrot, diced

1 medium onion, minced

1 stalk celery, diced

2 garlic cloves, smashed

One 750-ml bottle Malbec, or other fruity, full-bodied red wine

1 bay leaf

1 teaspoon fresh thyme leaves, chopped

1 teaspoon chopped fresh rosemary

1. Preheat the oven to 300°F.

2. Season the lamb shanks well with salt and pepper. Place the flour in a small baking pan, and dredge the shanks, shaking off any excess flour.

3. In a medium (preferably oval) Dutch oven set over medium-high heat, warm the olive oil until it begins to shimmer. Brown the shanks in the hot oil on all sides; this should take at least 10 minutes. Remove the shanks to a platter and set aside.

4. Add the carrot, onion, celery, and garlic to the pot and cook, stirring frequently, until tender. Nestle the shanks on top of the vegetables, adding whatever lamb juices have collected on the platter. Pour in the bottle of wine, bring to a boil, and cook uncovered, for 5 minutes, then add the bay leaf, thyme, and rosemary and cover.

5. Place in the oven and cook for 2 hours, spooning the sauce over the meat every half hour. Remove the cover and continue to cook until the sauce has thickened to a slightly syrupy consistency, about another 30 minutes. Don't strain the sauce; instead, drizzle it over the shanks, which should be served over polenta.

PAPPARDELLE WITH LAMB RAGU

Lamb ragu is by no means traditional. Ragu is usually made with ground beef, or even duck—but the meat's inherent succulent sweetness is a perfect foil for the addition of tart tomatoes to this thick, rich sauce, which stands up to heftier pastas like pappardelle or tagliatelle. Leftover sauce, should you have any, can be frozen for up to six months.

Serves 2, with leftovers

1 tablespoon extra-virgin olive oil

1½ cups shredded leftover lamb shank meat

1 cup leftover braising sauce with vegetables

One 28-ounce can San Marzano tomatoes

Salt

Pinch of red pepper flakes

8 ounces dried pappardelle pasta, cooked according to package instructions (1 cup of pasta water reserved)

Parmigiano-Reggiano cheese, for grating

1. In a large, nonreactive, straight-sided sauté pan set over medium-high heat, warm the olive oil until it shimmers. Add the shank meat, tossing it to coat it with the fat. Pour the leftover braising sauce and vegetables into the pan, and stir well to combine.

2. When the sauce comes to a simmer, pour in the tomatoes (with juice), stirring to break them up. Bring to a simmer, cover them askew, and cook for 20 minutes, stirring frequently, until the tomatoes and wine have melded into a thick, reddish brown sauce. Taste for seasoning, and add salt and red pepper flakes, as needed.

3. Add the cooked pasta directly to the pan and toss to combine; if it feels too dry, add tablespoons of the pasta water, and toss again.

4. Serve in warm, shallow bowls, with freshly grated Parmigiano-Reggiano.

CHAPTER 14

Christmas Dinner

My father was born into an Orthodox Jewish family on Christmas Eve, 1923, on a day so warm and beautiful that, according to my Aunt Sylvia, who was then five, the roses poked their heads out of the Bronx snow, in full bloom.

Our lives are filled with expectation and contradiction: You plan for a storm, and wind up with sun. You shovel snow, and beneath the snow there are roses. You plan to light a menorah, but all you have are eight Ikea tea lights in chipped jam jars. You expect plum pudding and a goose and a bottle of vintage Bordeaux, and you end up with old bread and an onion. My grandfather used to say *mentsch tracht, Gott lacht*: man plans, God laughs.

Years ago, on a day off from my job at Dean & DeLuca, I found myself in the neighborhood of the store, and, drawn like moth to flame, I walked in. Fighting the Saturday bridge-and-tunnel crowds to get to the tiny corner in the back where my in-box sat, I found a VHS tape wrapped in fancy letterhead, and rubber-banded in place, a scrawled note:

> *Hope you enjoy this—*
> *Best, Martha*

"She just dropped it off," my boss, Kevin, said. "She's hoping we'll carry it—Why don't you take it home and watch it?"

It was Martha Stewart's latest video—*Secrets for Entertaining*—

teaching viewers how to throw massive buffets and elegant dinner parties for friends. My memory is hazy, but if I recall correctly, it ended with her pushing a wheelbarrow filled with hay and dessert up to the table, in a nod to stylish Yankee rusticity.

I was responsible for buying the books for the store, and even though Joel Dean refused to let me carry the video—Martha had just aligned herself with Kmart and in no way did he want anything at Dean & DeLuca to be remotely connected to the down-market retailer—I was enraptured. I watched the video over and over again until I could imagine myself there, at Turkey Hill in Westport, dressed in red-and-white gingham in that old rambling farmhouse that Martha had bought for virtually nothing years before with her handsome husband, Andy. I imagined myself there, surrounded by space and high ceilings and ornate sideboards, a commercial Garland range and stacks of antique ironstone and vintage jadeite nearby, gray-muzzled black Labs and their owners, and, of course, friends from prep school wandering in and out, leaving their L.L. Bean boots in the mudroom, and shaking off their barn coats from the damp winter chill. Like Martha's, my buffets would be grand, elaborate affairs, with the long mahogany trestle table I inherited from darling great-grandmamma buckling under the weight of an entire poached Scottish salmon, its scales magnificently rendered in thin-sliced cucumber, and an immense glazed ham from a Gloucestershire Old Spot pig raised and slaughtered just for the occasion. The table would be set with vintage purple glassware dragged back from a winning haggle with a Gauloises-sucking dealer at the Porte de Clignancourt; my dessert would be delivered alfresco, on an old, forgotten barn-wood cart unearthed from an outbuilding in which, perhaps, a passel of feral kittens had been born only days before. I wanted all of it, and Martha's video enabled the dream, even though at the time I lived in a fifth-story walk-up with a bedroom facing an air shaft that was home to a flock of pigeons.

+++

In the years that I spent living alone in my studio apartment, I regularly hauled small groups of friends over for celebratory holiday dinners featuring pheasant wrapped in home-cured bacon. The birds, slightly smaller than chickens, took up little room in my twenty-four-inch-wide apartment stove, allowing me to stuff the rest of it with pies, biscuits, cakes, and, on one occasion, a plum pudding mold floating in the middle of a shallow brownie pan filled halfway with water, which was my attempt at a bain-marie. Once ignited, the pudding set off every smoke alarm on my end of the fifth floor. One year, I ordered a six-foot-square piece of construction-grade plywood from a lumber yard off Delancey Street. I had it delivered, and, settling it down over the top of the thirty-inch-square vintage Irish pine card table I used for dining, I suddenly had enough room to comfortably seat twelve for a formal holiday repast, which revolved around a Martha recipe: a roasted rack of venison laden with currants and cranberries. Between my eleven guests, the wine, the coats, my cats, my decorations, my furniture, and the suddenly enormous table, there was no room for anyone to get up to go to the bathroom. It took so much maneuvering for me to get to the stove to remove the main course when the timer went off that the venison I was serving was so dry it could have been used as dental floss.

"Delicious," my guests kindly said, nodding their heads, alternately smiling and chewing until their cheeks burned, while Nat King Cole's Christmas album played sweetly in the background.

But it didn't matter. After consuming nearly a case of wine under the softened, ambient light, we decided: it had been a good—even great—holiday dinner after all. The next year, aiming for drama, I smoked meaty Willapa Bay oysters over a pile of aged Lapsang souchong leaves I'd bought loose in a Chinatown tea shop, serving them as an hors d'oeuvre in their shells nestled tightly in a bright green, icy kiwifruit-granita seabed. Thick brown elm twigs that I had picked up in Central Park and soaked overnight in my bathtub until they were flaccid and soft as basket reeds served as kelp.

"This is just a tiny bit insane," my friend Betsy whispered to me, standing in front of my first-editions bookcase and sipping garnet-hued, baby grape–infused vintage Laurent Perrier in a Riedel flute as my other guests milled around.

"Am I supposed to eat the bark?" she asked, holding it up to my track lighting.

+++

The first Christmas I spent with Susan—just a month or so after we met—didn't exactly happen on Christmas. She celebrated the holiday with her mother, cousins, and aunts, and, even though we had slipped into the sort of bucolic, slightly saccharine comfort zone that made other people around us instantly nauseous, it was still far too early for me to join her family for their holiday dinner.

"Can you come up a few days before Christmas?" Susan asked. "Is that okay?"

I assured her that it was, and immediately set to work preparing a Christmas menu for two: there would be a small roast goose—a gosling, if one could be found—and persimmon-glazed Brussels sprouts, creamed pearl onions with baby peas, a trifle, or, if we had the time, a flaming plum pudding.

"Just for us?" Susan asked when I called to read my litany of Dickensian overabundance to her over the phone.

"Why not?" I said. "It's our first Christmas together—I'd like to celebrate."

"How about a small roast beef instead of the goose?"

"How about a standing rib roast?" I countered.

"For the two of us?" I could hear the weariness in her voice. "Can one rib stand up on its own?"

"Haven't you heard?" I answered snarkily. "One rib is a *steak*. We are not having an ordinary steak for our first Christmas dinner together; it's just not Christmas-y enough." I imagined one slab of meat balancing on its end, pathetic and alone.

"Let's just figure it out when you get here, okay?" she said. "We can go shopping together. There's a great meat market right down the road in Litchfield, and we can pick everything out, buy some nice wine, and spend the day cooking together. It'll be wonderful— I promise."

I swooned: the image of the two of us pushing a shopping cart up and down the aisles of a supermarket together in forty years was burned in my brain.

"Okay, honey," I responded, "whatever you'd like."

And really, it was okay, except for the snow that began to fall in vast dumpings when I got off the train in Hartford. Driving back to her house along Farmington Avenue, Susan's little Hyundai began to fishtail, and by the time we got to the house, there was nearly three inches on the ground, and by afternoon, a foot, making the roads impassible.

"I think we should go out now if we're going out at all," I said to her, as we trimmed the tree with the ancient decorations of her childhood. There was a faded, formerly red-and-green, pinwheel that she made from construction paper when she was five, in the late 1950s; there was a pipe-cleaner Santa that her cousin Rose had given her when she was not yet ten; there were mountains of vintage glass ornaments from the 1930s that had belonged to her mother—hollowed out, hand-painted jewels that put folk-art Pottery Barn ornaments to shame.

"I hate to tell you," Susan said, looking out the front slider into the yard. The car was now completely indistinguishable from the snow drift next to it. "I don't think we're going *anywhere* until a plow comes through."

"Don't you even want to *try*?" I whined.

"It's too dangerous," she said, "besides which, I think we'll be fine here. We can make onion soup—we have a little wine, we have some cheese and bread and onions. And each other—right?" She hugged me while I stood there flapping my arms, like a rag doll.

"Right," I squeaked, staring over Susan's shoulder out the slider, at the snow piling up in drifts in the backyard.

We sat together that night on the floor of the living room, the first Christmas tree of my life decorated in a mismatched hodgepodge of childhood ornaments, drinking bourbon Manhattans out of two etched glasses that Susan's father had won in a bridge tournament at the Knights of Columbus back in the mid-1960s. I sucked the sweet, burning smoky syrup into my mouth between my front teeth, thinking about New York and the Christmases of my youth, of chronic disappointment and the relentless urge I had to infuse celebration, however inauthentic, wherever I could.

"What is it?" Susan said softly, reaching for my hand.

"I just thought—"

"What?"

"I don't know, Susie—"

"That we'd do something a little *fancier*?"

"I guess—" I looked away, out the front slider window to the snowy street.

"You don't get it, *do you*?" she asked, putting down the string of lights she was trying to untangle.

I shuddered and half-smiled, and thought of the coils of balsam roping I considered buying at one of the tree stands down at the Union Square market, as a surprise.

"We have dinner right there," she said, nodding over to the kitchen. "And I have you. It's all I want for Christmas."

ONION PANADE

There could be nothing to eat in the house—no meat, no fish, no chicken, no pasta, no rice, no nothing—but if you have a big onion, some leftover bread, some cheese, and some broth of any kind (chicken or beef, but vegetable will do in a snap), you've got the makings for this dish, which is peasant food at its finest. Anyone who knows *soupe a l'oignon gratinée* understands that it's just an excuse to eat the soup-soaked bread, and bubbly, crunchy brown cheese that cascades over the sides of the bowl. This onion panade is exactly that: unctuously delicious onion soup, without the soup.

Serves 2 to 3

3 tablespoons extra-virgin olive oil

2 large Spanish onions, thinly sliced (about 3 cups)

2 garlic cloves, minced

Salt

6 slices day-old country-style bread or baguette

1 cup grated Parmigiano-Reggiano cheese (or, more traditionally, Gruyère)

2 to 3 cups stock (beef, chicken, or vegetable)

1. Preheat the oven to 325°F.

2. In a large skillet set over medium heat, warm the olive oil until it begins to shimmer. Add the onion slices to the pan, toss to coat them with the oil, and cook slowly, until the onions are golden brown and a bit sticky, about 10 minutes. Add the garlic and continue to cook another 5 minutes. Remove the pan from the heat and taste an onion for seasoning; add salt if you need to.

3. Grease an ovenproof, 2-quart soufflé dish, and line the bottom with 2 pieces of the bread. Spoon a thick layer of onions and garlic onto the bread—enough so that the bread is completely obscured. Top with one-quarter of the grated cheese, and another 2 pieces of bread. Make another layer until you have used all of the onions and the bread, but are left with ¼ cup of the cheese.

Slowly pour in the stock, a cup at a time, until it is completely absorbed by the bread. Once it begins to overflow, you've used enough. Top with the remaining cheese, and carefully place the soufflé dish on a baking sheet.

4. Slide the sheet into the oven, and bake until the panade has puffed up beyond the sides of its dish and the top is golden brown, about 1½ hours.

5. Serve immediately in warm bowls.

PART II

CHAPTER 15

Famous

There is a photograph of my mother that will always remain vivid and clear in my memory: In this picture, she is sitting at the edge of a vast, kidney-shaped saltwater pool at Caesar's Palace in Las Vegas, wearing a long-sleeved, turtleneck, navy-blue Emilio Pucci bikini. Her nearly white, sun-bleached blonde hair is pulled back in a sleek ponytail so tightly gathered that not one strand flies out of place, and her eyes are pulled, ever-so-subtly, back toward her earlobes. She wears ghostly white, chalky lipstick that glows like a harvest moon against her perfect, caramel tan. I'm seven years old, half in the water, hanging on to the round metal pool bannister, my dark blonde hair streaked a ribbony lemon yellow. Over my bathing suit I'm wearing a white T-shirt emblazoned with a picture of Flipper to protect me from the brutal desert sun that singed and bubbled my skin in the first few hours we were there, when I insisted on going swimming immediately, as children always do. My mother is tall and fashionable, thin and stunning, and behind her, over her shoulder and just faintly out of focus, men are staring at her, and she doesn't even seem to know it.

It is late spring, 1970, during a three-week trip that my parents and I took to the West Coast. Chez Panisse is just a glimmer in Alice Waters' mind. Janis Joplin and Jimi Hendrix are still alive, the Vietnam War is still raging, and Kent State is a fresh and bloody memory. Wherever we go—Las Vegas and San Diego, Beverly Hills and Carmel, San Francisco and Palo Alto—there are crowds in the streets and in the airports. My father takes pictures with his white Linhof pistol-grip camera, as bald men in robes hand me flowers, and young blacks march in sunglasses and berets. The air is thick with energy and rage, and even though I'm a young child, my parents expose me to all of it—to the fashions, the food, and even the fury: one afternoon, my father inexplicably drives us through a still bombed-out, depressed Watts in his rented, royal-blue Torino convertible while my mother screams and alternately laughs *noooooo*, a trail of capricious white suburban fear and anxiety careening around our car like a passel of empty Just Married cans clattering off the back bumper.

"We're really slumming it!" she bubbles, still giddy with danger, in a phone conversation with Gaga from the bathtub in our room at the Beverly Hilton Hotel.

Wherever we go on this trip, we are together; my parents have somehow managed to temporarily abandon the anger, silence, and disappointment of their real lives, and instead, they appear to be a contented—even *happy*—couple. We park the Torino and stroll around Nepenthe and San Simeon, and my mother, who believes that all squirrels are rabid, lets me hand-feed the ones at Point Lobos; we walk from Ghirardelli Square all the way to The Haight—which leaves her cooing with delight at paisley-draped stoners—and then back down to Fisherman's Wharf. We eat high food and low in fancy, Naugahyde-covered dining rooms and from the food concessions that dot Highway 1—everything from spicy cioppino and chewy chowder out of take-out cups to sole mornay to fish tacos and my first spoonful of gravelly granola, doled out of a vintage canning jar and into a small coffee bowl of thick, homemade yogurt, in the dining room of a tiny, jewel box of an inn, in Carmel-by-the-Sea.

Just for this trip, my mother has somehow lost her fear and loathing of food and the three of us dine everywhere together, from

Chasen's and Nate 'n' Al's to the Bantam Cock, the Brown Derby, the Mandarin. There are no attempts at rolling her food around on her plate to keep from eating it; there are no snide comments and sideways admonitions to my father, who wipes his plate clean with warm pieces of sourdough bread torn from the ever-present baskets on every table we're seated at. It takes me years to understand why: instead of focusing on what she's eating, my mother instead is in awe and not a little starstruck—every restaurant we visit in Los Angeles is packed with actors and actresses whose movie careers she follows, has memorized, the way a choir boy knows his catechism.

"Please, Rita," my father quietly begs over dinner one night in Beverly Hills when he catches her staring at a familiar, handsome man sitting at a banquette across from us with another man. "Don't say anything to them—*please*."

"For god's *sake*," she laughs, "don't you understand that they *want* to be recognized? Acting is a ploy to get attention—that's all it is."

✝✝✝

My mother, even now, says that the '60s and '70s were "her time"; she loved the music and the fashion and the hippies and the hair, even though she was already in her late twenties and looking back at a full professional life as the television girl singer on *The Galen Drake Show*—the predecessor to variety shows like Carol Burnett's—and as a high-fashion fur model in Manhattan. She is not like other mothers: she doesn't bake cookies, she doesn't bake bread, she doesn't make me sugared cinnamon toast when I come in from playing outside in the snow after school. Instead, we stand on checkout lines in the grocery store together and people recognize her.

"Didn't you used to be on television?" they ask, and my mother—standing there in her lace front, leather hip huggers, and midriff blouse, with the candy racks and piles of Hostess Twinkies and Hand

Pies stacked up on endcaps behind her—suddenly appears taller. She smiles and replies *yes*, she had been, and I gaze back and forth at the two of them in silence, *mortal v. model*; one grocery cart is filled with Mrs. Butterworth's and frozen Swanson's fried chicken and the kind of poppin' fresh dough biscuits that come in a cardboard roll that you have to smack on the counter, and the other cart filled with wafer-thin Pepperidge Farm Diet White, a toothpaste-like squeeze tube of red caviar, a long plastic see-through container of empty snail shells and a tall can of Roland escargot, tiny tins of white tuna packed in water, and a container of eggs, from which the yolks will be discarded. My mother, who sets lamb chops on fire every time she makes them for me, has taken a liking to escargot at a French soup restaurant on West Fifty-Fifth Street, and has attempted to re-create the dish at home: Shells, *check*. Snails, *check*. Pack snails back into their shells, stuff with butter and parsley, and broil. She serves this to friends when they come to the house for cocktails, while other mothers serve chips and dip made from onion soup mix and sour cream.

"There's absolutely *nothing* to them," she says to me one late weekend afternoon, forcing the escargot back into their shells with a long wooden skewer. "Not caloric at all."

A high-fashion princess, wherever she went or whatever the day had in store—whether she was walking the dog or buying a head of shrink-wrapped iceberg lettuce at the nearby Associated Grocery Store, run by Henry and his wife, a sad, blonde Holocaust survivor with green numbers tattooed on her arm—my mother refused to leave the house without full, heavily applied makeup. She was the first woman in our town to wear Mary Quant eyeliner, which made her look like a blonde Cleopatra; she wore false eyelashes so long that on our trip to California, Super-8 home movies show her at Seal Rock, her lashes fluttering and flapping in the strong coastal wind until the thin line of white glue gives way and they take flight into the breeze, like the tiny, body-less wings of an ortolan, while I watch, laughing until my sides ache.

✛✛✛

In our Queens, New York, town, the mothers of my friends typically wore zip-front polyester housecoats and flowered Dacron dresses that brushed the floor and hung over the sides of their red Dr. Scholl's exercise sandals. They did their grocery shopping and cooking wearing paisley silk babushkas wrapped around wire-mesh curlers until an hour before their husbands arrived home from work in Manhattan. But not my mother: one afternoon, I came home from school to find her alone in the living room, singing at the top of her lungs to a Peggy Lee album. I shuddered and cried; it was the time of big, happy, tidy, gentile television families, and I wanted my mother to be Livvy Walton, who would never be seen out of her apron, who would make me cinnamon toast or cream cheese and jelly sandwiches every day. I wanted to actually see my mother do things like laundry.

But she wasn't like the other mothers, who dressed their kids in triple-weave jumpers from Korvettes, bell-bottom jeans, or prim plaid dirndl skirts paired with Peter Pan blouses. My mother, with a metabolism like a hummingbird and a stack of her own studio recordings sitting next to my father's stereo, walked around town clad in leather hip huggers and miniskirts, fringed jackets and tie-dyed Wranglers, and dressed me the same way, like we shopped at a mother-daughter store managed by someone on an acid trip. She'd thrillingly send me off to school like that, and when she picked me up at the bus stop each day, would take me to our local luncheonette for a small snack of grilled cheese and bacon—like it wasn't fattening if someone else made it for me—and there I'd sit, revolving around and around on the counter stool, the fringe on my leather jacket flying every which way, while my friends—often the children of much older German or Dutch immigrant parents—looked on. Months later, when the weather became warm and every family in our building bought a membership to our local pool, the other kids would arrive dressed alike in one-piece bathing suits with modesty panels and ruffled white skirts. They gawked and whispered when they saw my mother, cooling her gold-sandaled feet in the chlorinated water, dressed in her navy-blue Pucci turtleneck bikini, take a long, smooth drag off her Virginia Slims, gazing through her blue-lensed Jean Shrimpton aviators at the suburban, tedious life she'd somehow managed to find herself stuck in.

CARMEL FISH TACOS

Depending where you eat them, fish tacos might be fried and topped with mayonnaise and rolled in a flour tortilla with all manner of accoutrement, from tomato to lettuce to onion. The thing that made these tacos so remarkable that they stick out in my mind all these years later was not just that they were served to me out of a weather-beaten shack on Highway 1 by a fringe-wearing hippie, but their unwavering simplicity; they require nothing more than corn tortillas (the fresher the better), the absolute freshest white fish you can find, and a squeeze of lime. Once I grew up, I started doctoring them with a few dribbles of Cholula hot sauce, but only a drop.

Serves 2

1 tablespoon grapeseed oil

½ pound fresh, flakey white fish (such as sole)

Four 6-inch corn tortillas

Lime wedges

Hot sauce of your choice

1. In a small skillet set over medium heat, warm the oil until it shimmers. Add the fish to the pan and cook until the fish is barely opaque, about 4 minutes per side. Remove from the heat, and set aside.

2. While the fish is cooking, heat a medium cast-iron skillet or griddle until a sprinkle of water sizzles when it hits it, about 3 minutes. Toast the corn tortillas until they begin to brown in spots, and then turn.

3. Wrap a bit of fish in each tortilla, hit it with a squeeze of lime and, if desired, a drop of hot sauce. Serve immediately.

CHAPTER 16

Diet White

We are sitting at Café Luxembourg on Seventieth Street in Manhattan during an early-spring snowstorm a few months after Susan and I met, when my mother observes, apropos of nothing, that she can't recall when food became so important in my life.

"I mean, when exactly did it happen?" she says, "You used to be so skinny?"

"I'm not exactly *big*, Mom," I say, under my breath.

"That picture of us at Caesar's Palace? My god, you were such a rail!"

"I was seven."

"I know that," she answers, taking a bite of a heavily seeded roll.

"And you were wearing a turtleneck bikini and white lipstick," I say.

"That was a *very* expensive suit, honey," she snorts, slightly humbled. "And the white lipstick looked fabulous!"

"You're right, Mom—it did."

And really, it did. She was gorgeous.

She still *is* gorgeous.

"But times and styles change, though, don't they?" I add.

"I know they do, honey, but it's all relative—don't you think? I mean, you were so tiny that I used to have to shake you into your leotards in the morning the way you shake a pillow into a pillowcase! It was all your grandmother and I could do to get you to eat. And now, all you do is talk about food: what you ate, what you're planning on eating, what you're cooking for a party. And all of those boxes of cooking tools in your apartment? I just don't get it. You should get rid of them—really."

I drum my soupspoon against the side of the metal-wire bread basket and order a glass of Gigondas.

My mother, even now, is a magnificent woman, with her Annie Lennox crop of platinum blonde, asymmetrically cut hair, her enormous velvet-brown eyes, and the clothes—always the clothes—that hang on her svelte, broad-shouldered, model's body. Instinctively, when we go to a restaurant, I give her the seat facing the mirror to give her something to do while she pushes food around on her plate: a head shake here, a reapplication of Shanghai Red lipstick there, a coy glance in a bistro-reflecting glass at long-dead Nathan Applebaum, her regular Stork Club date who she dumped for Dick Shawn after a weekend at the Raleigh Hotel in the late 1950s. They all make suitable substitutions for focusing on eating the meal that she will order, that I will pay for, and that she will leave virtually untouched.

But today, on this quiet, snowy late morning, I've mistakenly given her the wrong view, and all she can do is stare at me in silence through those gigantic black round glasses of hers that she started wearing long before Iris Apfel bought her first pair. My mother watches me closely as I nibble on a voluptuous hamburger sagging under the weight of cave-aged Gruyère, sautéed sweet onions, and a dollop of chutney.

"What's that?" she asks, reaching over with her teaspoon to scrape some dripping off the sides of my burger.

"Branston Pickle," I say, with my mouth full, holding up my napkin.

"But I don't see any pickles—"

"There aren't any," I say. "It's a chutney, for sandwiches—"

She licks the fruity paste off her spoon.

"Tastes sweet," she says. "I'm sure it's very fattening." She sighs, wiping her lipstick off onto her linen napkin. "Have you heard back from the headhunter yet?"

"No—not yet," I answer, staring out the window. My dot-com is about to fold and she's insisted I talk to a family friend about a desk job that I don't want at a publishing house with a reputation for chewing up their editors and spitting them out into tiny, little, bloody pieces.

My burger is getting cold and the onions are starting to congeal. But the thought of what would happen if I kept eating it—the glaring that will ensue, the sideways comments, the sudden desire to take me shopping so she can monitor what size jeans I'm now wearing—leaves me cold.

"Maybe he'd call," she says, "if you dropped a little weight?"

+++

For a lifetime, this has been the crux of the conversation for me and my mother, who turns heads wherever she goes. Lithe and elegant, as she's been as long as I've known her, the fact of food, of weight, really, is still there for her, flitting around like Tinker Bell, taking up exhaustive quantities of unconscious mental time and space with hummingbird-like energy. Constantly dieting from the day she turned fifteen—when it struck her that while no one could see how heavy she was as a 150-pound child radio singer, they certainly would see her on television, where she intended to perform, and did—her staunch enemy has been the food on her plate. She takes no comfort or joy in that food; it's an adversary meant to be manipulated and maneuvered. Restaurants are places not to eat but to be seen, and the Stork Club, El Morocco, 21, had been some of her haunts before she married my father. I ask her what she ate on those late nights after her performances at the Copacabana were over, and what kind of food they served, and she looks at me blankly. She can tell me what she wore, down to the most minute detail; the cut, color, material, designer—even the contents of her purse. But when asked about food she goes silent and vacant. She is so terrified of eating that she has no recollection of anything that might put an ounce of weight on her needle-thin body.

"Of *all things*," she cried, when I told her that I was going to work for Dean & DeLuca, "*that's* what you're going to do? I *paid* for you to go to college."

"But it's what I love, Mom," I whined.

She winces, like she's in pain.

"But will you have to eat *everything* you sell?" she squeaks, her voice getting higher and softer.

"I certainly *hope* not," I say, remembering the cans of smoked grouse the store carried in its British section, which were purported to contain buckshot.

"Well, thank god for that," she says. "I mean, surrounded by all that food, all the time, you could get fat just by *being* there."

So great is her obsession with weight—whether hers or mine—that whenever I stay overnight at her house, even now, she regularly checks the tags on my clothes to see what size I'm wearing, so I clip them off to avoid discussion.

✝✝✝

A year after I started working at Dean & DeLuca, when it moved from Prince Street to the corner of Broadway, we employees were allowed to invite two people each to the opening party: *Interview* magazine and Bill Cunningham were rumored to be coming, and knowing how much my mother and her second husband, Ben—the charming furrier who she'd gone to work for when I was in middle school shortly before my parents' divorce—relished the diamond-in-the-rough social scene that was SoHo in the 1980s, I gave them the tickets. I stood at the back of the store in my starched, white apron watching while Ben shmoozed Lauren Hutton at the door.

"I think your mother has a new friend," my colleague Gordon said, motioning over to where she was standing, five feet from me, near tall Metro shelving piled high with stacks of French copper from Villedieu.

Impeccably dressed in a dark gray chesterfield coat, his reading glasses perched at the end of his nose, Craig Claiborne stood chatting with her, her sable jacket casually draped around her shoulders. She looked fabulous.

"Come, my dear," Craig said to my totally oblivious mother, linking arms with her. "Let's go visit the lamb chops."

They strolled over to the meat case, bent down, and peered in. Craig—whose *New York Times Cookbook* my father had prized as a bachelor, and whose every word he scoured in the *New York Times* food section each Wednesday of my childhood like it was the Talmud—gazed at the prenatally tiny lamb riblets, while my mother, not sure what she was looking at, or with whom, stared down a pork loin.

"I met the nicest man tonight," she told me later as we walked down Prince Street toward Raoul's, where Ben could have a steak and my mother, a salad.

"He says he's a food writer. *But you're so thin!* I told him."

+++

"So," she says, putting down her fork, having made small piles of the lentils du Puy that are sitting on her plate. "Are you going to tell me?"

"Tell you *what*, Mom?" I ask, sipping my wine.

"What's in Connecticut. Because there's definitely *something* in Connecticut—"

She opens up her compact, fixes her hair, clicks it shut, and puts it away.

My heart begins to pound.

"Look," she says, "I'm no fool. You're never around on the weekends anymore, so I know that *something's* going on *up there.*" She reduces me to a teenager whose parents have just discovered a joint floating in the toilet.

From the day I came out to her in the mid-1990s—when I finally let on to my glamour-puss mother that her daughter liked ladies—we've never spoken about the people I've dated or been involved with. She never asked if I had met anyone, or if there was anyone special in my life.

But by now, I'd been leaving the city every weekend, for months, and my mother had no idea where I was going, or why. I'd wanted to keep it that way for as long as possible for the simple reason that I'd wanted to keep my relationship mine, untainted, and unfettered.

"Fine, Mom," I say to her, looking away. "I met someone."

"Boy or girl?"

"*What?*"

"Boy or *GIRL?*"

"Mom, what do *you* think?"

"If I knew, I wouldn't ask, silly, now would I," she coolly snaps, pressing her napkin against her lips.

"So you actually managed to forget that little lesbian thing I told you about a few years ago?"

"*Shhhh,*" she hushes, like a burst steam pipe. She looks around, deflated.

"Why are you shushing me?"

"Gay," she whispers. "I prefer gay. It's just classier."

"What*ever,* Mother."

"Does she like food, too?"

"Yes, Mom, she likes food, too—"

"So she's fat, then?"

"Why on earth would you think that? Because I said she likes food?"

"I just think that if a person really likes food, odds are, they're going to be—you know—*fat*. I mean, Julia Child is fat—"

"She's a big woman, Mom—that's all."

"*F-A-T*," she whispers to me, spelling it out, mouthing the letters, silently, like when my Aunt Sylvia leans over to her partner during duplicate bridge and mouths that *Doris Goldberg's sister-in-law has c-a-n-c-e-r*.

"Will you STOP already?" I plead.

"So, she is or she isn't?"

"For god's sake!"

"So she is, then—"

"Just stop." I'm almost in tears. "She's gorgeous, Mom."

If she wants to know, I'll tell her, I decide. My mother looks at her nails uncomfortably as I give her selective details: that Susan is a book designer who owns a home in Connecticut and loves dogs and photography and looks like Jean Seberg and keeps her sea salt in a small ceramic bowl on her counter next to her stove. My mother drifts away; I feel it, like I've become white noise. I'm in love, and even though she was the one who asked, she doesn't want to hear it. She flares her nostrils, snorts her disapproval, rolls her eyes, and together, we stare at each other for thick minutes that drip with tension, that feel like hours, staring out the window, as the waiter picks up the breadbasket. My mother dives for it, breaking the silence.

"Just *one more little* roll," she coos at him, plucking it out of the basket to change the subject, to redirect it back to food and weight.

"I just can't figure it," she says, adding "—you were *so* painfully skinny as a child."

No matter the outrageousness of her rambling commentary, I always listen closely to her repeated concerns that perhaps, as a food writer, I would eventually wind up like poor, stout Suzanne Muchnik, who grew up across the street from me.

"They'll have to bury that poor girl in a damned piano case," Gaga would say, shaking her head when we found out that, as a ten-year-old, Suzanne was suffering from diabetes so bad that she was having to take shots every day.

"*In the leg*—that's where," Gaga would add, clasping her heavy hands together and shaking them like a prizefighter who'd just won a heavyweight title.

So I grew up terrified of becoming Suzanne Muchnik and having diabetes and getting shots in the leg. And while my mother watched *Name That Tune!* on our little black-and-white television and my father read the paper and drank his Scotch in silence, I refused to eat the fatty lamb rib chops that she had mindlessly shoved under the broiler and set ablaze while the dog and I ran off to hide in my bedroom from the conflagration. On Friday nights, there was my grandmother's roast chicken, which I picked at. There was almost always canned asparagus, off-season cranberry sauce, and rye bread from our local Jay-Dee Bakery on Queens Boulevard. I nibbled on everything like a gerbil, barely making a dent, but when my mother produced her lamb chops and they caught fire, sending angry flames shooting and licking up the front of our Chambers stove until my grandmother beat them back with a greasy kitchen towel, I'd go on a hunger strike. Igniting our dinner over and over again said it all: food was not love in my house. Food was dangerous, and deadly, and something to be beaten into submission, right after it was immolated.

There was nothing convivial about our meals—there was no gorgeous routine, no cozy, chattering lessons from my father about mother sauces and what turned a sauce espagnole into a bordelaise. There was no attempt at a mornay or a bourguignon, and the last time the copy of Craig Claiborne's *New York Times Cookbook* had been cracked open was in my father's East Seventy-Ninth Street bachelor apartment, before he and my mother were married; now, it sat on the top shelf on my parents' Danish modern bookcase, sandwiched between his collection of Frank O'Hara poetry and Henry Miller's

Tropic of Cancer, dusty and forbidden. While I loved the secret, illicit La Côte Basque lunches that he and I shared on the sly, I hated our silent, heavy dinners at home that reeked of my discontent and ancient angers and the sweet, gamey odor of charred baby lamb. Still, despite my resistance to eating at the family dinner table and my Biafran physique, my mother made my school lunches on thin-sliced, Pepperidge Farm Diet White, which fell apart into stark white crumbs by ten in the morning; and if the neighbors were having a fondue party at the end of the week, Phillips' Milk of Magnesia showed up in the fridge, kept icy cold between small bottles of Tab and Fresca.

CHAPTER 17

Fish

"Hello," the Peter Pan Bus driver announces over the loudspeaker. "My name is Peter, and I will be your driver to Hartford this evening."

I laugh out loud, alone.

Peter. Peter Pan. Hah.

I am sitting in the front seat with no one next to me because, on my lap, in a large plastic shopping bag, sit four gallon-size ziplock bags containing two pounds each of ground whitefish and pike; various fish heads, tails, and bones; and three quarters of a pound of pulverized onion. I can't smell anything, the way ladies who drench themselves in Shalimar can't smell it after a while either.

In all the years I'd been cooking, I'd never once baked (and froze) two matzo meal pound cakes (one for the first night of Passover, one for the second), or made vats of chicken soup, or braised briskets. I'd never made matzo balls or roasted a shank bone for the seder plate, or prepared three different kinds of kugels. That was always Lois's job, and one she willingly took on. Lois is the family party maven, possessed of remarkable organizational skills, who could undoubtedly have orchestrated the Allied landings at Normandy without getting a run in her panty hose.

The year before I met Susan, a few days before Passover, Lois called me from her home on Long Island to ask if I wanted to learn how to make gefilte fish, from scratch.

"You mean like with live carp, swimming in the bathtub?" I asked.

"No one does that anymore, silly," she said. "Be here at noon, and wear old clothes."

The next day, I was standing at Lois's immense kitchen sink, using the heavy ceramic pestle that our great-grandmother had schlepped over from the Old Country to pound fish heads in a huge stainless colander set over a mixing bowl. Every window in the house was cranked open.

"That's what makes the fish jelly," she said, as I pounded and pounded, reducing the fish heads to a thick, grayish pulp.

Within a few hours, we had formed and shaped somewhere in the neighborhood of thirty fish balls, which were simmering away in a tall aluminum stockpot; in a separate fish poacher, the bones and pulp and an onion burbled underneath the poaching tray, and the aroma of boiling fish and steaming bones filled air and engulfed the entire house. Every cat in the neighborhood showed up at the front door. Odd bits of mashed whitefish clung to the undersides of the golden oak cabinets, having been catapulted into the air like small, fishy missiles by my exuberant pounding.

"All this to avoid buying the stuff in the jars?" I asked, my arms burning.

"You'll taste one," Lois explained, "and you'll know why I make it from scratch."

It was the most exquisite, delicate, tender gefilte fish I'd ever tasted, anywhere, and absolutely worth the effort and cost, including having to throw away my favorite sweatshirt, which still reeked though it'd been laundered seven or eight times to get the stench out.

+++

"I think *we* should make it from scratch," Susan said to me one night on the phone, when I described my fish head–pounding tale. "It probably is so much better than the stuff in the jar."

"How would *you* know?" I asked, laughing.

"Are you kidding?" she balked, "I *love* gefilte fish—"

"You *love* gefilte fish. *You?*"

"I do," she laughed, "and tongue sandwiches, kishka, and kasha varnishkes."

This woman—freckled, green-eyed, salt-and-pepper-haired, and as Irish-looking as Maureen O'Hara—loved Jewish food. But gefilte fish?

I couldn't believe it. I assumed she just wanted to make a good first impression on my family, when she'd suggested we make gefilte fish from scratch, but she actually loved the stuff.

"Since I'm meeting everyone for the first time," she suggested, "I think we should just pull out the stops. It'll even be cheaper than buying ten jars of it." This was mostly true: my cousin's Passover seders were grand, extensive affairs, with her own children bringing stray friends, Ellen and Peter and their kids coming from Washington and Michigan, and my father with his longtime girlfriend, Shirley. Dinner could easily wind up being for twenty-plus. That's a lot of bought gefilte fish, if you figure two fish balls per person.

"Is there a fish market up there somewhere?" I asked. Harwinton, where Susan lived, was a good hour away from West Hartford and the nearest big Jewish community.

"There's Value Mart."

"No way. All their fish has rigor mortis. For gefilte fish, it needs to be fresh—super fresh. And I want the fish guys to grind everything. Lois says that's what they're supposed to do."

"Why don't you just bring it up from the city this weekend?" she asked. "We can make it on Saturday, and then cart it back down to Long Island for the seder."

"Bring it up to bring it back down?"

"Honey, I really want to do this, okay? *Please?*"

Susan got very quiet when she said please, like a five-year-old asking for candy because she's been such a good girl. I could never say no.

"Okay." I sighed. "You win."

✛✛✛

On Friday at lunch, I jumped into a cab and headed uptown to my fishmongers on Beekman Place. The shop was a few blocks from Arnaud's, and bar none, the most expensive fish market in the city; every day, Sundays included, they received fresh deliveries directly from the city's wholesale fish market, and virtually every good restaurant in New York bought their seafood from them. When I arrived, Salvatore handed me a slightly damp plastic shopping bag filled with ground fish, pulverized onion, bones, and a separate baggy packed with crushed ice. I handed him my credit card and winced as I signed the bill.

That afternoon, after work, my bag of fresh-ground fish, bones, and onion and I raced up to Penn Station and bought our Amtrak ticket to Hartford, only to discover that the trains weren't running. Together, the fish and I ran outside to search for a taxi. It had started raining and people were flinging themselves onto cab hoods in order to hail them. The only option was Port Authority and finding a bus that would take me up to Hartford in more or less the same time frame, since the small fortune of fish I was toting along with me couldn't be risked.

"Do you have the fish?" Susan asked when I called her cell from the last available cab in the city, hurtling toward the bus station.

She made it sound like heroin.

"Of *course* I have the fish," I assured her.

"Is it warming up? Maybe you can jump off at one of the stops and get another bag of ice."

"I'm not jumping anywhere," I told her. "It'll be fine."

And when I arrived in Hartford, two and a half hours later, it mostly was fine: I smelled of onions and pike and my lap was soaking wet, but nobody had dared sit next to me the whole way up.

The next morning, we lowered the heat in the house to keep the furnace from going off every few minutes, cranked open every window, gave the dog a huge bone to distract her, rolled up our sleeves, and made homemade gefilte fish from scratch for twenty people. Susan gingerly formed and shaped each fish ball, alternately dipping her hands into ice water to keep them from warming the mixture; she gently nudged and caressed each oval into a size and shape identical to the previous ones she made until there, on her largest Anne Hathaway's Cottage platter, sat forty-one matching ovals, ready to be cooked in her mother's hand-me-down RevereWare stockpot. The extra one was for us: it was tender, sweet, and the absolute ideal of what gefilte fish should be.

"Even Eric Ripert would be proud of these," I said, my mouth full.

Susan stood back in her apron and inspected the platter.

"I think we did a great job." She put her arm around me and together, we stared at the result of our first collaborative cooking attempt.

"Happy Passover, sweetie," Susan cooed, kissing the side of my head. "When do we have to fast?"

+++

My cousin Lois's house on Long Island was perfect for large parties. A contemporary built in the early 1980s, it was open, airy, with high ceilings and a dining room big enough to comfortably fit twenty around the table, its only small drawback being the step down from the living room to get to it. At least once every party, someone would forget that the step was there and take a header toward the table, which was heavily laden with holiday food and more silverware than the White House uses for state dinners. But no matter how much room there was in the rest of the house, everyone always gathered in the French Provincial–style kitchen, which is where they were when I walked Susan in through the garage door to meet my entire family, all at once, for the very first time.

Just before, driving down their street, we were both quiet.

"You nervous?" I asked, looking over from the passenger seat.

"No—they'll be fine."

"What?"

"The fish—they'll be fine. I wedged the dish between two rolled-up towels, so no worries."

"I was talking about meeting my family—"

She pulled the car up the driveway, shut it off, and took my hand.

"You need to stop worrying so much, honey," she said. "I'm not taking you to the prom, you know."

Susan was dressed to the nines that night, in a long dark gray silk pencil skirt and a black cashmere V-neck sweater. When we walked in, carrying an enormous soup terrine containing forty homemade gefilte fish produced from the most expensive whitefish and pike in the city of New York, my sea of cousins turned around, in silence.

"This is Susan, everyone," I announced, setting the dish down on the kitchen table.

Everyone smiled. Ellen and Peter got up from where they were sitting in the family room and gave her a hug like she was a long-lost friend. Someone handed her a Waterford goblet of non-kosher Sonoma-Cutrer Russian River Chardonnay.

"Are they here?" I could hear my father, who was standing in the dining room talking to Lois's husband, Stuart.

"Dad?"

He shouldered his way over and into the kitchen and wrapped his arms around me in a bear hug.

"Ishu—" his nickname for me when I was a very young child, "it's so good to see you, honey."

"Daddy, this is Susan," I said to him, pulling away while my cousins looked on. "We made the gefilte fish." I was so proud.

He looked at the two of us, taking a step back as though he needed distance to see us more clearly, and to size up this woman I'd finally brought home to meet my family. And he burst into tears.

MATZO BREI TARTE TATIN

Some like it savory (with onions, salt, and pepper), and some like it sweet (sugar, cinnamon), but however you like it, the fact of matzo brei—the traditional Passover, pancake-like amalgam of eggs and matzo—but made with apples and then flipped, like a tarte Tatin, cannot be underestimated. Created years ago by my Aunt Sylvia, the dish, which I have adopted, has achieved almost mythic notoriety, and people from far and wide will somehow find their way to her kitchen table on the mornings when she makes it. And if she doesn't make it, they beg her to. I am among them.

Serves 4

6 unsalted matzo boards

4 eggs, beaten

2 tablespoons unsalted butter

2 large apples, peeled, cored, and thinly sliced

3 tablespoons sugar

1 teaspoon cinnamon

Maple syrup, for drizzling

1. In a large bowl, crumble the matzo boards and combine them with the beaten eggs. Set aside.

2. In a large, nonstick skillet set over medium-high heat, melt the butter. When the foam subsides, add the apples to the pan, decrease the heat to medium, and cook until they begin to soften, 5 to 8 minutes. Sprinkle in the sugar and cinnamon and continue to cook until the apples begin to caramelize, turning a soft, sticky golden brown, about 10 minutes.

3. Pour the matzo mixture directly over the apples, and distribute it evenly using a wooden spoon. Cook until the egg mixture begins to pull away from the sides of the pan, about 5 minutes. Cover and continue to cook for another 8 to 10 minutes.

4. Remove the cover and give the pan a few good shakes. Carefully place a large dinner plate over the skillet, and invert it. Slide the brei back into the skillet and continue to cook for another 5 minutes, uncovered, apple-side up.

5. Slice into wedges and serve with warm maple syrup.

CHAPTER 18

The Guy on the Cross

Susan had gotten off easy, since the first holiday we'd celebrated with my family of extended cousins was Passover, and there's a section in the Haggadah that says *You shall not oppress a stranger, for you know the feelings of the stranger.* It's in the official rule book, and therefore against the law. But my family didn't exactly oppress; they just smiled and stared a lot, over the bowls of soup and the plates of matzo and *moror*, over the roasted shank bone and the bitter herbs. The woman I brought home to meet my Jewish family—they loved her at first sight—reached across the table for the vat of gefilte fish that we had made from scratch, dolloped a fish ball with enough horseradish to melt granite, and read every prayer when it came her turn. In English, but still. My father listened to her from his place at the end of the table, and cried again. But then again, my father had even been known to cry at supermarket openings.

And then, a week or so later, it was my turn to dine with her family.

Easter is a peculiar holiday for Jews, and it can be a little nervous-making. The more secular among us may put up Christmas trees and swear up and down that it's really just the solstice we're celebrating, but no Jew I know of is going to put a palm cross in the window and a trail of Easter eggs for the kids to find in the backyard. We're okay with a small, fat German man in a red suit breaking into the house and leaving Tiffany boxes and gold Schwinns under a tree, but when it comes to nailing a Jewish guy to a cross and waiting around for a few days until he dies—that's pretty much the rock bottom of our celebration scale.

But when I was invited to Susan's family's Easter celebration, I couldn't say no, and so I tried to look at it as more of a cultural experience. Easter was Susan's holiday—her favorite one, she told me, ever since she'd been a baby, when her father used to wait for her to fall asleep and then leave a trail of chocolate eggs through the house.

"Did you have to wear a special outfit?" I asked. I was an Easter ignoramus.

"Of course; I got a new spring coat every Easter," she said.

How nice, I thought. I got a box of waxy Manischewitz chocolate lollipops for finding a piece of the hidden matzo—the *afikomen*—accidentally left over from the previous Passover buried in the recesses of my grandmother's yellow-striped Duncan Phyfe sofa.

And Susan got a coat.

I'd been gypped.

"You're sure they even know you're a Jew?" my mother asked on the phone, when she called me at Susan's to find out what I was wearing. It was Easter morning, and the outfit I'd cobbled together for myself—a kelly green cable-knit sweater and pedal pushers covered in pastel hot-air balloons—hung off the bedroom closet doorknob.

"Of course they do—they must," I responded, but then I asked Susan while I was getting dressed. She smiled sweetly, hugged me, and told me not to worry.

"They're not without their prejudices," she promised, "but I'll be right there."

"*Great*—" I sighed, rolling my eyes.

I turned around and glanced at the mirror: I looked like the result of an explosion at a Lily Pulitzer factory.

"You look perfect," Susan said.

"I look like the spawn of Dina Merrill and Molly Picon."

"Honey," she soothed, "you'll be fine. Worse comes to worst, we can always stay in the kitchen and cook."

"And drink," I added.

Every family has culinary holiday rituals to which they adhere; there were always ancient stories rattling around about my great-grandmothers on both sides vacuuming out the most minute bread crumbs from every crack and crevasse in the kitchen before Passover, but no one followed suit after they died. Instead, my Aunt Sylvia used to slave for weeks on end, making a traditional Eastern European Jewish Passover menu—gefilte fish, mushroom and barley soup, brisket, and tzimmes. Then my cousin Lois took over, and started pulling the skin off skinny, hapless Cornish game hens, butterflying and roasting them for hours under a pungent, aromatic layer of orange peel soaked for days in brandy. Eventually, when I took over on a few occasions, my menus were fanciful, restaurant-style affairs filled with French and Sephardic dishes that most of my family just stared at, like potato pancakes topped with mousseline of salmon and a tiny boiled quail egg. They ate in silence: the Israelites did not eat mousseline on their forty-year hike through the desert. Game hen, yes. Mousseline piped out of a French pastry bag with a number-six star tip, not so much.

But when it came to Easter, Susan's family were traditionalists; there was no wiggle room for creativity or culinary experimentation. I considered ordering an artisanal country ham from Arnaud, and surprising them with it, but Susan shook her head. I suggested rigging up a spit in the backyard to roast a whole baby lamb, Greek-style, brushed tenderly with avgolemono sauce, but Susan said *no*. I wanted to make an Italian Easter bread, braided with colored eggs embedded in the dough, but Susan said *forget it*. These people were strict super-market ham folk, and they were not going to trust any Jewish New Yorker to either buy or bring it.

"How about something French? We don't have to do the whole spit-roasted lamb—we can just do seven-hour leg of lamb, with some braised white beans and rosemary. They'll love it." I envisioned perfect boneless slices of watermelon-pink, rare-cooked, garlicky lamb, arranged in a perfect circle atop a timbale of the beans and drizzled with persillade, presented to everyone on the gleaming white fourteen-inch chargers I'd stockpiled from my catering days.

No.

"They want what they want," Susan said, "and they want regular ham, and Polish bologna. It has to be simple, and it has to be what they know, otherwise they won't go near it."

"What the hell is Polish bologna?"

"Kielbasa," she said, laughing. "And they'll *never* eat the smoked stuff, so don't even go there."

"Why not?" I asked.

"Too fancy."

✝✝✝

That Easter was a combination of firsts: First introductions to people I'd never met before. My first experience with a visceral, unsettling sort of Hebraic terror. And my first attempt at impressing Susan's family. From the time we walked in, I had already secretly planned to squirrel myself away in Susan's mother's kitchen, along with the ham and the Polish bologna. Not taking any chances on ingredients for the glaze I had invented for the occasion, I packed for the trip in a striped L.L. Bean boat bag: bourbon, honey, Colman's English mustard, soy sauce, orange juice, and allspice. When we arrived at her house, I made a beeline for the kitchen, where I found a gigantic, ninety-nine cents per pound Cook's ham in the sink, floating in milk to remove some of the salt.

My ankles immediately began to leach over the sides of my shoes.

"Come," Susan said, taking me by the hand. "Let me introduce you."

She herded me into the living room, which was covered from one end to the other in small, stuffed bunnies and jelly beans that had been scattered hither and yon over the lime-green broadloom. In a small bowl set on the coffee table were three magnificent red, black, and white Ukrainian Easter eggs that Susan had painstakingly painted years before.

I stood there in my hot-air-balloon outfit, meeting a small crowd of aunts and cousins, who, when you added their ages, totaled 271. One by one, I said hello, and shook hands. One of the smaller ones looked at me and frowned like she'd just had a sip of sour milk. She leaned over to the aunt sitting next to her, who was adjusting her hearing aid.

"She shouldn't wear that color green—she looks *fat*. Doesn't she look *fat*?"

"Shhh, for gawd's sake, Sally, she can hear you," the hearing aid aunt said.

They can hear you in Warsaw, I muttered to myself, downing a glass of 15 percent alcohol Zinfandel, and fleeing for the kitchen, where the Polish bologna had been boiling for an hour, exploding out of the confines of its natural pork casing like it was a ripped condom.

✝✝✝

"They hate me," I muttered to Susan, tying on a flowered apron.

"They don't hate you. They don't even *know* you." She put her hand on my shoulder.

"Sally thinks I'm fat."

"Sally thought Twiggy was fat."

I dug up a small saucepan from the cabinet and started to put together the glaze, since I refused on principle to use the brown mucous-y stuff that came shrink-wrapped to the pig. It had been in the oven for an hour, so I took it out, scored it, lowered the oven temperature, and began to baste. And drink.

Another hour went by, and the ham started to emit a sort of burnt sugar aroma, like the time that I walked away from melting caramel during a dinner party and only realized what I'd done when the smoke alarm went off and the cats hid under the bed.

I opened the oven door and instead of pulling the rack out for one last baste, I bent down and reached in all the way, right up to my kelly-green shoulders. The glaze had burned and hardened like the outside of a candy apple that had been dipped in sugared bourbon.

"What in the *hell* are you doing? Take that ham out right now!" Sally was behind me, shrieking.

I peered over my shoulder from inside the oven, and all I could see was the flowered hem of her dress, her dark tan support hose, and her black bump toe shoes.

"I've been making Easter hams for *seventy years*, and I know when it's burnt, and *it's burnt*. So take it out, *now!*"

I could just hear the family stories: Susan brings home a Jew who carbonizes the milk-soaked Easter ham, winds up with her head in the oven, and half a dozen Polish octogenarian aunts lose several teeth while trying to navigate the glaze. Happy holidays.

But once we sat down, all anyone could do was eat and talk. There was a constant flurry to make sure that everyone's glasses were filled, and stayed filled. Questions were fired at me from around the table; Susan's mother and aunts spoke in a dated, slightly formal manner that made me squirm amid the clattering of silver.

"Where are your people *from*?" one of the aunts asked, passing around a footed silver-wire basket of dinner rolls so white they glowed.

We're New Yorkers, I answered.

"Susan says that you live in Manhattan, just like Marlo Thomas in *That Girl*—"

I nodded *yes* and smiled weakly.

"Well, you must be *very* rich—" another of the aunts mused dourly.

Susan gasped under her breath, looked at me, and mouthed the words *I'm sorry*.

"Elissa," Susan's mother interrupted, "where is *your* family celebrating Easter today?"

"They're not," I answered, buttering my roll. The color drained from Susan's face.

"*Why* not?" her mother asked. Everyone had stopped speaking. I sat there at the table and looked down to make sure I had remembered to put my pants on that morning before leaving the house.

"Because—" I couldn't think of a way to put it to this group of very devout, older Polish ladies who thought that Vatican II was some sort of left-wing radical conspiracy perpetrated by a crazed pack of Roman rabbis with a plan to take over the world.

"But *why*?" she repeated, cutting me off and staring at me long and hard.

"Because they don't *celebrate* Easter—" I answered, ripping my roll into tiny, buttered pieces until it sat in a pile on my plate, like I was getting ready to feed the birds in the backyard.

"They don't celebrate Easter? I've never *heard* of such a thing," Sally whispered to Et.

"I *know* it—" Et responded quietly.

"We all need more wine," Susan's cousin Richard chimed in, popping up from his seat and pouring me another enormous glass of Zinfandel. He patted my shoulder, leaned down, and whispered in my ear, "They're a tough crowd, kid. You're doing great."

That afternoon, Helen's table creaked under the weight of ancient family platters lined with crazing and blue-and-white, oven-to-table

Corelle ware: There was green bean casserole with the little crispy onions on top, and mashed potatoes thick with milk and butter. The kielbasa, sliced in rounds and eaten with a drizzle of yellow mustard, was basic and bland, but delicious. The ham, once you chipped off the coating, was sweet and tender.

Easter being Easter, all was forgiven.

CRISPY BRAISED EASTER KIELBASA

Kielbasa is a lot like sex—when it's good, it's fabulous, and when it's bad, it's still pretty good. But the idea of boiling a whole kielbasa in a pot of water for a few hours or until it explodes in celebration of one of the holiest Christian days of the year seemed to me to be, at best, suspect and, at worst, sacrilege. The version I prefer involves two cooking methods—braising and grilling—and the result is spectacular, and can be applied to virtually any mild sausage. If there are leftovers, slice them up and toss them into a frittata (see page 208) along with their onions.

Serves 3 as a small main course, 4 as an appetizer

Two 16-ounce bottles of very dark beer (such as stout or porter)

2 medium red onions, cut into rings

2 whole Polish kielbasas (smoked or fresh, about 1½ pounds), each poked twice with the tines of a fork

5 black peppercorns

5 juniper berries

2 allspice berries

1. In a medium Dutch oven or large saucepan, warm the beer over medium heat until it begins to foam rapidly. Place the onions in the pan, decrease the heat to medium-low, and cook until the onions have softened, about 10 minutes.

2. Place the kielbasas in the pan with the onions, and add the peppercorns, juniper berries, and allspice berries. Set the lid on the pot askew, and cook at a low simmer for 1 hour. Remove from the heat and, leaving the onions in the beer, transfer the kielbasa to a plate or platter.

3. Preheat a gas or charcoal grill to medium-high.

4. Grill the kielbasa over indirect heat, turning frequently, until it begins to blister and crackle, and the skin darkens, about 10 minutes.

5. Slice and serve, topped with the cooked onions, on warm toast or buns, accompanied by grainy mustard.

CHAPTER 19

Party

My father was a crier, a weeper, our family's Emmett Kelly, a known producer of endless tears that could erupt like Vesuvius with the slightest provocation. When my cousin Rebecca got married and I was in the wedding party, I asked permission to come down the aisle carrying tissues for him. And right there, on the video tape of the black-tie affair, recorded for posterity, is me, dressed from teased-blonde-head to toe in full-length lavender organza, marching down the aisle at the Mayflower Hotel in Washington, D.C., with a matching box of Kleenex tucked underneath my arm; I passed it off to my dad like it was a football and I was Joe Namath.

It never mattered the occasion. Dad once came for dinner to the Chelsea apartment I shared with Julie, and from a height of two feet, I drizzled his salmon with a bright green sorrel sauce until it was sitting in a small, perfect puddle. I used the corner of my towel to wipe the stray droplets, and presented him with his plate.

"It's beautiful," he cried, red-faced and choking on his words.

He was even known to sob when the news came on—it didn't matter if it was good or bad—suddenly appearing apoplectic and in need of his handkerchief. God forbid he saw a television show involving a lost puppy, or that Folger's commercial where a college kid surprises his parents by coming home in the middle of the night on Christmas Eve. At funerals, he was utterly inconsolable—he didn't even have to know the person well—and on the day in 1989 when he was listening to NPR on his commute home from work and heard that Vladimir Horowitz had died, he had to pull over to the side of the road to rest his head in his hands. As a devoted fan of classical music, my father's crying jag went on for an hour before he was able to get back on the road and head home, by then depleted and spent.

+++

When my parents were married, and until the day they divorced in 1978, my father lived a life of precariously guarded emotion, as though his sadness was so deep and exquisite that once released, it might never be reined in. Given to sudden rages that were there and then gone like fleeting summer storms, his otherwise ironclad, Danish Modern, Brooks Brothers, ad man exterior kept a tight stranglehold on anything that was untidy or unseemly. He poured his energies into his work, into taking care of his aging parents, into making sure that his wife was always dressed to the nines, and into the illicit food affair he had with me.

Manhattan's hushed halls of haute cuisine were my father's temples of peace and reason, where he went to shake off the detritus of disappointment and the fury it sometimes evolved into. Before marrying my mother, he was engaged five times to five different women he loved in five different ways, ending each relationship when his mother voiced her disapproval of them, as if they were sirens luring him away from his family: this one was too fat, that one was cross-eyed. This one wasn't worthy, that one was ugly. Off my grandmother went, again and again, until finally my father was introduced to my mother on a blind date and he knew his search was over. The polar opposite to his stocky, short, bespeckled self, she was tall, thin, blonde, stunning, a singer, a model, a clotheshorse, a trophy his family would be unable to find fault with. So after a short engagement, they were married, and nine months later, there I was: four pounds, as big as a Bresse chicken because my mother, not wanting to "balloon out," watched her weight while she was pregnant.

Dressed up and ready to go out, my parents made a gorgeous couple, and I regularly swooned over them on Saturday nights, when they headed into Manhattan leaving me at home with Gaga. But beyond the fancy dinners and the expensive clothes they wore like psychic body armor, my parents' sixteen years together were mostly cantankerous, alternately rage-filled or bitterly silent, with a few détentes here and there. They had absolutely nothing in common beyond me, and inevitably they drifted apart: a year after the Summer of Sam, when blackouts and garbage strikes paralyzed the city and Elvis, puffy as a fugu, was found dead on his bathroom floor at Graceland, my mother—who had gone to work for Ben-the-furrier the year before stopped coming home for dinner a few nights a week. My father had lost the magazine he'd quit the ad agency to launch; there were accusations of infidelity and gross financial incompetence on both sides. His business had gone bust, and my father could no longer support the lifestyle we were used to. My mother could no longer tolerate his failure.

As my parents' sixteenth wedding anniversary approached, there was no discussion of a fancy meal out in Manhattan, or a romantic vacation alone together. So, taking on the mantle of reason and convinced that I could save them, I secretly called their closest friends one night after dinner.

"I'm having a small anniversary party for my parents," I whispered into the bedroom phone, cupping my hand around the receiver so they wouldn't hear me from the dining room.

Their friends were mostly noncommittal, and uncomfortably *umming* and *ahhing* their responses.

I gathered the fifty dollars I'd saved from a year's worth of allowance, walked down to Ben's Best Deli on Queens Boulevard one day after school, and arranged to have three catering platters of meats—tongue, corned beef, and pastrami—delivered on the afternoon of the celebration.

The day before the party, I watched my father as he stood in the kitchen, making himself his favorite comfort food—salami and eggs—in an ancient, scuffed Teflon pan. He was taking a break; all afternoon, he had been sitting on the living room floor in front of his stereo, with our dog at his side, making separate piles of record albums. Trini Lopez, Shirley Bassey, Simon & Garfunkel, Peggy Lee, and Tom Jones lay in a careless heap, under the piano bench. Shostakovich, Chopin, The Modern Jazz Quartet, Yma Sumac, and The Music of the Moiseyev sat neatly arranged and organized by style of music, and then, alphabetically. On top, like the cherry on a sundae, my father placed his Mohammed El-Bakkar album, *Port Said*, his favorite. The cover featured a picture of a mostly naked Anne Baxter look-alike wearing pasties and dancing in front of a hookah. My father picked up his albums, gingerly placed them in a small grocery carton, and pushed them off to the side. His books—the Frank O'Hara, the Henry Miller, the copy of *Portnoy's Complaint*, Norman Mailer's *Marilyn Monroe*—were collected in a white-and-blue Alexander's shopping bag. The only book left on the shelf was his 1962 edition of Craig Claiborne's *New York Times Cookbook*.

I answered the door that afternoon to find the deli's delivery man waiting, cradling three huge platters of cold cuts draped in sheets of jewel-toned plastic, tied at their tops with a contrasting ribbon.

"I'm so sorry for your loss," the man said, trying to hand me the platters, each one labeled with a three-inch white sticker marked SHIVA.

"What are you doing? No one died—it's for my parents' anniversary," I whispered, stepping out into the hallway and closing the door behind me.

"Who is it?" my father called from the kitchen, putting down his plate and walking to the door, wiping his mouth with a paper towel. "Who placed this order?"

"Your daughter did," the delivery guy answered, nodding at me.

"You've got the wrong day, dammit—" I fumed. "Dad, it was supposed to come tomorrow, for your party—"

"*What* party?"

"I'm making you an anniversary party, for tomorrow—"

"You're *what*?" bellowed my father, his face angry and twisted like a character in an Edvard Munch painting.

"I ordered them a few days ago—"

My father took the platters and set them down on our foyer bar. He reached into his back pocket for his wallet but the man shook his head, no, and handed him the receipt.

Paid in full.

"There's not going to be a party," my father said quietly, handing me half a pastrami sandwich from the platter. "Your mother won't be home until later tonight. Have some mustard."

My stomach lurched in the familiar way it did when I was a young child suffering the queasy-making, jittery pangs of Saturday night separation anxiety, when my parents went out for dinner and left me home with Gaga. I was convinced in the murky, terrified recesses of my mind, as children often are, that they would never come home again. Sitting there in the safety of my childhood apartment, the laugh track of *Love, American Style* howling in the background, my life—I was sure of it—teetered on the precipice of abandonment and sickening, uncontrollable change. There was nothing I could do to halt it in its tracks, and pull it back from the edge. A party would make things right, I was sure, like a pubescent Mrs. Dalloway.

Fighting back tears, I put the pastrami sandwich back down on the platter, grabbed my tennis racquet and a ball from the hall closet, and left my father in the apartment with his piles of albums and books. I spent the rest of the day whacking the ball hard against our local middle school's paddleball wall, a few blocks way, until tears cascaded down my cheeks and into my shirt and the early-autumn daylight faded, and my arm burned with exhaustion.

✛✛✛

A week later, my parents formally announced their plans to me: my father would be leaving in the morning. Together we stood in our narrow galley kitchen, my father's face flushed an apoplectic red.

"Where is he going?" I addressed my mother, as if my father wasn't even there.

"I don't know yet," he answered.

"How could you *not know*?" I pictured him sleeping on the street, or at the Y, or jumping a freight train in some far-off Midwestern town.

"It's not important," he said quietly.

"How am I supposed to find you?" I asked, choking on my words.

"I'll let you know as soon as I know, Liss," he said, putting his hands on my shoulders.

"But what will you eat?" I asked.

I thought of all the Brooks Brothers–clad men dining around and near us during our secret lunches at La Côte Basque and Le Perigord, the ones with their gorgeous socialite wives and their sack suits and their monograms emblazoned in midnight blue on their pressed, white cuffs. None of them, I was sure, lived with the mess of not being able to tell their daughters where they were going to be living, or eating, or sleeping. Their lives were delicious, and tidy; I was certain of it. There were country clubs and vice presidencies and shopping at Best & Company; there were private schools and navy blazers, French lessons and station wagons, country houses and mother sauces. There were supple, sweet voices never raised beyond the quiet timbre of a whisper, and the soft, affection of parents who loved each other.

There were English biscuits and Tiptree jams, escargot and tournedos Rossini, veal Orloff and quenelles Lyonnaise.

There was safety, and order.

"I don't know," my father said. "It doesn't matter right now—"

I reached for the phone in slow motion, like my hand wasn't attached to my arm and my arm not connected to my body; some-body—was it me?—called my best friend, Lucy, from down the street, and in minutes, she and her mother were at our front door, coming to pick me up and take me back to their house so that, at fifteen years old, I wouldn't witness the very end, the last possible minutes of my parents' disintegrating marriage.

"Don't leave," my father suddenly implored, trying to grab the phone out of my hand. "Please—" he begged, like a child clinging to his parent's leg.

"I can't stay tonight," I said, trying not to cry. I took nothing with me; I walked out through the kitchen, past our Chambers stove and half-eaten boxes of Entenmann's donuts and cakes, and left.

The next day, when I returned home in the early afternoon to check on the dog, I walked in on my father dumping drawers of clothes into a dirty tan suitcase that still bore the travel stickers from my parents' last trip to Europe, four years earlier. They had been to Italy, where my mother performed every single night, getting up to sing at every restaurant they dined in, from Rome to Florence to Capri. My father had watched her, glowing, bursting with pride that this stunning woman who had caught the eye of every man in the room actually belonged to him. But that afternoon in their bedroom, surrounded by the trappings of his former life, my father sat down on the side of the bed that he had shared for sixteen years with his wife, and sobbed.

From that point forward, he never really stopped.

SALAMI AND EGGS

Some people turn to macaroni and cheese, or chocolate, or Ho Hos when their lives are crumbling around them; my father, despite an educated, sophisticated palate that eschewed nothing and savored everything from stuffed, roasted pig's trotters at Maison Troisgros to brains in red wine sauce with onions, went native and craved only one thing: salami and eggs. So important was the dish to him that long before he was married he was thrice arrested for smuggling chicken fat across the border into Canada when he was living there so he could make the dish for himself; it became an iconic security blanket that he would eat with his eyes closed, swooning. A note to the healthy: my father's use of chicken fat was like gilding the lily; the salami has enough fat in it that the additional is not necessary.

Serves 2, or my father

1 tablespoon chicken fat

8 ounces kosher salami, cut into rounds, then into quarters

2 to 3 eggs, beaten

Salt

1. In a medium skillet set over medium-high heat, melt the chicken fat. Add the salami, decrease the heat to medium, and cook until the salami begins to brown, tossing frequently, about 8 minutes.

2. Pour the eggs over the salami and stir frequently. Remove the pan from the heat when the eggs are cooked through.

3. Season with salt and eat immediately, right out of the pan.

CHAPTER 20

Cheese Food

My friend Abigail and I were sitting in a bistro on Third Avenue one night after work, drinking tall thin flutes of Prosecco, while trucks thundered by and onto the lower level of the Fifty-Ninth Street bridge.

"Look at you," she said, tossing her long, blonde hair. "You're so cute, I want to throw up."

"I'm just happy, Abs," I answered. "When was the last time you saw me *this* happy?"

"It must be the sex," she said, winking. "I think you've dropped some weight."

"*Stop*—it's like talking to my mother." I blushed.

A perfume-drenched woman sitting next to us sipping a margarita looked me up and down. I could feel the heat beaming off my face like I'd just awakened on a beach after falling asleep in the Florida sun at high noon.

"Look," Abigail said tersely, "I'm glad you're having a good time with her. But seriously, what are you going to do—*move*? Because I certainly don't see her coming down *here* too often."

She had a point, and I was trying really hard not to think about it. Eventually, if things progressed, one of us was going to have to make a change, and if neither of us was willing, what was the point? Abby, the only other person in my life who is a bigger New Yorker than I am, was skeptical. She'd seen me through long strings of bad dates, of attempted fix-ups with straight men by well-meaning but delusional cousins, and through an office crush that was so hideous and all-consuming that I would go into ventricular tachycardia whenever I passed the woman at the water cooler.

A publicity director at my dot-com, Abigail had flowing, dyed blonde hair and wore more makeup, higher Jimmy Choos, and shorter skirts than anyone I knew at any age. Her own love life, checkered though it was, left broken-hearted men littered from SoHo up to the Bronx and everywhere in between. Still, her advice was peerless.

"You know what's going to happen? You move up there to Green Acres, and there are no Jews, no Chinese food, no Williams-Sonoma, no Dean & DeLuca, no restaurants, no stoplights; you give up your apartment, you get bored, you break up, and *then* what?"

I suddenly felt queasy.

"I think you should slow down a little bit," she added. "Stop with the every-weekend-in-the-country thing. Make her come here instead. You need to be more mysterious."

"But I'm not mysterious. I don't want to be mysterious. I just want to be with her—am I *crazy* for that?" Margarita lady was staring at me.

"Fine," she said. "Don't be mysterious. I'm thrilled for you both," she said, sighing, "but take Valentine's Day off. Trust me. Make her work a little. Let's order."

At the beginning of any new relationship, there's a fine line between hormonally driven lust, the promise and possibility of love, and jumping out of a plane with a broken parachute, metaphysically speaking. Susan was worth the risk, I knew. But still, with Abby's voice careening around in my head, I decided not to mention to Susan that our first Valentine's Day together was falling on a Monday, and that if we were going to be together, I was either going to have to take a day off from work, or suddenly develop a strange and violent illness that would prevent me from returning to the city on Sunday night.

But I took it one step further: as a sort of despicable, sophomoric test, I didn't mention Valentine's Day to Susan *at all*, even though it was very much on my mind.

"What are we doing next Monday?" Susan asked when she called later that night.

"What's next Monday? I don't have a calendar," I said in what I hoped was an innocent voice, though I had to dig my nails into my own thigh to stay cool.

"Oh—"

"*What—?*"

"I just assumed that since it was Valentine's Day, you'd stay in Connecticut on Monday instead of going home on Sunday night." She cleared her throat.

"Of course I will!"

"I was worried for a minute—are you sure?"

"Of course I'm sure. I just lost track of things," I said.

So much for cultivating an air of mystery.

+++

At work the next day, I fantasized about what I'd cook Susan for Valentine's Day. Chocolate was too obvious.

Abby came over to my desk to consult. She was still dubious, but trying to be helpful.

"How about red velvet cake. It's red—Valentine's Day food is supposed to be red. Right?"

"Forget it. What else?"

"Something with pomegranates? It's the original love apple!"

"I don't think so."

We were reviewing my options when one of the mailroom guys

walked over to me carrying a small box. The postmark said it was from Penzeys Spices, in Norwalk, Connecticut.

I opened it while Abby looked over my shoulder: it contained three bottles, one each of vindaloo spice, pequín chile, and cayenne pepper.

All very hot and all very red. The card read, *See you soon. Love, S.*

Abby and I just stared at each other blankly.

"Maybe she just wants to do a lot of cooking," she suggested, matter-of-factly.

"Maybe she just likes a lot of heat," I responded, refusing to make eye contact with her, instead turning the bottles over and giving one of them a shake.

"I think I should get back to work," Abby snorted, and walked away.

✝✝✝

I would keep it simple. Or at least my version of simple.

Oysters and lobster and tarragon-infused beurre blanc and Champagne. Why hadn't I thought of it earlier?

I called information in Torrington, Susan's neighboring town, where there were actual food stores.

"I need the number of a good seafood store."

"Sorry, ma'am. No seafood stores in Torrington."

"How about the supermarket?"

"Hold for the number, ma'am."

I asked for the seafood manager. When was his oyster delivery coming in?

"Maybe three months or so, give or take."

I hung up and Googled "seafood, Torrington, Connecticut." And all I got was a small operation named Fish-Is-Us. I called the number, and a man answered the phone.

"Do you have any Pemaquid oysters and lobster?"

"We have oysters. Don't really know what kind they are, though. How many do you need?"

"A dozen, and two large, female lobsters. I'll pick them up next Monday morning."

"Here's the address—cash only."

On late Monday morning, Valentine's Day, I developed an acute, indefinable illness that prevented me from leaving Connecticut to go into the city and back to work. I called in sick. Then Susan and I got dressed, jumped into the car, and started driving around northern Torrington, looking for what the Fish-Is-Us proprietor had described as an "old brick Tudor-style colonial with hanging gutters," which described at least 80 percent of the houses in town.

"This can't be it," I said, as Susan slowed down. There, in the cracked asphalt driveway, was a once-black, rusted-out, late-'80s pickup truck with the words *Fish-Is-Us* stenciled on the side and a bumper sticker bearing the slogan:

KEEP HONKING . . . I'M RELOADING

"We're going to die. Your mother's going to find us in the kitchen tomorrow with lobster bibs tied around our neck."

"Go knock on the door," Susan said. "You called them, right?"

"I'm not sure my shots are up to date," I replied. "We can't eat shellfish from this place."

"Pick the stuff up. We'll decide later—"

I knocked on the screen door, and a bleached-blonde, middle-aged woman in a pilling, lime-green acrylic turtleneck sweater motioned me to come around the back. Then a man opened the back door, strode over to the truck and jumped into the flatbed, from which he pulled out a plastic bag containing the lobsters and oysters. He held his out his hand, and I gave him twenty-seven dollars and fifty cents in cash.

"I don't think we should do this," I said when we got home, stuffing the seafood into the fridge. "Oysters and two lobsters should cost a lot more than twenty-seven dollars and fifty cents, at least where I come from."

"Let's just start cooking, okay?" Susan said reassuringly. "If anything looks funky, we'll just go out."

"Where will we go?" I asked her.

"How about Red Lobster?" she offered, smiling.

+++

I made three sauces for the oysters: mignonette, cocktail, and an Asian ponzu sauce. I filled Susan's largest stockpot and set it on the stove for the lobsters, which were resting in the fridge in the stainless hotel-catering pan I'd hauled up from the city. And then, I started to shuck.

Hunched over Susan's farmhouse sink with my oyster knife, I worked and pried and only stabbed myself once. And that was just the first oyster.

"I'm impressed," she said, wincing. "Should I get the peroxide?"

Sweat started to drip into my eyes.

Two hours later, I'd managed to shuck all dozen oysters, which we gulped down seconds after I plunged the lobsters into the stockpot to cook for fifteen minutes. I shelled each lobster, propping up each cracked claw against the dense tail meat that was perched, dramatically aloft, in the center of two small white platters I'd unearthed from Susan's cupboard; I whisked together the tarragon infusion and the beurre blanc, and drizzled each platter with the gorgeous, light yellow froth. I carefully wiped down the rim of each plate, carried them over to the coffee table in the living room, popped the cork on a bottle of Laurent Perrier Brut, and, forgetting about Fish-Is-Us and the health department, we fed each other the lobster while sitting on the couch in the living room. It was delicious.

"I made something for you, too," Susan said when we were done, walking into the kitchen after we'd finished the Champagne.

"I love it when you get mysterious," I whispered, getting up to follow her in.

She smiled, opened the fridge, reached into its cavernous depths, and pulled out a round Tupperware container with a warped, stocking-colored lid.

I pried it off and carefully extracted its contents. I was expecting a truffle, or maybe two truffles.

But there, wrapped in plastic wrap, were three symbols that Susan had expertly carved out of a block of family-size Velveeta:

I ♥ U

CHAPTER 21

Farmers' Market

The first time I actually noticed the Greenmarket in Manhattan—the big one, down in Union Square—was in the early 1990s, more or less the same time that Alice Waters started extoling the virtues of Meyer lemons, which she once described as falling somewhere along the continuum between a Eureka lemon and a Mandarin orange. It seemed that in every one of her books, there the damned things were, and there was nothing you could do about them if you lived outside of Berkeley. I'd be lying in bed late at night, surrounded by the Chez Panisse cookbooks, which dangled these delicious globes of goodness right above my mouth like the starving and thirsty Tantalus, who was forced by Greek gods to live out eternity with a delicious bunch of seasonal and organic grapes just out of reach. I desperately yearned to taste and cook with this prized fruit. But even in the city of New York, where almost anything was possible, I was, as they say, shit out of luck.

In New York at the time, if you wanted exquisitely small Brussels sprouts just picked the day before, you could find them. Or chanterelles, still covered with the dirt of the primordial forest floor? No problem. But there were no Meyer lemons anywhere to be found. Lying in my sad, little single-girl bed, in my small, dark apartment, I thought about how I could make any dish Alice's cookbooks threw at me, unless they called for this particular fruit, which seemed somehow torturous, spiteful, and cruel. But then one afternoon, on my way home from Greenwich Village, there—diagonally across the street from the gigantic Paragon Sporting Goods—I noticed a small jumble of little white tents emblazoned with the word *Greenmarket*, set up on an oddly shaped spit of sidewalk at the north end of Union Square Park, which my father, when I was a child, used to compassionately refer to as Needle Haven.

It was late March, cold, and bone-chillingly damp in the way that only an early spring day in Manhattan can be; the wind sliced right through me, and I snapped the chin-warmer closed on my coveted Barbour jacket that, years earlier, I had smuggled through customs after a few months spent studying in England.

"Excuse me," I asked one of the vendors, a wide, tall guy in a too-small woolen tweed newsboy cap and Dickensian-style half gloves, who was warming his hands over a small, smoking garbage can, standing next to a sign that read ORGANIC FRUITS AND VEGETABLES. "Do you happen to have any Meyer lemons?"

He just glared at me, unsmiling, the earflaps on his cap knotted tightly around his chin. His nose was running.

"You're fucking *kidding* me, right?" he grunted. "Does it *look* like I sell fucking *Meyer lemons*?"

I peered into the blue plastic milk crates behind him, which contained piles of dusty storage carrots and dirty parsnips that had clearly just been pulled out of an in-ground root cellar in upstate New York somewhere. There were maybe half a dozen waxy rutabagas the size of small basketballs and a basket of huge, purple-tipped turnips that were overwintered and probably as flavorful as cardboard. No Meyer lemons to be found.

"Do you know when you'll have them?" I asked inquisitively.

"Yeah, miss," he said. "If you fly out to California, pick them, put them in a bag, fly them back to New York, get on the R train and bring them down to me, *then* I'll have them."

My relationship with farmers' markets had long been rocky, so that I'd managed to stir the ire of the Union Square vegetable salesman was the rule, rather than the exception. When it came to fresh green-market shopping—the kind where you have to engage with the farmer or the seller, I was a bumbling idiot. It had all started many years before, when I was a college student on my very first trip to France, when I was physically accosted on a beautiful Wednesday afternoon in the ninth arrondissement by a tight-lipped, chignoned, grandmo-therly woman in a gray wool dress and sturdy patent leather pumps, who swooped down out of nowhere to whack my sorry wrist as I gently—I thought—perused and lovingly caressed some beautiful, tiny apples that had just come down from Normandy, or so the sign said. Nobody had bothered telling me that in France, you don't just sidle up to a seller and thump their honeydews. You don't touch their produce, at all. You tell them what you want and when you're going to serve it, and then they choose what they think is the right fruit or vegetable for you, based on its ripeness. I learned this the hard way, when the apple seller angrily grabbed them out of my hand, spat "stu-pid American child," put them in a small brown bag, thrust them at me, and demanded payment. Later that afternoon, lazing around my tiny hotel room romantically, wearing a red-and-black-striped French sailor's shirt, looking like I'd just fallen out of a *Gourmet* magazine photo shoot, I wistfully nibbled on a warm demi-baguette and a round of cheese so stinky and ripe that it oozed all over the pink poly-ester bedspread. The apples—meant for jam and requiring a very long, slow simmer under mountains of sugar—were bitter, inedible, and made me violently ill that night.

Sometime later, while studying at Cambridge University, in England, I was lucky enough to be assigned two rooms: a small bed-room facing a courtyard, complete with a sink and towel warmer, and a huge study that looked out over the Cambridge outdoor market-place, where you could buy everything from a 1901 edition of

Shakespeare's *Twelfth Night* to a World War II–era, dark green, Frederick Forsyth–style woolen trench coat; tied-and-larded veal roasts that had come from a neighboring dairy farm to gigantic, unwrapped wedges of raw-milk Stilton cheese so aggressively piquant that shoppers would regularly gawk at each other to make sure that the stench was, in fact, food and not human. One warm afternoon, I bought a pound of the raw Stilton and a thick slab of a kind of *pâté de Campagne* that had been made with a combination of local meats instead of pork-just-pork, brought it back to my study, and shared it with the chemistry professor who lived at the far end of my hall. Dr. Naylor, who had a shock of white hair and a long beard that he man-carved every morning into the shape of an arrowhead, was delighted by my willingness to sample local East Anglia fare.

"Very few young Americans will eat this pâté," he said, cutting a sizeable slab with his boyhood pen knife from his days at Eton that he carried in his back pocket. He placed the garishly dark, gunmetal-gray meat onto a hunk of crusty bread.

"How come?" I asked, popping a small, earthy piece into my mouth.

"Well, my dear," he said gravely, leaning in close, "there's been a horse rumor for years—"

Seven hours later, I was lying, chilled and feverish, on a gurney in the emergency room at the Cambridge City Hospital with an IV bag hanging next to me. A handsome, young, balding resident leaned over me.

"You Americans," he whispered. "You'll try anything. Next time, stick to the supermarket and Wimpy's."

And that's what I had been taught, for years, by both my grand-mothers and my Aunt Sylvia: if the lettuce wasn't shrink-wrapped ice-berg, you shouldn't buy it. If it doesn't come from a hyper-sterilized supermarket, fancy specialty store, fancier gourmet shop, butcher, or fishmonger, don't eat it. If you have to wash the dirt off it—the actual dirt—put it back and buy something *clean*-looking instead. If it's alien—like Meyer lemons, or an unidentifiable pâté de pony sold by a slightly rangy-looking, manure-coated farmhand out of a stall at the Cambridge City market—stay the hell away.

"Farmers' markets," my Aunt Sylvia said when I came home from England and told her the story, "aren't meant for Jews. We like things to be *clean*—it's in the Talmud."

So I stuck to "clean" food, sharply limiting my few vegetable purchases to upscale shops like Dean & DeLuca or Agata & Valentina, where everything was magnificently displayed in a dizzying, kaleidoscopic array of color and texture so inviting that it would compel even the most vegetable-hating cook to drop ten bucks for a perfect, organic Romanesco that, once home, would lie forgotten, buried behind that big tub of discount cottage cheese.

We were never big vegetable eaters in my family—I was raised eating asparagus and Brussels sprouts out of a can or a boil-in-bag pouch. Dining at a restaurant with my parents as a child, I once sent back a red leaf salad because I was sure the leaves were rotting. When prim and tiny steamed vegetables and pasta primavera became all the rage in the mid-1990s, I girded my loins and started making weekly trips to the greenmarket, where I'd pissed off the turnip man years before, to peruse overpriced infantile squash that I could afford exactly two of, just like everyone else shopping there—aspiring foodies, gapemouthed at the prices, clutching two or three spongy-looking morel mushrooms, a handful of fava beans, a few tiny peppers, a couple of Rocambole garlic bulbs.

I continued to search the market for the Meyer lemons that Alice Waters tempted me with, but those shopping excursions usually ended with me taking the subway home carrying an odd, incompatible combination of vegetables; a wedge of rare, hard-to-find sheep's milk cheese from a ewe named Matilda; and a loaf of heavy, dense brown bread so weighty that it could have been used as ballast on the

Titanic. Most of those purchases would end up rotting in my salad crisper.

Once farmers' market shopping became trendy, one of the things that made me so uncomfortable shopping at them was that everyone was so goddamned earnest and pure, and from my vantage point, close to the earth. Gorgeous, sober-faced twenty-year-olds in dirty T-shirts, vintage Red Wing boots, and mushroom-colored torn corduroys that I cannot afford sat cross-legged in the cargo boxes of ancient, rusting Ford pickups, reading Foucault and William Burroughs, and when they noticed you were there—*if* they noticed—picking at their long, thin organic breakfast radishes or the shishito peppers that they'd marked down at the end of the day to fifteen dollars a pound, you would wind up listening to a well-rehearsed soliloquy about growing conditions and permaculture and Wendell Berry, and when you asked them how to prepare what you were buying, they'd scratch their heads and say *dunno, man.* Everyone had the politics down pat; that was the easy part. It was the actual cooking that no one bothered with.

"You *could* stuff them, I guess," one blond, dreadlocked guy said when I bought a half pound of his sweet, delicate peppers, tapered and thin as knitting needles. So long and lanky that it would have been like trying to hollow out a string bean with a toothpick in order to fill it with cocaine for smuggling purposes, the peppers broke and buckled when I tried to use a plastic drinking straw to fill them with soft, creamy young local goat cheese. Once under the broiler, they exploded into smoky, dripping, green blistered rivulets while my friends sat in my living room, drinking glasses of cava, unaware.

Farmers' markets in Manhattan were all about fashion and food—the gorgeous, expensive, rare stuff that costs as much as the gross national product of some small African nations, and signified your dedication to the people around you and to your table—even though no one, not even the hipsters who were selling it, had a clue how to cook.

+++

During my first spring weekends with Susan at her house in Connecticut—even with snow still on the ground and the odd, middle-of-the-afternoon squalls well into April—vegetable stands began to crop up everywhere, rich with the promise of warmer, sunnier weather; knotted, decrepit-looking radishes and lush lettuces; and enough root vegetables to feed most of Soviet Russia in the 1970s. Few of the stands had a connection to any specific farm; instead, they were run by local residents who happened to have a surplus to sell from their backyard vegetable patches that, at the height of the season, threatened to overtake their kids' dilapidated, faux-cedar swing sets. Piles of early fruits and vegetables invariably sat on old card tables alongside rusting, metal mailboxes enshrouded in vinyl wraps depicting puppies and kittens, or the American flag—gnarly-looking baby turnips with their greens wilted and sun-dried, a few stalks of new pencil-thin asparagus, too early to be fat—and, if you happened to pass by, you could stop your car, take what you wanted, and leave your cash behind in an old cigar box marked with a sign that said LEAVE CASH IN HERE, without worry that it would be stolen. Some of the bigger, seasonal farm stands—like the one at Krell's Farm, which had been in business for over seventy years just a few miles down the road from Susan's mother's house—sold in much greater volume and were the places to go should you be in need of enough rutabagas to feed an army. Gryzyck's Farm, owned and operated by a family whose children had gone to grammar school with Susan's mother, was the biggest farm stand by far, providing local customers with a steady bounty of fresh vegetables, fruits, and sweet corn from the moment the ground was workable, until the first killing frost decimated their late-fall squash, pumpkin, kale, and collard greens. There was no organic this, or trendiness that, or dogma or local politics; it was just fee (your money) for a provided service (chemical-free vegetables pulled from the ground), and if you were lucky, the vegetables you carried home with you would be sweet and tender. Mostly, they were. If they weren't and you complained the next time you were there, Old Man Gryzyk would simply tip the peak of his filthy John Deere cap up on his head and say things like, "Ground never got cold enough to sweeten anything up this year. Just add a little sugar."

+++

"I hope never to have to shop in a supermarket at all this season," Susan said to me excitedly on the phone one night. A few of the local vegetable sellers had just started to pitch a few tents together every week in a neighboring town not too far away from her house, and were selling overwintered potatoes, onions, carrots, parsnips, and the season's very first microscopically small, overwintered baby kale leaves no bigger than an inch across, that had just started poking up out of the snow.

"You mean *microgreens*?" I asked Susan that night, when she called excitedly to tell me that after the long and harsh northern Connecticut winter, with snow still on the ground, one of these spur-of-the-moment, unofficial markets was actually open.

"No—I mean the season's first baby greens."

"You *do* mean microgreens! I just bought a handful for fifteen dollars a pound uptown at a stall in Union Square. I'm puréeing them for dinner tonight with smoked garlic and olive oil, and topping them with orange-glazed, pan-seared diver scallops I picked up on the way home from the market."

"You're kidding—"

"I'm not," I said. "How much were they at your market?"

"You'll hate me," she sighed.

"Come on Suze, *tell me*," I begged, genuinely curious about the markup for vegetables sold in Manhattan versus at the ragged little farm stand on the outskirts of a town that had just gotten its first stop-light a few years before. The manager, Mrs. Krell, at eighty-five, weighed in the neighborhood of three hundred pounds and oversaw the entire market operation from an ancient, extruded-aluminum folding deck chair; she held court with a clamped-off central venous catheter dangling out of her neck—it would flop back and forth like a fish out of water every time she turned her head to talk to a customer, of which there were many. What there were not were pallid, flannel-shirted, vegan babes skulking around, drinking homemade kombu-cha out of scuffed Nalgene bottles while reading Pema Chödron on finding peace in times of war.

"The baby kale was seventy-five cents—"

"Each?" *Really?* Per *leaf?* Per *half pound?*

"Not quite." She laughed. "A big *bagful.*"

By rough estimate, a *big bagful* of microgreens purchased at the Union Square greenmarket would have set me back more or less half a mortgage payment.

"And what, exactly, are you making with your precious bagful of baby kale?" I asked.

"Oh," she said, "I'm sautéing them with some garlic and a pinch of hot red pepper, and then I'm having them on some nice toast rubbed with a little bit of olive oil. I baked some Cuban white bread the other day."

"And what else?"

"That's it."

"Nothing else?"

"Nothing else."

SPICY BABY KALE ON GARLIC TOAST

There's a lot that Susan has taught me about cooking, but one of the most important is the fact of toast; toast is the saving grace of otherwise humdrum food everywhere, and, rubbed with a clove of garlic and drizzled with a bit of olive oil, almost anything that you set down upon it will be delicious. In this case, Susan did nothing more than cook down her beloved microgreens—specifically, baby kale—in a tablespoon of olive oil with some garlic, a pinch of red pepper flakes, and a splash of red wine vinegar. We've served this as an appetizer at dinner parties, and we've topped it with fried eggs and had it for dinner. If we can't get kale, we use spinach, chard, and, sometimes, even arugula. Note: Baby kale is so tender that there's no need to stem it; just give it a short swim in a sink full of water to rid it of sand, and a thorough drying.

Serves 2

2 tablespoons extra-virgin olive oil

1 garlic clove, halved; one half minced, the other kept whole

3 cups packed cleaned baby kale leaves

Pinch of red pepper flakes

1 tablespoon good-quality red wine vinegar

4 slices country-style bread

1. In a large, straight-sided sauté pan set over medium heat, warm 1 tablespoon of the olive oil until it shimmers and add the minced garlic. When the garlic begins to take on color, add the kale leaves to the pan in batches, grabbing and rolling them with each addition, using tongs. Add the red pepper flakes, toss well, and cover. Cook until the kale has completely wilted to a dark green tangle, about 8 minutes, and drizzle with the vinegar.

2. Toast the bread, and rub each slice with the garlic half, and then drizzle with the remaining olive oil. Top with the kale and serve immediately.

CHAPTER 22

Foraging

Where I grew up, we didn't have a whole lot of nature, per se, beyond Forest Park, Kissena Park, and Flushing Meadow Park, all of which were officially off-limits in the 1970s, because of Son of Sam.

So my experience in the great outdoors was sharply limited to seven summers spent at Towanda, a sleepaway camp that my parents sent me to in Honesdale, Pennsylvania. The food at camp, by any standards, was stellar; we had an outstanding chef named Bill Alexander, who made things like London broil and a reasonably good pizza and pepper steak with sirloin tips. When I told this to Susan, who went to a local camp called Happy Hill run by the Lions Club, she ended my waxing rhapsodic by telling me about having to blow the fly carcasses off the hamburgers she'd cook over a leaking propane grill outside her flammable nylon tent, the summer that she was seven.

One year at Towanda, there was a guy on staff who'd been hired to run the nature den and take us all on hikes. His name was Henry, or Hirsch, or something like that, and he was a doughy sort of fellow— like a cross between Euell Gibbons and Newman from *Seinfeld*—who wore torn clothes from Kreeger's Camping Supply, and an old army shirt with his name tag suspiciously ripped in half. He liked to take us on hikes through the perilous woods just beyond the camp boundaries. It was thrilling to hear him say things like, "See kids, *that's* a scrub-oak Lycidum, which is the Latin for acorn bush," and "if you eat the flowering bud of the Pennsylvania swamp mug, you'll be protected from mosquitos for an *entire* season!"

We were transfixed by his knowledge, even though we knew, deep down, that he was lying through his teeth.

One day, Nature Guy—we started calling him that after our first hike—took us out to hunt for some wild edibles. This was something of a conundrum for a lot of us, since we had perfectly fine edibles back in the dining room, and our parents had paid twelve hundred dollars for us to eat there for eight weeks. But Nature Guy wanted to show us that you could eat straight from the forest floor, and subsist on some pretty wondrous stuff. We watched with rapt attention, but he had no takers when he asked if any of us wanted to try a mysterious purple flower that looked exactly like a Venus fly trap. I'll never know what it was for sure, but Nature Guy disappeared from camp the next day, and we never saw him again.

So the idea of foraging for my own food has always been a little fraught for me, between Nature Guy and being a New Yorker. Maybe it's because my idea of foraging involves making it to the olive bar at Fairway on the Upper West Side without getting elbowed in the head. And although in the '90s, it became very trendy to march around Central Park with a guide picking bags full of weeds and mushrooms to take home and make into ragouts of every earthy variety, I was always skittish about that. What happened if you went out stalking wild asparagus and wound up stalking poison oak, instead? My people, I was certain, didn't forage, unless they were being chased by the Nazis. They didn't make it all this way just to wind up eating eat shoots and leaves. My people don't forage. We shop.

One Friday, when Susan was in the city meeting with clients, she called me to say she'd picked up a surprise for us at the greenmarket in Union Square: two huge bunches of ramps that she'd gotten a break on because the hipster child selling them at the market thought they were scallions, and Susan hadn't corrected her. She also bought a dozen quail eggs and an expensive loaf of Jim Lahey's *pain pugliese* from the Sullivan Street Bakery. She had splurged—really splurged—and that night, when we got back to Harwinton, we sautéed the ramps in a little bit of olive oil with some minced garlic, draped them over a few pieces of the bread toasted and rubbed with half a sliced garlic clove, and topped them with the very tiny, very adorable poached quail eggs.

"I wish we could do something with these," Susan said, cradling the delicate, tan and brown speckled shells in her hand.

"Like what?" I asked. "A craft?"

+++

In New York, no one knew what the hell ramps were until they started showing up at high-end restaurants in the late '90s. Invariably tortured into altered states—early on, they were foamed, pickled, puréed, turned into gelato—ramps are best left alone, like infantile green peas. Most food people want to gild the lily, and tart them up in all sorts of self-congratulatory ways, but that's mostly because no one really knows how to cook them whole. Really just a wild leek that most often can be found in rich, moist, deciduous forests, ramps taste like a mild cross between baby garlic and a very young spring onion; the entire plant is edible, assuming you can find it, or afford it. Once they became more popular and entered the Manhattan gourmet vernacular, the greenmarket started carrying them by the crate-load, foraged everywhere from as far north as upstate New York and as far south as West Virginia. They were astronomically expensive, and rich New Yorkers bought them by the grocery bag full.

As we ate our little ramps and eggs on toast that night, we decided how lucky the folks down in West Virginia must be, to have ramps growing all over God's green earth, right out there in the middle of forests and lawns everywhere in that state. And we bemoaned the fact that since they're such a rarity, like truffles, they were just far too expensive for us to have all through the spring, especially since it was becoming more and more apparent that my dot-com, where I was spending my weekdays writing and editing travel and entertainment content, was on the skids.

That weekend, Susan took MacGillicuddy out for a walk while I stayed back at the house, nursing the kind of early allergies that light up my nose like Rudolph, and make me sound like Brenda Vaccaro with a head cold. Susan opened up the slider and stepped into the house, beaming.

"I'm not sure," she said, subversively, "but the neighbors over on the next street seem to have ramps growing near their front yard. They look like the same things I bought on Friday."

"Impossible," I said, putting my teacup down and looking up from the newspaper. "They must be lilies. Did you try one?"

"Of course not—who knows *what* they are. They could be lilies, like you said."

"Well, let's not get excited," I said. "Ramps don't just grow anywhere in rural Connecticut. They're a rare delicacy limited to upstate New York and West Virginia. And probably Berkeley, where Alice Waters wills them to grow, like the Amazing Kreskin bending a spoon."

Still, what if they *were*, in fact, ramps? We would go over to the house around the corner. We would pull a few up. We would nibble. We would pray that they weren't lilies, or sprayed with anything that came from a bottle emblazoned with a skull and crossbones, like most of the bottles sitting in Susan's mother's garage since the Truman administration.

But I'd be breaking my own foraging rules set in stone the morning Nature Guy didn't show up at camp lineup before breakfast, the day after he'd eaten the fly trap. And, we would be removing something from Susan's neighbor's property without his knowledge, and, of course, there are some very basic rules about that.

Still, we were in love with ramps, so exceptions could be made.

"I have an idea," Susan said. "I'll get the dandelion weeder." And off she went, into her shed, emerging moments later with the tool concealed in the sleeve of her bright red anorak.

"Shouldn't you be wearing, you know—*black*? Like Peter Graves in *Mission: Impossible*? And maybe a knit cap?"

"Let's go," she whispered, like the neighbors could actually hear her. She slipped the collar back onto MacGillicuddy, and off we went, trying as hard as we could to look like normal people going for a stroll around the neighborhood with their dog, weeding tool and ziplock bag safely hidden from view.

"Bring the dog over here," Susan motioned to me, as we approached the spot where she thought she'd seen the ramps.

Great, I thought. *Now we're involving the dog.*

Gilly nosed around the tree for a while, and I came to the realization that a big, sweet, happy dog is a pretty good foil for almost anything. Susan bent down, and dug and pulled, and dug and pulled, and in seconds, we had a bagful of what were, in fact, outrageously valuable ramps that would have cost a small fortune in the city.

"I can't believe it!" I held the dog's leash while Susan brushed the dirt off her knees.

"I *told* you!" she laughed, standing up.

When we got back to the house, we filled Susan's big farmhouse sink with cool water and immersed the ramps, gently rolling them around, and bits of dirt and sand and the odd bug sank to the bottom. We rolled up the ramps in a clean kitchen towel, swaddling them like a newborn, to let them dry.

"Wine?" Susan asked, taking a bottle of cold Pinot Gris from the fridge.

She pulled the cork, poured us two small juice glasses, and sat down at the counter while I went to work, separating the leafy greens from the thick, white bulby stems. I rummaged around the storage drawer under the oven and pulled out one of Et's prized, jet-black cast-iron skillets, heated it up, and melted a tablespoon of the bacon fat that Susan had reserved in a small can on the shelf above the sink. When it sizzled like rain, the ramp stems went into the pan, along with some freshly ground black pepper. It took not much more than a minute or two for them to begin to turn translucent. When I added the ramp tops and turned them over a few times with a wooden spoon, a dense cloud of onion-y, garlic-laden goodness filled the room.

"God—" Susan swooned, looking at me and then at the stove.

She was right; there was nothing in the world, at that moment in time, more spectacular than the smell of smoky bacon and the softening of tender, wild, garlicky aromatics releasing their essence into the hot, salty, splattering fat. There was nothing in the world, at that moment in time, more spectacular than sharing that simple headiness with this woman I met online by sheer luck, and who I loved, in her tiny house in northern Connecticut. We did nothing more to the ramps that night than beat six sizable local eggs—the kind with yolks so vibrantly red that the Italian name for them is *rosso di uovo*—pour them over the ramps, and bake them until the eggs were lightly set. We ate a simple frittata for dinner with glasses of cold, herby wine, and went to bed early.

RAMP FRITTATA

Ramps often pose confusion for people, who try to prepare them the way they would scallions; they use the bottoms, or the root, and discard the leafy greens. Unfortunately, they're missing out on the entire point behind the wild edible: that they're entirely delicious, from tip to top. To prepare ramps for cooking, give them a good wash and dry to rid them of any dirt or sand; then slice them into halves if they're young, or thirds if they're not—one-third about where the bulb begins to turn white, and another third midway up to where the leaves begin. Start by cooking the bulbs first; when they soften, add the middle third, and then, the leaves. The result is onion-y and earthy, and worth every penny (especially when pulled out of your neighbor's front yard). This recipe is a slightly fancified twist on the version that Susan and I made that night, only it's a bit richer.

Serves 4

1 tablespoon extra-virgin olive oil

1 bunch ramps (about 8 ounces), cleaned and prepared

Salt and freshly ground black pepper

1 tablespoon heavy cream

6 eggs

1. Preheat the oven to 350°F.

2. In a large sauté pan set over medium heat, warm the olive oil until it shimmers, then add the ramp bulbs. Cook, tossing frequently, until they begin to soften, about 5 minutes. Add the middle portion of the ramps, and then the leaves, tossing and rolling them in the hot fat, using tongs. Cover, and continue to cook until the leaves have completely wilted, 5 to 8 minutes. Taste for salt and pepper, and season as needed.

3. In a small bowl, beat the heavy cream together with the eggs, and pour them over the ramps. Shimmy the pan around so that the eggs are evenly distributed, and place the pan in the oven.

4. Bake until the eggs are set, about 10 minutes.

5. Remove from the oven, slice into wedges, and serve right out of the pan.

RAMPS ON TOAST WITH EGGS

Prepare this dish by cooking the ramps exactly the way you would before pouring on the egg-cream mixture. Fry the eggs (we prefer quail eggs with ramps for their delicate flavor) and serve atop garlic toast, as in the kale on toast recipe on page 200.

PART III

CHAPTER 23

Bitten in the Garden

I am an allergic person—the kind who attracts all manner of mosquito, gnat, and blackfly. Even if I'm surrounded by people sipping sweet tea and eating honey cake, I'm the only one who gets stung. My doctor once said it was because my cholesterol is high, as if saturated fat is as alluring as simple syrup. But even as a small child, I was like flypaper. Once, when I was four and my mother and father and I were staying at the Marco Polo Hotel in Miami Beach, I went to sleep in my hotel bed and woke up the next morning with my eyes swollen shut and looking like a short, white Leon Spinks after a few rounds with Muhammad Ali. Every goddamned mosquito on the eastern coast of Florida had found their way to our room, flying through the window screens, which were dotted with holes like Swiss cheese, and right past my sleeping parents, to chew on my face. To ensure against accusations of child abuse, my mother went to the gift shop in the lobby and bought me a pair of big, black, square, wraparound sunglasses—the kind geriatric cataract patients all over Boca wear right after surgery—and together, my parents and I went to the beach, where I watched my father squirm around in the sand, having his private man parts gnawed on by sand flies before they set their vicious sights on my runty Coppertone-covered, prepubescent arms.

So while I love the romantic promise of outdoor endeavors of the type that recall checkered, French picnic oilcloths; Gidget and

Moondoggie playing Frisbee in the sand; boating in Central Park when spring is finally gone and the air has an undertone of the dense sweetness that forces every New Yorker out of their office buildings at lunchtime; the Barbour- and wellie-wearing, high-ass appeal of Vita Sackville-West and her gardens at Sissinghurst, in order to participate in real life I either have to spray myself with enough DEET to kill every bug on the Mekong Delta, or stay inside. Which, conveniently, makes doing any sort of yard work next to impossible.

+++

Before Susan and I met, I never thought much about planting anything because Manhattan was dotted with farmers' markets everywhere, so if it was great produce I was after, it was never very far away and almost always available somewhere, at a price. I never had any particular yen to grow flowers either, since they were available at every Korean grocery store on every corner of the city. And when I once brought tiger lilies home, my cat, Viola, ate them and had to be hospitalized, her little white chin stained bright orange for weeks from the pollen.

But love does strange things to people. Some people skydive because it's their partner's favorite pastime. My friend Dave, a nice Jewish dentist from the Upper East Side of Manhattan, married a Southern girl from rural Alabama. The weekend before his nuptials he found himself sitting in a tree with a shotgun, waiting to pick off raccoons with his intended's brothers Earl and Bubba, all because he was in love. These things happen.

Starting in late winter, I arrived every weekend at Susan's house to find new piles of seed catalogs sitting in every room, including the bathroom. Some were gorgeous, four-color magazines with production values high enough to rival French *Vogue*. Others were very obviously meant to appeal to the Birkenstock-wearing, peace-loving among us, and were printed on crushed-wood-pulp paper and hand-lettered with a smeary, dreamy sort of black ink, like the vegetarian cookbooks printed on brown paper back in the early '70s. But in the depths of the winter, they were a lure, and we would sit side-by-side at Susan's kitchen counter, wondering how successful we might be at growing yellow summer squash, Charentais melons, and black, sweet Paul Robeson tomatoes, our eyes wide with want and desire and the self-confidence generally reserved for the delusional.

"You're going to grow a melon?" my mother gasped in disbelief on the phone when I told her about our plans. "I could just *buy* you a melon—"

"You know," Susan said one morning, thinking out loud as we flipped through catalogs over breakfast, "if we amend the soil well and take this seriously, we won't have to spend a dime on vegetables this summer."

This summer. The words hung in the air like a banner being dragged by an airplane.

This summer.

She was thinking ahead.

"And if we plant enough perennial herbs, we'll have a lush herb garden *next* summer—" she went on, taking a sip of tea.

Next summer.

"But if we want to put in asparagus," she said, looking at a catalog page containing at least ten different varieties, "it'll take much longer: you can't harvest them for three years. Look at these—they're *gorgeous!*" She held up a two-page spread with a picture of thick, fat purple asparagus at full size.

"Really? Three years?" Who knew?

Where would we be in three years? Would I even be in the picture? Would I still be spending hundreds of dollars every month on Amtrak tickets? Would we take the time to put in the asparagus crowns—finding someone with a backhoe, digging the trench, tending them until they produced something we could harvest—only to break up in a year?

"But we could put them in if you like them—there's nothing as delicious as freshly harvested asparagus. Have you ever had them? You just steam them and top them with a fried egg. Nothing better, unless you pan-roast them and grate a little truffle on them. For special occasions, of course."

No, I told her, I hadn't ever had fresh asparagus. With or without a truffle. I'd grown up with the grayish-green canned variety, and then when they showed up at the farmers' markets in the city, I'd buy great fat bunches for ten dollars a pound to wrap up in blankets of prosciutto di Parma and drizzle with Silver Palate raspberry mayonnaise. But now, the words *backhoe* and *crown* and *trench* careened around my brain. And as I wondered where we would be, and what we'd be doing in three years in this tiny house in this tiny town with one stoplight and a bear that was eating from the neighbor's bird feeder every morning, I looked out the window at the backyard, and imagined digging deep together, putting down roots.

+++

"Why would *anyone* plant vegetables if they don't absolutely have to?" my father asked when I told him that we were starting to sketch out plans for a garden.

To him, vegetable gardening was only for people who couldn't afford to eat any other way. It was okay to buy the results of what other people grew, at lush, hydrangea-covered farm stands out on Long Island and at greenmarkets, and maybe, if you had the space and the romantic inclination, to grow some ineffectual and cottony patio tomatoes, just to say you had. But the actual act of vegetable gardening was a little bit embarrassing and off-putting to him, like buying cans of generic vegetables labeled BEANS and SPINACH in big black block lettering against a stark white background, and hiding them at the bottom of the grocery bag so that if you ran into your neighbors, they couldn't see them. If you were truly serious about being a vegetable gardener, it meant other, unsavory things, my father said, quoting Dickens, like "loss of situation."

And I *had* lost my situation: the dot-com I'd been working for had imploded. The day our CEO showed up to smugly inform us that the business would be closing immediately and there would be no severance pay because the funders, Louis Vuitton Moët Hennessy, had pulled the plug after mind-bogglingly gross financial ineptitude—*sorry folks,* he simply said—was the same day his wife, Patricia, came barreling into our tiny meeting space carrying four overstuffed shopping bags from Armani Exchange, across the street.

"Did you tell them yet, Daddy?" Patricia stage-whispered, bursting in through the glass double-door. She always called him *Daddy,* while half of us turned around and stuck fingers down our throats in disgust.

In response, Daddy shoved his hands into the pockets of his Brooks Brothers pin-striped trousers and blushed a deep crimson.

"Just come up, honey," Susan comforted, when I called her that afternoon as I was cleaning out my desk. "I bought some graph paper, so we can sketch out our garden boxes and order our seeds—okay?"

I went home, threw a week's worth of clothes in a bag, headed for Penn Station, and took the next train north.

+++

On the first warm day in Harwinton, when there were still errant patches of snow here and there but the grass had turned bright green and was already begging for a trim, Susan and I ventured out into the backyard with the dog to size things up. Hidden behind a tree, in a corner of the yard, was a small shed that I hadn't really noticed before, and attached to it was a crumbling greenhouse whose glass roof had collapsed over the winter under the weight of more than sixty inches of snow.

Susan unlatched the broad wooden door. It creaked open and there, lining all four spider-webbed walls, were ancient tools in varying states of disrepair: short-handled hand rakes; a scuffle hoe; a Hori Hori—a Japanese knife meant for splitting plants and digging up weeds; a manual rotary mower; two gas mowers; a child's rake kept specifically for the task of getting fallen leaves out of the ground cover without destroying the things around it; a leaf blower; a cord trimmer; shovels of every shape and size; a lightly rusted, formerly dark green–painted pitchfork like something out of *American Gothic;* and a long, very heavy silver-colored metal pole with a flattened end, which Susan aptly dubbed "the thing with the thing on the end of it," used to jimmy up the rocks that litter Connecticut soil from one end of the state to the other. Every home in the northern part of the state has one of these rock-plying tools—you can drive through Litchfield County during growing season and see scores of people in their yards using them—and no one has any idea what they're called.

I stood in the middle of the shed, gesturing in awe. "Holy shit! You didn't tell me about all of *this*—"

Susan calmly pulled out a red plastic gas container with the word *mower* scrawled on its side in thick Sharpie.

"Have you ever mowed a lawn before?"

"Where would I have mowed a lawn on Fifty-Seventh Street in Manhattan?" I responded. I followed Susan outside as she dragged her beaten-up green push mower out onto the grass, added a little gas, and then began the painstaking process of priming and pulling what I referred to as the *rip cord.*

Once she got the lawn mower going, it rumbled and belched and shook and threatened to take off on its own, like the brooms in *Fantasia,* which always reminded me of chickens running around without their heads. I grabbed the handle, released the clutch, and began pushing and schlepping, hauling the mower from one side of the yard to the other and back again, round and round, in giant rings the diameter of the inflatable wading pool in the next-door neighbor's backyard, around which they had just built a deck. By the time I was done, three hours later, Susan was already freshly showered, lounging on the deck sipping a Hendrick's martini, and admiring the series of concentric crop circles I'd carved into her backyard.

"I wonder if you can see them from outer space—" she yelled down to me.

"Very *funny*—"

"Next time, *I'll* do it," she offered encouragingly, as I trudged up the back deck stairs, drenched in sweat.

✛✛✛

By the middle of the summer, Susan and I had built six, ten-foot-by-three-foot garden boxes in her backyard. I found that I could sit out there contentedly for hours digging around, pulling weeds, staking and tying tomato plants just the way Susan had shown me, using old panty hose just soft enough so as not to cut through the plant stems. Now without a full-time day job in Manhattan, I'd started coming up to Connecticut for four days a week, and during that time, we planted everything that we could think of: exotic Asian greens meant to be eaten raw or cooked, summer squash, winter squash, cue-ball squash, tomatoes, cucumbers, radishes, kale, Nantes carrots that wouldn't come in until early fall, spicy mustard greens, four different kinds of tender lettuce, wax beans, sugar snap peas, and even two varieties of magnificent, ruby-red beets—though I *loathed* beets. By the time the weather turned warm, we could have sustained ourselves, as well as Susan's entire town, plus all thirty-seven members of the King Family, on what we had produced. When our summer squash began to run up the side of the rope ladder we fashioned from pieces of garden bamboo and twine to keep the vegetable from lying in the dirt, we found ourselves awash in baskets full of luscious squash blossoms, which we stuffed with softened, herby goat cheese, battered, and then pan-fried as predinner snacks for weeks on end. Eventually, cooler-weather greens like kale, chard, and mustard started to come in, and one night, while the dog barked loudly enough to awaken the entire state, we discovered our neighbor, Laurie—whom we adored—sneaking into our yard in the wee hours of the night to pilfer the overflow.

"I can't believe she wants *our* vegetables," I said sleepily. But she did.

Even with all of the planting and tending and harvesting I was doing, unless a vegetable was stuffed with cheese, battered, and then fried, I still wasn't really a fan. I was raised to believe that vegetables were a side dish, and never deserved anything more than second billing to meat, like a B actor who nobody pays much attention to when George Clooney is on the screen. So more often than not—and even as our neighbors were swiping the bounty of our very successful gardening efforts—the only evidence on our dinner table of something that had come from the ground was my artfully placed handful of perfectly trimmed haricots verts crisscrossed atop the filet mignons I'd brought up from Arnaud, which would, in turn, be sitting up tall and mighty on a potato timbale, which I argued also came from the ground.

"Maybe we could actually have something *green* tonight," Susan said one night in frustration. "Like, from the garden—I mean, that's why we planted it. Right?"

She had a point: I had grown to love going out to the yard with the dog to see what was coming in, to find carrot tops peeking through the soil, and green, cue-ball squash dangling from the vines. In the city, I'd have paid a fortune for them at the greenmarket, shopping shoulder-to-shoulder with chefs and flannel-shirted beautiful people who were comfortable dropping inordinate sums of money for stunningly colorful, precious vegetables destined for dinner. But here, where I could just pluck them from the ground for free plus the cost of the seeds and sweat equity, I had absolutely no idea what to do with them.

"What did you have in mind?" I questioned Susan one Saturday afternoon, after she proposed a dinner only of items coming straight from our garden.

In response, she picked up a pair of cheap gardening scissors and an old, deep basket that had belonged to one of her aunts, and gestured to me to follow her outside.

In the backyard, Susan walked around the boxes, examining what we had, what looked good, and what was not yet quite right for harvesting. She snipped voluminous, lace-edged mustard leaves big as palm fronds, pulled up narrow, bullet-shaped French radishes, a few finger-size baby carrots, a six-inch-long yellow squash, and a perfectly round, softball-size head of Boston lettuce.

"*This* is what we're having for dinner," she pronounced, holding her basket out proudly for me to see.

"*Nice*," I said weakly. "Why don't I also go into town and get a chicken to put on the grill."

"You will *not*," she insisted, as we climbed the stairs back to the deck. "I'm making us a garlic salad. I used to have it all the time when I visited my friends' farm back in the '70s."

Garlic salad had been invented by Susan's friends Katie and Val, who left Manhattan in 1976 to move to a fifty-acre tract of land in upstate New York. It was not far from the near-comatose Borscht Belt, which had once been inhabited by wall-to-wall hotels like Grossinger's and The Windsor, but had fallen into disrepair as the older Jews who'd spent every summer there, playing shuffleboard and laughing with the *tummlers* in the lobby on rainy days, began to die off. Some of the properties were sold as ashrams; others just faded away into oblivion.

The acreage was cheap, and Katie and Val took full advantage of it, moving their lives north, and stocking their new, lush property with goats and chickens, which would supply milk, cheese, and eggs. It was a blissful existence for about eight minutes until they realized that they were actually poor and without any feasible way of earning a living. They definitely had enough food, though, so long as they stuck to what was growing in their garden. Thus, their infamous salad was born.

Garlic salad had to have three key ingredients, the primary one being enough garlic to wilt a redwood. The garlic was squeezed through a press and tossed together with incendiary raw mustard greens and radishes, which were the other key components. Sweeter vegetables—carrots, summer squash—could be thrown in, assuming one had them. The salad combination made for a pungent, eye-tearing concoction, which Susan dressed with hefty tablespoons of cider vinegar and a bit of olive oil. The result was a wet, spicy tangle of vegetables that not only assured me a seat on the train by myself back to New York, but that I now dream about in the steamy days of summer, when leafy mustard greens are tumbling out of gardens everywhere.

"But you don't even *like* vegetables," my father said to me when he called Susan's house to say that he and Shirley were going to stop by the next day on their way back to New York from their annual vacation on the Cape. Susan and I were standing in the kitchen, doing the dishes when the phone rang; I answered and went on about this pungent, delicious invention that Susan had just fed me, and that cost us not one red cent.

"For god's sake, Cy—" I heard Shirley yell in the background. "She's in love."

+++

The next morning, Susan and I took our cups of tea and coffee, climbed down the back deck steps with the dog beside us, and strolled into the garden to discover that all of our beets and beet greens had been destroyed. Left behind were tiny, chewed-up, reddish spindly nubs standing at attention where the lush vegetables had lived and grown only hours earlier. *How could this happen?* I raged, while Susan set her mug down on the edge of the garden box.

"Sometimes," Susan replied calmly, bending over to pull up what was left of the vegetable, "stuff just dies. It gets gorgeous, it looks perfect, everything is fine and great, and then other things decide that it's just as gorgeous as *you* think it is, and they get there first. It is what it is."

Sweat trickled down her face but she kept pulling, tossing the ragged ends of the beet greens into a nearby bucket meant for the compost heap on the far side of the shed.

Forget about the fancy-ass greenmarkets that dotted Manhattan, where wealthy New Yorkers dropped insane sums of money for their exquisite produce; the act of vegetable *gardening*—of growing food for actual *sustenance* rather than *trend*—was an unpredictable labor of love that didn't always turn out the way it was supposed to. It was shrouded in romance and fashion and allure, but involved a vast amount of work under constant threat of disappointment; no matter how hard you tried, you still might conceivably lose the things you'd worked so hard to grow. And there wasn't a damned thing you could do about it.

"Look at you, Miss Gardener," my father yelled out the window of his Toyota when he and Shirley pulled into the driveway later that afternoon. I was in the front yard, deadheading my new addiction—climbing roses, which I'd planted all along Susan's front picket fence when the local nursery had a sale—in an enormous straw hat that made me vaguely resemble a thumbtack.

"You look like Lillian Gish in *The Whales of August*," he said, walking in through the front gate and hugging me hard. "But you look happy—"

"I am, Dad." I beamed, pulling off my gloves and stuffing them into my back pocket.

In just a few months, I'd tossed the idiot overalls and the fancy clogs and the leather work gloves I'd bought at some haute couture garden shop in Manhattan, and now worked while dressed in an old pair of khakis that I'd picked up at the local Goodwill. I wore rubberized gloves that Susan's mother had found in a box in her basement. I had even become adept at composting, the very definition of which is pretty much taking dreck and turning it into more dreck. Because vegetables, and roses, I discovered that summer, really love dreck.

"So what's next for you—a John Deere?" my father teased. It was: a few weeks later, I was driving around Susan's backyard on a green-and-yellow lawn tractor instead of pushing the crop-circle mower around like a lunatic for three hours at a time.

That afternoon, the four of us considered going out to eat at one of the nicer restaurants in Litchfield, just down the road, where Armani-clad New Yorkers with summer houses in the country would go when they wanted tall, mediocre, wildly overpriced food.

"We *could*," my father said, thinking out loud, "if that's what you want. I just thought we'd stay here." He looked out into the backyard, at the garden, gorgeous in the late afternoon sun.

Susan and I went back out into the garden and pulled masses of tiny, tender yellow summer squash and snap peas from their vines and gently boiled them for a few seconds, before showering them with a rich, peppery green olive oil, topped with handfuls of fresh herbs and sea salt. We made a pot of simple, peppery bouillabaisse with fresh white fish and spot prawns that I'd brought up from the city a few days before, and toasted thick slices of garlic-rubbed French bread over Susan's father's ancient, patent-pending avocado-green Weber kettle grill.

The four of us sat at the kitchen counter with the early evening sun streaming through the slider behind us. We drank glasses of cold, dry rosé, and dipped the grilled garlic toasts into the spicy soup, peeling the succulent tomato-drenched prawns with our fingers, and making the kind of happy, lip-smacking noises usually heard from children. Shirley and Susan talked garden talk—what we were growing, what worked and what didn't, and why, while my father just stared at me, wiping his hands and his face with his fifth napkin.

"This is *good*," he mouthed to me, picking up his wineglass and clinking mine gently, his blue eyes welling up.

A month later, Susan and I were out in the garden, up to our knees in dirt. It was a hot, sweaty day, and we were both soaked to the skin in damp, compost-covered T-shirts and shorts. We'd gone into the house to get a glass of water when the phone rang.

"Lissie—please come now!" Shirley's son, Robbie, cried frantically. "There's been an accident."

We left the tools in the garden and grabbed the car keys, and without bothering to change, raced to New York, where my father and Shirley had been in a car accident just a few miles from their home. At the hospital, I sat with him in the emergency room for what felt like an eternity. Under the sharp, metallic glare of surgical lights I looked down at my mud-covered hands not letting go of his—at my nails, my legs, my feet, my shirt, caked with dirt and the lifeblood of the sweet and earthy food we'd shared with him a few weeks before.

When he hugged me tightly before saying goodbye that last time I'd seen him in Connecticut, he whispered in my ear as Shirley climbed into the front seat.

"You're home, Liss," he breathed, kissing the top of my head. And then he got into the car and drove away.

CHAPTER 24

The Land of Lost Contentment

My father loved *Walkabout*, the movie about a young teenage girl and her little brother who are dumped in the Australian outback, where they are abandoned. It's a brutal film about filial love; coming of age; sudden, shocking loss; and emotional disorientation. It's about a relentless searching for home and for safety, and the discovery that the place that you knew as home is gone.

It was years before I realized why my father loved the movie as much as he did: he saw himself, always, as that little boy in the wilderness with no one but his sister to protect and care for him. When he was three, his mother had famously—mythically—walked out on the family, leaving my grandfather to care for him and his eight-year-old sister, who took it upon herself to never let him out of her sight. His mother did return eventually, but for my father, things were never the same. Those easy, youthful days of feeling nothing can harm you, that the world was perfect and delicious—for him those days were gone forever. Once my grandmother came back, my father and my aunt spent much of the rest of their lives trying to somehow ensure that she would never leave them again, draping a thin veneer of imaginary perfection over her—she was a good, no, a *great* mother, they would say—and trying to fix whatever they had done wrong that might have compelled her to walk out in the first place. She died at the age of ninety-two.

Her leaving him at such a young age turned my father into an eternal searcher—always walking, always moving and hoping and looking for something he was never quite able to find, or to nail down. During World War II, he became a night fighter pilot, joining the navy because, he half-joked, the food was supposed to be the best of all the branches of service, and the uniforms were nicer. And he flew planes, he told me, because he could see more of the earth all at once, and *have a better grasp of things.*

There he is, in his 1941 Lafayette High School yearbook photo—*Member of Arista, Biology Club*—and two months later, he was off at preflight school in Del Monte, California. Once he earned his wings, he'd spend every evening after dinner taking off in his little Grumman F6F Hellcat from the deck of the aircraft carrier USS *Enterprise* as it lumbered around the Pacific. It being wartime, the carrier never dropped anchor; it moved here and there in the middle of the vast ocean, in absolute pitch darkness. My father, when his midnight runs were over, had to land his little moving plane on this massive moving ship, which, he said, was like trying to thread a needle blindfolded while being tossed around in a hurricane. He accomplished this feat by the ancient art of celestial navigation, with help from a set of round, plastic star charts that sat on his lap as he flew. Guided in the dark by the Pythagorean and the mythic, on the other side of the world, he was completely alone—free, like Saint-Exupéry's pilot, floating above the unholy brutality beneath him—and not yet out of his teens.

We are looking at the same stars that will bring you back to your ship tonight, my grandmother wrote to him on thin, blue onionskin from her hallway phone table in Brooklyn. It was her only comfort, that after washing up their dinner plates, she and my grandfather would push up the sash and climb out onto their fire escape right off the kitchen window, and Orion's Belt—the stars Alnitak, Alnilam, and Mintaka—that she craned her neck to see beyond the flickering lights of the Coney Island parachute drop in the distance, was the same Orion's Belt that would guide her nineteen-year-old son to safety.

The only time my grandmother knew exactly where my father was during the war was on the day his service ended, and he flew himself back to Brooklyn, to Floyd Bennett Field. He told her to be out on her apartment roof at exactly three o'clock in the afternoon, and at the precise hour he flew over the borough, passing their kosher butcher and their fish man, the shoemaker and the Orthodox synagogue, eventually turning his plane east and flying long and low over the entire length of Ocean Parkway. Over their apartment building, he ventured down, as close as twenty feet over the roof, where he could see his mother standing, watching for him in her flowered apron, smiling, waving a dish towel in the air. In a final salute, he tipped his wings and made a second, closer pass. That image of my father's watery, sea-blue eyes inside his goggles stayed with my grandmother for her entire life.

"Otherwise," she mused, "I never would have believed it was really him flying the plane, the damned fool."

You are home at last, my grandfather said to him that night after a dinner of boiled chicken and noodles speckled with wisp-thin strands of dill, stubbing out his cigarette in the foyer ashtray. *You've been away for years, and now you owe it to us to stay.*

And he did for a while, coming home from college classes in Manhattan to sleep every night in his childhood bedroom with his star charts tacked to the wall next to his tiny bed, still searching. He left a year later, settling first in Boston, then in Ontario, then in Manhattan, and always taking jobs that required he be on the road by himself, constantly. When I was a little girl, I listened to the storybook tales he'd tell me over our meals together: the hangtown fry he'd share with a vacationing Oregon logger while driving north from San Francisco to Seattle; the pastrami sandwich he shared with Zero Mostel—a friend of my grandfather's from his Jewish newspaper while eating at a deli in Los Angeles; eating a twenty-ounce porterhouse at the Pump Room in Chicago during a storm so bad that the windows were obscured by snowdrifts piling up outside on Michigan Avenue. By the time he met my mother, he had been everywhere, he had eaten everything—charting his travels by what he ate, where, and with whom.

When my parents married, he continued searching, and the road trips we took together were extensive, romanticized ordeals that ran the gamut from long Sunday drives in the country gazing at enormous estates in Westchester or Long Island to spur-of-the-moment dinners at extravagant restaurants where my mother would push the food around on her plate while my father gorged himself.

Years later, after my parents' divorce and after he had moved back into his mother's Brooklyn apartment, his tiny bedroom with the star charts still intact, my father and I began to log hundreds of hours in the car together, ostensibly to visit colleges all along the Eastern Seaboard and up to the farthest reaches of northern New England. Each Friday after school, he drove up in front of my high school's rotunda in a long series of leased cars—the ones my mother never let him have—the silver hatchback with the wide racing stripe and the promise of Formula One talent emblazoned on the hood; the brown, wood-paneled station wagon—and off we'd go, driving for hours, arriving late in the evening at our bucolic, New England destinations: Hanover, New Hampshire, or Northampton, Massachusetts, or Auburn, Maine. Together, we searched for the same serenity we had always found in Manhattan's temples of haute cuisine, places of our secret past he could no longer afford.

One cold October night in Burlington, Vermont, we parked the car off Church Street and walked along the redbrick pedestrian mall looking for a place to have dinner. It was absolutely freezing; the wet wind blew off Lake Champlain so ferociously that it cut through me like a knife. We ended up in a tiny bistro—beef Wellington for me, and lobster Thermidor and a dry Gibson for him—at a round table set close to the front window, on a pair of wobbly, old bentwood Thonet chairs. Familiar classical music played through a tiny bookshelf speaker hanging in a corner, near the ceiling.

"That's a mazurka," my father mumbled while buttering a roll, pointing at the speaker with the tip of his knife.

I recognized it—he'd often hummed it in the car when we were together—as the music of his childhood.

+++

"I love this place," my father said to me at Susan's house, the last time I saw him. Standing on the deck and looking out at the back-yard, he had shown up, with Shirley, dressed like someone else's father: gone were the whipcord trousers and the navy-blue English duffel coat that made him look like an aging schoolboy. Gone were the pressed Brooks Brothers button-down shirts with his initials embroidered onto the cuff, the rep ties, the cordovan wingtips. Instead, he arrived wearing jeans—not the fake, triple-weave polyester kind that he infrequently donned in the '70s to exhibit his furtive hipness, but real, honest-to-goodness, stiff-as-a-board Wrangler jeans rolled up twice at the bottom—black leatherette sneakers with Velcro closures, a polo shirt, and a baseball cap with the name of his aircraft carrier and his year of service—USS *Enterprise* 1944 emblazoned on the front. He had been fancy all the years that I had known him, shoe-horning himself into outfits and fashions, as though the clothes possessed the power to keep him safe.

That day, Susan and I took Shirley to a local nursery to buy some perennials for the tiny front garden she attempted to plant every year at the condo where she and my father lived. True to her Yankee profile—she had grown up outside of Boston and had been taught the lessons of Depression and wartime frugality early on—Shirley held off on buying her seasonal plants until coming up to the country, where there were real Agways.

"I'd rather stay here," my father yawned, unfolding a dark green camping chair on the deck so that it faced away from the house and into the yard. "Why don't you gals go"—he always called us *gals*—"and I'll sit with the dog."

We left him there that afternoon with MacGillicuddy stretched out alongside him, the two of them just beginning to snore in unison as we closed the door behind us. Two hours later, we returned and found them still fast asleep in the late afternoon sun, in the exact same position, my father's baseball cap pulled down low over his face, the smallest hint of a smile on his face.

"A boy and his dog," Shirley whispered, smiling.

I reached over him to put my hand on his shoulder and shake him awake.

"Don't, Lissie," she said gently. "He's content."

+++

My father, who had flown planes off a moving aircraft carrier at night in the Pacific during World War II, was running a simple errand two miles from his house on a magnificently sunny August morning just a few weeks after his visit, and was broadsided by a bunch of speeding kids in an uninsured, rusted-out Honda, with Shirley sitting next to him. She, with lesser but still severe injuries, was taken to one hospital and he to another; after twenty inseparable years, she would never see him alive again. Susan and I and my cousins sat at his bedside for a week waiting for a sign that any brain function might return, but it was gone forever. Days before he died, before the doctors and other family members decided when and under what circumstances I needed to remove him—my father, my friend—from life support, I was already planning his funeral with the help of my cousin Lois while he was still very much alive.

The ground had shifted beneath me, the way it suddenly does during an earthquake; I felt woozy and drunk, the way I once did when I got off a cruise ship, and like my legs weren't really attached.

"I just want to go home," I whispered to Susan, clutching her hand in the limousine after the funeral, tears pouring down my face.

"To your apartment?" she asked softly.

"*No*—" I shook my head.

"You see that?" my father once asked me when I was a teenager, pointing up at the ceiling of Grand Central Terminal, sparkling with illuminated constellations. We had taken the IRT into the city one weekend morning shortly after my parents' divorce, when it became too expensive for him to drive in and park in a garage, and when our secretive meals at La Côte Basque and La Grenouille had given way to carbohydrate-laden lunches at local greasy spoons that he still managed, somehow, to fetishize. We stopped together in the middle of the Main Concourse, near the round information booth decades before the National Guard presence and the bomb-sniffing Labradors. It was quiet that Saturday morning; we stood side-by-side, and looked up.

"The people who built this—they made a mistake; the constellations are backward," he said, taking his plastic aviator glasses off and wiping them down with his handkerchief.

"Does that mean the world is upside down?" I asked.

He looked at me hard, and put his hand on my shoulder.

"Isn't it?"

CHAPTER 25

Craving

"Honey—Susie?"

"What—what time is it?"

"Three, I think. Honey, I want tongue."

"*Now*? I'm *asleep*," she groaned, rolling over, her eyes closed.

"God, Susie, *not that*—"

"It's the middle of the night—"

"I know."

I stared at the ceiling. I couldn't get it out of my head: the rich, dense, salty sweetness of sliced pickled beef tongue on rye, painted with a thin coating of pungent yellow mustard between the tender meat and the bread—it was driving me crazy.

It was months before my father's accident; when I called him the next morning to complain, he was sympathetic but practical.

"You're not exactly in the big city anymore, honey," he laughed. "Not having deli is the price you pay for falling in love with a country girl."

"So what am I supposed to do?" I whined like a child.

"Call the local rabbi," he responded sensibly. And then he hung up.

✝✝✝

I never had any particularly debilitating hungers—gastronomical or otherwise—until I started spending four days a week in Connecticut.

For a while, the biggest problem for me was waking up on a Sunday morning and feeling a weird sort of intravenous drip–like sensation that occurred when I stumbled down the stairs, opened the door, and the *New York Times* wasn't there. It was a slow burn, like the radioactive dye they shoot into you before you have a CT scan, that wouldn't dissipate until I got into the car, drove a mile to the local convenience store, picked up the paper—caressing the front page like a lunatic as I sat alone in the parking lot—and drove home. The newpaper delivery truck couldn't make it up the hill to Susan's house in the winter—its antilock brakes had once jammed and the truck slid all the way back down the street to the main local road—so the residential route had been permanently canceled.

At least, though, that situation was fixable. I could just get into the car and buy the *Times* in person. My bigger problem was my insatiable midnight craving for what I called *Jew food*, and knowing there wasn't a damn thing I could do to satisfy it until I got back to the city.

But the morning after my three A.M. tongue obsession, when I couldn't stand it anymore, I decided to heed my father's advice. I strode into Susan's studio, picked up the phone book, and dialed the local reform synagogue.

"Excuse me, Rabbi—could you tell me where there's a Jewish deli around here?" I was very apologetic.

"Can you call back later? I have services in half an hour and I need a tenth for a minyan."

Finding the quorum of ten Jewish men whose presence was required by Talmudic law to begin Sabbath services was no easy feat in that part of Connecticut.

"I'm really sorry, Rabbi," I pleaded, "but it's a little urgent. I need to find tongue."

He sighed.

"I need a minyan, and you need tongue. In this part of the world, good luck to both of us. You'll have to go to the Crown," he offered, before hanging hung up.

But New England's largest kosher supermarket was, I knew, an hour away, in West Hartford, and closed for Shabbos.

"Couldn't we just *buy* a tongue and make it ourselves? We have everything for the brine—all we need is the meat," Susan asked logically, sipping her tea.

"Where the hell am I going to find a whole tongue? And even if I did," I said, "it's just weird to buy a tongue. It *looks* like a tongue. Jews don't just buy an entire tongue and boil it themselves, unless they're from the shtetl."

She looked at me blankly.

"I have an idea," my father announced. He had called back the way he always did on sleepy late Saturday afternoons while he was doing the crossword puzzle—he'd bellow *Hello there, Cy Altman here*, like I didn't know who he was without that grand pronouncement—and I moaned and complained to him about the fact that his rabbi idea was a good one, but had yielded me nothing. And if I didn't have some tongue, I was going to drop dead exactly where I stood.

"I understand," he breathed, heavily. "Imagine me in Kansas during the war. There was no Federal Express, you know. By the time your grandmother's *halupches* made it to my barracks, they could have killed every Nazi in Germany." My father had a particular lust for these small, savory cabbage rolls, and my grandmother was determined to make sure that he had them, even while he was in the navy, stationed on the other side of the world, in Kansas.

The next day, while I was out working on the roses in the front garden, my father showed up alone, out of the blue, at Susan's house with a pound of tongue from Ben's Deli on Long Island. A separate shopping bag held two loaves of thin-sliced Jewish rye, a container of half-sour pickles, a jar of mustard, and a foil loaf pan of kasha varnishkes—bow-tie pasta tossed with kasha and fried onions. I wept exhausted tears of chemical relief, the way an addict might after a shot of methadone. We sat at the counter, made some sandwiches, heated up the kasha varnishkes, and the dog drooled like she'd swallowed someone's shoelaces.

+++

A little while after he died—after the papers were filed and the stone was designed and the insurance claims started coming in and I had cried so much that I didn't think I could ever possibly cry again—I developed a sudden and insatiable craving for lox, eggs, and onions, which my father made for me almost every Sunday morning when I was growing up, when he wasn't cooking Spam. He would have gotten up early, taken the dog out for a long walk, and stopped at the local bagel shop where he'd pick up a half pound of Nova Scotia, a dozen eggs, an onion, and two bialys. Though still in bed mostly asleep, I would hear his keys jangle the door open, and the clatter of the dog's toenails on the hard parquet floor. Within minutes, I'd be lured from my bedroom by the sweet, burnt aroma of caramelizing onion, which he'd chopped as precisely and perfectly as Susan had done for her mirepoix; a dab of salted Breakstone butter would sizzle in my mother's Teflon sauté pan and my father would add the onions, tossing them like a television chef by jerking the handle of the skillet back and forth—flipping the hot contents of a pan without a spatula was one of the "fancier" cooking techniques he prided himself on being able to do. The butter and the onions would begin to turn a light, golden nut-brown while he tore up the slices of Nova—he claimed that chopping actually bruised the fish—and added it to the pan. Beaten eggs would be poured over it, and in seconds it was done and plunked down in front of me on top of a toasted, lightly buttered bialy, on my little white melamine Mary Poppins plate.

It was all I could think about, and for months after he died, I found myself sitting at Susan's breakfast counter obsessing about what my father used to cook and how he cooked it. Had he used Nova, or was it lox? Was it thick, salty belly lox? Atlantic or Norwegian? Was the onion sweet, or the more pungent red onion? Was the bialy actually onion pletzl, or was I just imagining it? Every Sunday, I stood in Susan's kitchen, trying to replicate that breakfast every way I could think of, while she sat at the counter having her tea and watching in silence. By the time it was finally done, Susan was usually in the garden and I sat at the counter, eating breakfast alone.

Weeks later, I began making a dish that my grandmother had first fed my father when he was a boy, and which I knew he'd loved. I opened a can of skinless and boneless sardines, drained it, and mashed the sardines together with cottage cheese, which I spread on some Scandinavian crackers I had on hand that had all the flavor and delicacy of foam packing material. I ate this combination every morning for a month, sometimes just spooning the mixture straight from the bowl into my mouth.

Eventually, I began having short, vivid dreams about the palacsinta my father and I would order for dessert at the Czech restaurant Praha, during our subversive lunches when my mother was still modeling. It wasn't so much the taste of the food itself that I was dreaming of, but rather, how we sat together in the usually empty restaurant, and sliced into the thin, featherweight pancake wrapped around warm apricot preserves, and dusted with confectioners' sugar and crushed hazelnuts; it was a dish that outclassed anything else on the menu, and my father frequently raced through lunches of veal paprikash to get to it. The dreams stopped when, in the city one night, I took my mother out for a special birthday dinner at Felidia, and there it was, on Lidia Bastianich's dessert menu; Lidia came out of the kitchen in her whites to say hello, and I swooned.

When the palacsinta arrived, warm and seductive and dripping with apricot sweetness, it was set down between us; I reached across the table to cut into it, while my mother groaned her displeasure at my ordering dessert. She glared at it and then back at me, flaring her nostrils.

As the summer wore on, I became completely fixated on Holsteiner schnitzel, the heavy egg-and-anchovy-laden fried meat dish that so delighted my father and so terrorized me as a child. In the August heat, I stood in Susan's kitchen, cooking dinner, and out of the corner of my eye, I could swear I'd caught a glimpse of my father sitting at the counter, looking a little bit younger and a good bit heavier, about to dive in to a plate of perfectly golden schnitzel, topped with a sunny-side up egg crisscrossed with anchovies just the way Luchow's used to make it for him when he took me there to see the Christmas tree.

"I think you're exhausted," Susan observed, when I finally confided what I'd "seen." We were in the car, driving the dog to her favorite hiking spot.

"I could tell you exactly what he was wearing," I told her, "the Black Watch tartan tie I brought him from the Scotch House in London, in 1983. And his gray Harris tweed jacket with the little dark-brown leather buttons. He looked like he was about to say something."

She reached for my hand from the driver's seat.

+++

In the deepest, hottest part of the summer after my father died—it was late August, when nighttime temperatures begin to cool but the days are still long and oppressively humid and steamy—I stood in Susan's kitchen, pounding boneless pork loin, and, when we could afford it, veal, until it was thin as grade-school oak tag. The dog ran upstairs with every hard, violent whack, creeping back down to the living room only when the fresh lard I'd brought up from Arnaud had melted to the exact point where the meat, dipped first in chestnut flour, then beaten egg, then fine bread crumbs to affect the puffy, delicate outer Holsteiner schnitzel coating achieved by long-closed Luchow's, could be slid into the hot fat for a few minutes. I'd turn it once, carefully, move it to a warm plate, and top it with anchovies and a fried egg, the way my father adored it. Steam coated the window above the stove, where I'd deftly roll a diaphanous crêpe out of its sizzling pan, and fill it with warmed apricot preserves, to make the palacsinta that we had shared, alone, at Praha.

The entire state was in the midst of a heat wave when I conjured up the dish that my father talked about nonstop after eating it in Rome. I went on a fettucine Alfredo binge, hand-cutting the noodles on the kitchen counter—flour everywhere, on the walls, the floor, the dog— and tossing them with the thick, creamy cheese sauce that my father could only dream of after his first heart surgery, and which he had been forbidden from eating ever again. One night, after a high-end seafood market opened up in nearby Litchfield, I stood at the kitchen counter, chopping pickles, whisking homemade mayonnaise, and thinning batter I'd made from the buckwheat flour I'd unearthed at a nearby health food market to make blini and caviar, and shrimp rémoulade and oysters Rockefeller, which my father and I had once shared at L'Espalier in Boston, when he was dropping me off at college.

"*Uncle*—" Susan implored, holding her stomach when I spooned the rémoulade over the shrimp and poured her a cold Chablis into one of the two tall Riedel glasses I'd carried up from the city, wrapped in towels. "Can we have something not quite so fancy tomorrow? Please? Like maybe a *salad* and some garlic toast?"

I obliged, and instead made all of my father's favorite homestyle foods. There were the dumplings and chicken paprikash that Gaga used to make for him, which we ate, sweating, perspiration running into our eyes. There was duck confit cassoulet brimming with fresh, unsmoked pork kielbasa I'd found at a nearby, old-time butcher shop in New Britain; there was my grandmother's Liptauer that she used to feed him on challah while he sat underneath her piano on those long Brooklyn afternoons of his childhood; and there was cottage cheese mashed together with sardines, and flakey French fig tarts oozing with chèvre and fresh herbs from the garden. Stacks of cookbooks were beginning to pile up everywhere, frantically, around the kitchen and into the living room, and, once pulled from the bookcase in Susan's studio, wouldn't be shelved again.

One Friday night, I left Susan in the house with the dog and drove twelve miles away to attend services and to say kaddish, the Jewish memorial prayer for the dead, in a tan, brick, modern-esque temple tucked back into a thicket of pine trees. When the choir began to sing the songs I recognized from the services I attended at sleepaway camp every Friday night during my childhood, I craved the food that followed them. That night, I drove back to Susan's past Value Mart and stopped there for a chicken and matzo meal. By nine, we were sitting at the counter, eating chicken soup with matzo balls. The next day, while Susan squirreled herself away in her studio and finished designing a book for a New York publisher, I set to work on the leftovers: I pulled the chicken off the bone, minced it together with shallot and parsley, added a beaten egg white, packed it into the oval ring mold I'd brought up with the wineglasses, baked it, and drizzled my little lumpish hunk of leftover poultry with a velvety béchamel so thick and smooth that a wooden spoon, propped up in the middle of it, would have stood at attention.

I dripped a little bit of the sauce on the broad rim of the plate, grabbed the napkin that was hanging off my apron, carefully wiped it down, and formally set the plate in front of Susan, who just stared at it—a pathetic, bastardized version of *quenelles de volaille*, the dish that my father always ordered at Le Pavillon and that generally takes four hours and an army of Lyonnais chefs to prepare correctly. I stood back, waiting for applause, like a petulant child possessed of too little talent and too much hubris waits for audience applause at the end of a dance recital.

"You know, honey, the garden is bursting—the German Stripeys are ready. It's really *so* hot to be eating this kind of food," she begged, rolling the chicken around mindlessly in its plaster-white sauce. "We could just have a big salad—"

I remembered my father sitting in the dining room in Forest Hills on a hot August night after I'd returned home from sleepaway camp. *It's too hot to cook,* Gaga would say, as she put down an angular, oversized modern teak bowl in the middle of the table. Dripping beads of sweat, my father dispassionately tossed the salad—mostly flaccid white iceberg lettuce and cottony pink tomatoes sliced into quarters—and dumped some onto our plates, passing around a bottle of viscous blue cheese dressing.

Rabbit food, he'd mutter under his breath.

"My father hated salad," I said to Susan, shaking my head *no*, my appetite suddenly gone.

HOLSTEINER SCHNITZEL

The concept of topping meat with an egg was lost on me as a child, as it likely would be to most children. But of every dish I had ever witnessed my father eat—the foie gras, the palacsinta—this was, by far, his favorite. You couldn't actually talk to him while he was eating it; it was though he was having an out-of-body experience, eyes closed, swooning, like a religious zealot. The first time I made this dish accurately—with eggs and little crisscrossed anchovies—was the year I lost him. That night, Susan and I ate it in silence, washed down with small gin Gibsons. We saved the pickled onions—his favorite part—for last.

Serves 2

Two 4-ounce veal cutlets, pounded to ¼-inch thickness (ask your butcher to do this)

Salt and freshly ground black pepper

Chestnut flour, for dredging

3 eggs

½ cup fresh bread crumbs

¾ cup grapeseed oil or other vegetable oil (not canola)

4 anchovies, soaked in water for 2 minutes and drained

2 lemon wedges, for accompaniment

1. Sprinkle the cutlets on both sides with salt and pepper, and then dredge each one in the flour, shaking off any excess.

2. Beat one of the eggs. Dip each cutlet in the beaten egg on both sides, and then in the bread crumbs.

3. In a large skillet set over medium-high heat, carefully heat the oil until very hot, but not smoking. Gently slip the cutlets into the hot oil and cook until golden brown, about 3 minutes per side. Remove to a platter and cover with an overturned plate to keep warm.

4. Carefully wipe out any excess oil from the pan, and crack in the remaining two eggs. Cook them until the whites are firm and the yolks still tender (sunny-side up), about 3 minutes. Top each cutlet with an egg, and then crisscross them with 2 anchovies each.

5. Serve immediately, with the lemon wedges.

CHAPTER 26

The Heat

Susan's mother, wearing a long-sleeve white turtleneck purchased from the sale bin at Goodwill, stood in our backyard under a floppy pink-and-green flowered hat, waving at us while we finished tall, Tom Collins glasses of iced coffee on the deck.

By ten in the morning, Helen had already push-mowed her own acre-size backyard from one end to the other. She'd spent an hour picking up sticks, and then trimmed every stray blade of grass with a Weedwacker and a pair of children's blunt plastic school scissors, like she was giving a haircut to a *Vogue* model during Fashion Week. At a little bit after eleven, her white '83 Buick rattled into Susan's driveway, and there she was, ready to start all over again. She opened her trunk and pulled out a threadbare canvas duffel bag of ancient but pristine hand tools, a broadcast spreader with one working wheel, a twenty-pound bag of grass seed, and her Weedwacker. We were still sitting at the counter reading the paper and sweating when she arrived.

"You girls have *got* to learn to get out there earlier in the day, before it gets hot!" she shouted through the front slider, cupping her hand up to her mouth like a megaphone. The metal vintage barn thermometer hanging on the side of the house read ninety-one degrees.

"She's kidding—isn't she?" I mumbled to Susan, who was wearing an old T-shirt and a pair of Cat in the Hat boxer shorts.

"Unfortunately, she isn't—"

"Isn't it a little too warm for her to be doing this? I mean, the woman is eighty-two—"

"She loves this weather—she'd work outside for hours in it if I let her."

Great, I thought. *Happy days.*

And with that, our glasses landed in the sink, we put on gardening clothes, and minutes later, we were out there—me, bent over, pulling weeds in the exploding herb garden, where clumps of carpet thyme undulated around and over heavy stones and the French tarragon was being threatened by the Greek oregano; Susan, tying up the tomato plants that were bending and breaking under their own weight— sweating through our T-shirts and shorts while this Polish octogenarian Yankee was dragging open the shed door and hauling out Susan's mower. She primed it and pulled the cord, hard, seven or eight times before the engine turned over. And then she began to mow the huge, flat, backyard. For hours.

At noon, while I took a water break in the kitchen, Susan came in and riffled around in the fridge and came up with a large, half-empty jar of Hellman's mayonnaise and a loaf of Pepperidge Farm Sandwich White bread, whose doughy blandness possessed all the culinary nuance of foam packing peanuts.

"She's not going to take a break. I'm bringing her lunch," Susan insisted, taking a dinner knife out of the utensil drawer. And then she pulled open the slider with a free hand, and tramped down the wobbling back deck stairs to the garden, her arms full.

From where I stood, with my back to her farmhouse sink, I watched as Susan forcibly pulled the mower from Helen's hands, killing the motor. Helen followed her daughter over to the box with the tomatoes—some just ripening, some starting to split—and twisted one off the vine. Together, they sat down on the side of the vegetable box, opened the jar of mayonnaise and the package of bread, and dragged the knife from one edge of the crust to the other, on both pieces. Susan cupped the tomato with one hand and sliced it into rounds with the other, arranging them on the four slices of bread balanced on her knees. She assembled the sandwiches, handed one to her mother, and together, they gorged themselves lustily, like they were eating fresh black truffle butter on a still-warm crusty Poilâne loaf at some country chateau in the Dordogne. Rivulets of tomato juice ran down their chins and onto their shirts. Susan tossed her head back and together they laughed at a joke I couldn't hear, and when the sandwiches were finished, Susan handed her mother a white paper napkin, picked up the jar and the knife and the bread, and headed back across the yard and up the stairs to the kitchen.

"Want one?" she offered, pulling another mottled German Stripey from her pocket. "I wasn't sure—I remember you telling me you hate raw tomatoes."

"Cool—I've never been involved with anyone who carries vegetables in her pocket—" I smirked, mildly appalled at the idea of eating what I was sure would be a squishy, wet sandwich thrown together with nothing but supermarket white bread, mayonnaise, and the raw fruit. "But since you went to the trouble of bringing it up here—I'll try it."

Still warm from the sun and from Susan's body heat, the tomato's thick, beady innards dribbled across the old wooden apple-shaped cutting board that was usually propped up behind the kitchen faucet. I thought of my first bite of a cherry tomato at my Aunt Sylvia's house when I was three, and the way its furry insides had exploded out of my mouth and onto the white carpet beneath me. Susan handed me the sandwich country-style—uncut—and I took a bite out of it; sweet tomato juice cascaded down my chin onto my T-shirt, and the marriage of soft, spongy, store-bought white bread with the oily, creamy mayo, which I normally loathe, topped with brightly flavored fruit just picked moments before, was glorious, refreshing, and wildly comforting, all at once.

"I bet it'd be great with a slice of really sharp Cheddar on it—and maybe some pesto—" I said with my mouth full.

"You can't leave well enough alone, can you?" Susan laughed, handing me a napkin. I have loved fresh tomatoes—pulled off the vine and sliced moments later—ever since.

+++

By five in the afternoon, it was over ninety degrees, and Susan and I had come inside to shower and change while Helen was still out there.

"Exactly how *long* is she going to keep this up?" I asked, pointing down to the yard, where her mother was trimming with her Weed-wacker.

We stood together on the deck, side by side, drinking tall gin and tonics with wedges of lime; we were freshly showered, already damp with perspiration, and utterly guilt-ridden watching Susan's elderly mother energetically work in weather that rivaled summertime in the jungles of Vietnam for sheer comfort.

"For as long as it takes," Susan laughed, rolling her eyes. "You think I should tell her she missed a spot?"

"Don't you *dare*—"

"Mom," Susan shouted down to her from the deck. "*Mom*—enough! Give it a rest!"

Helen put the wacker down, removed her floppy hat, and waved it at us vigorously, like she was in a small boat and yelling *AHOY.*

"Almost done!" she shouted.

"Well, thank bloody god," I muttered under my breath, watching as she killed the motor on the wacker. She dragged the silent mower back to the shed, pulled it up the tiny wooden ramp and inside, and emerged, a minute or so later. Helen walked up the driveway to her car carrying the wacker and the spreader, and dumped them into her trunk before climbing the stairs to the deck.

"Dinner is on *me* tonight, girls," she beamed, drinking the immense vodka tonic that Susan had handed her as she came in.

I'd never seen Helen in such a good mood; since I'd first met her, she rarely looked at me without scowling, or so it seemed.

"Endorphins," Susan whispered.

"Wouldn't you like to shower first?" I asked helpfully. "I'll go get you some towels. We can make dinner here." Susan nodded in agreement.

"No need," Helen replied, shaking her head. "I'm hungry! Let's have Chinese!" It was like the idea was exciting and novel and maybe even just a little bit dangerous. I smiled weakly at the thought of eating what would probably be gunky, brown-sauce faux Chinese food, replete with crunchy chow mein noodles and packets of orange, Day-Glo fake duck sauce, which, when I was in college and regularly eating cheap Chinese food during middle of the night study sessions, I called *fuck sauce.*

Helen put her empty glass down on the counter, grabbed her purse, and motioned for us to follow.

"Where are we going?" I whispered to Susan, stuffing my cell phone into my pocket.

"Back to her house," she replied, turning around. "We'll pick up takeout on the way."

"She has air-conditioning?"

Susan barked a loud laugh. "Are you *kidding* me? Never in a million years. It's just a *lot* cooler where she eats in the summertime—"

"Where's that?" I asked, a little worried, pulling the front slider shut.

"In the basement, silly," she answered, matter-of-factly, like I had just dropped through the earth's atmosphere on my way in from Mars. "Where *else?*"

When we arrived at Helen's with our brown paper shopping bags of Chinese takeout from a local establishment called, appropriately,

Chinese Takeout, the house was dark and warm. Giving it a nudge with her hip, Helen shoved open the heat-swollen door from the garage into the family room, and a cloud of dank humidity poured out of the house into the garage like a cloud. Climbing the two steps from the garage into the room, I could see that the mustard-gold crepe de chine curtains were pulled tightly closed, and the venetian blinds drawn taut beneath them. I walked over to the window to let a little dusky light into the living room and both Susan and her mother simultaneously shouted *"NO!"*

"But it's dark as a *cave* in here—"

"It's Yankee air-conditioning," Susan explained, putting the bags of food down by the basement stairs while Helen marched ahead into the kitchen. "You throw open the windows and blinds and curtains all night to let the cool air in, and then close them at dawn. It seals everything inside—"

"Right," I muttered under my voice. "And leeches cure the common cold."

Helen methodically pulled three flowered stoneware plates from the cabinet above the sink, three rime-coated beer mugs from the freezer, and a jumble of silverware from a drawer under the toaster oven. She toddled down the creaking basement stairs, her arms full.

"Bring the Schlitz, honey," Helen yelled back up to Susan. "I put it in the freezer to cool down before I left—"

Eight hours ago? I mouthed to Susan. *She'll put her eye out.*

But there, in the murky shadow of a thousand-gallon oil tank, boxes and crates of ancient Christmas tinsel, and shelves of enough store-brand, thirty-year-old canned goods to last through a nuclear winter, we sat together at a yellow, faux marble–topped kitchenette set—identical to the one that Gaga had in her own kitchen in Forest Hills—and poured ourselves mugs of the kind of explosively carbonated, refreshingly cold hoppy beer that actually tastes like *beer* instead of the overpriced artisanal fruit brews that are the rage in every food-loving upscale bar in America. That night, with the temperature outside still hovering in the low nineties and the humid air hanging stagnant like damp sheets on a clothes line, Susan, Helen, and I dined on heaping bowls of hot, salty wonton soup laden with unidentifiable, dark, slippery greens. White cardboard takeout containers sat side by side on the table, filled with luminous ruby fried chicken chunks enveloped in sweet-and-sour sauce; there was house-special fried rice heavy with bits of *hong shao lo*—addictively delicious red-cooked roasted pork of the variety that lurks in the folds of fried egg rolls served by every takeout joint in America—and tiny shrimp that had gone mushy in the Chinese kitchen's reheating process. We spooned out the gummy, MSG-packed food onto our plates, and as I took a taste of the sticky, glowing meat I remembered in the farthest recesses of my brain why I used to love sweet-and-sour chicken as much as I did as a child, and why most children do: it was just plain *good*. It was almost frighteningly unnatural in color, true, but it was also an alluring textural mosaic of crispy, tender, and sticky, and the sweet saltiness sated every taste bud. It wasn't fancy, experimental, tall, or expensive.

It was *just delicious*.

Helen handed me a fistful of crispy noodles to stir into the heap of fried rice sitting tall on my plate—*this is how* I like to *eat them*, she said, dumping the crunchy bits out on top of the pork and shrimp and working them in with her fork. I remembered, just for a small moment, dinner at the soaring Mr. Chow's on Fifty-Seventh Street in Manhattan with my mother and her second husband, Ben, in the early 1980s. Sweet-and-sour pork and fried rice could set you back fifty bucks a head, and Bianca Jagger and Andy Warhol might conceivably be sitting next to you, feeding each other slices of velvet chicken. Eating cheap Chinese food in the basement of my girlfriend's mother's house was a very long way from dining at Mr. Chow's; the thought made me smile.

"Don't forget your fortune cookie," Helen said, reaching across the table and handing it to me. "But you have to read it to us." Glowering, she folded her arms and waited.

I cracked it open and extracted the small sliver of paper; a jumble of magic numbers printed in black stretched across one side. I laughed when I turned it over and read my fortune out loud:

The night life is for you.

ASIAN MUSTARD GREENS DUMPLINGS

I had never made Chinese food until I started spending entire weeks in Connecticut, unable to find so much as a decent egg roll within a thirty-mile radius of Susan's house. This recipe was born out of the deep sadness I felt while experiencing that particular food-related ennui. Instead of pork or the nameless/shapeless mass that invariably gets jammed into the bright green dumpling wrappers that are meant to pass for vegetarian, I stuff my dumpling wrappers (which I buy previously frozen in a local Asian supermarket) with spicy, bitter greens tossed with sesame oil, chile oil, grated ginger, and scallions. The result is light, tender, crunchy, and remarkably delicious. I haven't been out to our local Chinese restaurant since I started making these. Note: They freeze for up to 4 months.

Makes 2 dozen dumplings

DUMPLING FILLING

2 tablespoons grapeseed oil

4 cups loosely packed mustard greens, cleaned of dirt and chopped

1 tablespoon grated fresh ginger

4 scallions (white and light green parts only), chopped, tops reserved

4 garlic cloves, minced

1 tablespoon toasted sesame oil

½ teaspoon chile oil

1 tablespoon tamari

Flour, for dusting

24 Shanghai-style round dumpling wrappers

Water, for sealing dumplings

SWEET-SPICY DIPPING SAUCE

¼ cup tamari

Reserved liquid from the greens

Reserved scallion tops, chopped

¼ teaspoon prepared roasted chile sauce *(nam prik pao)*

¼ teaspoon sugar (optional)

2 tablespoons grapeseed oil

½ cup water

1. To make the dumpling filling: In a large, straight-sided sauté pan set over medium-high heat, heat the 2 tablespoons grapeseed oil until it shimmers. Carefully add the mustard greens, tossing them with long-handled tongs, until they just begin to wilt. Add the ginger, scallions, and garlic and continue to cook, decreasing the heat to medium-low if it begins to dry out. Add the sesame and chile oils along with the tamari, and continue to cook until the greens have completely wilted and the garlic is opaque, about 8 minutes.

2. Remove the pan from the heat. Set a small colander over a medium bowl, and let the greens rest in it, pressing them with the back of a large spoon to extract as much liquid from them as possible. Strain out the liquid through a fine-mesh sieve, and reserve.

continued

3. Place the wrappers side by side on a lightly floured work surface and set a small bowl of water close by. Using a dinner teaspoon, place a small amount of the filling mixture in the middle of each wrapper. Dip your finger in the water, and lightly dampen the outer edge of the wrapper. Fold it in half to make a half moon, and press to seal it. Repeat, until the filling is used up. (At this point, they can be frozen.)

4. To make the dipping sauce: Combine all the ingredients in a small bowl and set aside.

5. In a large skillet over medium-high heat, heat the 2 tablespoons grapeseed oil until it shimmers. Add the dumplings and do not move them. Don't shake the pan, don't stir, don't flip them around. Let them brown for about 3 minutes and then carefully pour in the ½ cup water. Quickly cover the pan and give it a few violent shakes before letting it rest. Continue cooking the dumplings until cooked through, another 3 to 4 minutes.

6. Serve immediately with the dipping sauce on the side.

WARM TOMATO SANDWICH

Besides the sweltering, the lack of air-conditioning, and the eating-of-dinner-in-the-basement, an elemental tomato sandwich made from a tomato that has just been snatched from the vine, still warm from the sun, is Susan and her mother's idea of what summer really ought to be. There are specifics, though: the bread has to be Pepperidge Farm Sandwich White; the mayonnaise has to be Hellman's. If there's a slice of bacon hanging around, terrific; if you add a slice of very sharp orange Cheddar, all will be well. Either way, the goal of this truly extraordinary snack is to wind up with tomato juice running down your chin and onto your shirt, and so besotted am I with its existence that I wait all summer just to have one. When no one's looking.

Serves 2

4 slices Pepperidge Farm Sandwich White bread

3 tablespoons Hellman's Real Mayonnaise

Salt

1 burstingly fresh tomato, just picked, sliced into rounds

1. Spread each slice of bread on one side with enough mayonnaise to reach the crust from top to bottom and side to side, and sprinkle with salt.

2. Top 2 pieces of bread with slices of tomato, and cover with the remaining bread. Serve immediately, preferably outside in the garden.

CHAPTER 27

Summer Birthdays

When I was a small child, my parents threw me a succession of over-the-top birthday parties at Jahn's, a local ice-cream parlor decorated in 1920s red-velvet bordello chic. Each one resulted in my tearfully crawling under the table when one of our neighbors, an itinerant amateur magician, produced a basketball-size fireball from the depths of his magic top hat. First came a bunny, then a pair of baby doves that flew up to the gold sparkle–coated popcorn ceiling and hid behind some wood-grained stereo speakers, then a string of jewel-toned pocket scarves tied end-to-end like a narrow rope of brightly colored bratwurst, and then, finally, a burst of yellow-blue flame. I slithered down underneath the table, curled up on its cool iron base, hugged myself in my own tiny arms, and hid my face while the muffled shouts of my friends yelling *Again! Do it again!* echoed distantly around the room. I've suffered from a fear of fire ever since.

A few years later, when I turned twelve, my father rented a tour bus that pulled up in our apartment's little cul-de-sac to take me and fifteen schoolmates to a now-closed Manhattan pasta vomitorium called the Spaghetti Factoria; it was the sort of disco-era, brightly lit place where you could match any number of bland, pasta-y sauces to sticky, parboiled macaroni kept warm in large chafing dishes dotted with beading condensation, set up along the perimeter of the restaurant. I didn't much like being the center of so much attention, and when the restaurant's resident clown, dressed like Bozo with a shock of cherry-red hair that stood horizontally away from the sides of his head, said, "Say, little girl, what magic trick would you like me to do for you?" I thought about it for a moment and asked him to disappear.

As I got older, and I finally grasped the culinary and financial ramifications of all the secretive gourmet dining dates I shared with my father while my mother was at work, my birthdays always involved high food. One year after the divorce, when he could scarcely afford to put gas in his car, he took me and two of my classmates out for *homard a l'Américaine*—partially shelled lobster braised in a pungent, garlicky sauce of wine, shallots, and tomatoes—at a French restaurant in the theater district whose walls were severely upholstered in cushiony crimson silk dupioni. When one of my friends accidentally catapulted a chunk of lobster knuckle meat out of its shell, across the room, and onto the wallpaper, the captain came over to have a word with my father. Moments later, our plates were removed, only to be returned by the server with the meat cleanly extracted and formed into the fanciful shape of a fleur-de-lys, in the middle of which sat dollops of black caviar flanked by golden toast points. The erstwhile tomato sauce was gone and the lobster shells had vanished, probably simmering at the bottom of a tall stockpot in the kitchen, being readied for bisque.

During the four years I was in college, each of my birthday celebrations culminated in dinner with my father at a window-side table on the 107th floor of the World Trade Center. Windows on the World had opened to great fanfare in 1976, and the following year, when I was fourteen, on a Saturday while my mother was at work, my father and I drove into Manhattan and took the elevator up to the top-floor restaurant.

"This is *it*," my father whispered as we emerged from the elevator, pointing down the hallway toward the expansive, floor-to-ceiling windows from which, he assured me, I could see Massachusetts if I looked north. I felt myself sway a little bit that day, like the ground beneath my feet wasn't quite strong enough to hold me, like I was floating on a raft.

The restaurant was closed—it was between lunch and dinner service—but the maître d' waved us over to the windows to get a better look; I stood where I was able to press the length of myself against them, raising my hands high above my head like a diver getting ready to jump into a pool. My forehead touched the cool glass and I stood stock-still, terrified. That day, years before my first birthday meal there, I looked down at the ant-size humans walking down the street a block or so away, and I couldn't understand for the life of me why the idea of eating a meal 107 stories in the air would appeal to anyone, for the same reason that I think dining in those hotel rooftop restaurants that spin slowly while you eat their tarted-up commercial-food-service fare is completely sickening.

That afternoon, after we left the North Tower, my father and I crossed the airy white lobby and took the elevator up to the outdoor observation deck on the 110th floor of the South Tower. It was a quiet, windy day—virtually no tourists were there—and my father pushed open a side door labeled: WTC EMP ONLY, grabbed my hand tightly, and out we walked, onto the barren observation deck with the wind howling around us.

"I DON'T THINK WE SHOULD BE OUT HERE," I yelled, as the wind flattened us to the side of the elevator housing.

"I JUST WANTED YOU TO EXPERIENCE WHAT IT'S LIKE TO BE UP THIS HIGH," he shouted back, his thinning black hair standing on end. "IT'S LIKE FLYING." He flung his spent Benson & Hedges butt into the air and it sailed off into the stratosphere.

"I WANT TO LEAVE," I yelled, and pulling the door back open, we struggled to get back inside, to safety.

But that afternoon, my father had already made up his mind: as soon as he could afford it, my birthday dinners would be at Windows on the World, and eventually, they were. They were window-side meals that always seemed to involve conspicuously large, melting blocks of fatty foie gras and masterfully seared filet mignon set down upon gold-rimmed, steering-wheel-size chargers drizzled with port wine glazes and dried cherry sauces; there was always the rare, delicate toro that had been flown in overnight from the Tsukiji fish market in Tokyo and flecked with an unidentifiable fruit concasse; there was always cherries jubilee flambéed tableside; and great, fish-bowl-size crystal goblets of vintage Stags Leap Cabernet Sauvignon, each single glass costing the same as a bottle of a great Oregon Pinot Noir. There was the credit card, palmed to the server without even an examination of the bill, and the inevitable, ever-so-slightly regretful gasp when it came back to be signed.

"You don't have to do this," I said to my father uncomfortably, the year I turned twenty-two. Even though I was celebrating my college graduation and my birthday at the same time—it was really two dinners for the price of one very expensive one—it seemed so completely over the top and lavish for a man who was living at home with his mother, and forced to sleep on the couch whenever I came to visit him on the weekends. But there we were that night, all dressed up, sitting in his little chocolate-brown Subaru station wagon, hurtling through the Brooklyn Battery Tunnel toward lower Manhattan. When we emerged in the city, the towers loomed large in the rearview mirror behind and above us, like immense geishas walking on our backs.

"Birthdays only come once a year," he justified, depositing the car in an overpriced parking garage next door to the Downtown Athletic Club. He slammed the door and we walked out into an orange, glaring sunset that reflected off the side of the North Tower, forcing us to squint as we looked up.

+++

Susan's birthday and mine were almost exactly a month apart, and we both possessed the stereotypical hallmarks that define Cancerians, if one actually believes in zodiacal clichés: we both lived in the kitchen and had an almost preternatural instinct to feed people. We both were close to our families, crazy and sane, immediate and extended. We both had a tendency to cry easily if provoked, and even if not. We pulled on layers of emotional armor if we thought we were at risk of being hurt. And given the option of staying in or going out, we almost always preferred the former. Short on funds to do anything elaborate to celebrate Susan's birthday that first year, I was forced to be creative: I logged on to the then-new auction website called eBay and impulsively bid on a set of *Gourmet* magazines from the year of her birth. They arrived individually slip-cased in plastic sleeves, and I wrapped each of them separately and presented them to her, one by one, while she squealed with the delight of a child on Christmas morning. I fed her breakfast in bed—slow-cooked French toast, its center rendered soft and creamy, and enveloped in a blanket of caramelized crispiness, dripping with pure maple syrup—while she read through each issue, cover to cover, the dog snoozing on one side of her and me on the other, dozing and reading until late in the afternoon. That night, we rubbed a two-inch-thick porterhouse with garlic, olive oil, and coarse salt, and grilled it on her father's ancient Weber. Trying to effect a bistecca alla Fiorentina—the gigantic Flintstone cut of magnificently marbled beef produced from Tuscany's prized Chianina cattle traditionally cooked in the embers of a very hot, live olive-wood fire—we grilled it black and charred on the outside and crimson within, and fed it, sliced and drizzled with a squeeze of fresh lemon juice, to each other with our hands. When the sun set late in the evening, we pulled Susan's old, green Therm-A-Rest camping mattresses onto the deck, wrapped ourselves up in a single, unzipped sleeping bag, and fell asleep in each other's arms, under the stars, facing the garden.

When the weekend before my birthday finally rolled around, we still hadn't planned anything.

"We could hike in Litchfield and have a picnic," Susan suggested, "and then maybe go out for dinner?" Years later, she would riff on that theme, taking me on a slow, sweet kayaking trip and picnic on the Farmington River near her grandmother's home, a small, cream-and-white clapboard farmhouse that housed eleven children until 1948 when Susan's mother, the last one, got married and moved across town. The place still stands, its roof now sagging dramatically and sadly, hovering over the river like a sentinel.

On my birthday, I was instinctively drawn back to the city; I wanted to introduce Susan to Arnaud, to show her my favorite places, to plait geography to memory to food for her so that all of the stories I shared with her had some sort of physical, tactile context. I wanted to spend part of the day in Brooklyn, walking it from end to end, from Coney Island—where my grandparents had lived in the shadow of the Cyclone and the parachute drop, and where my father had flown over the apartment house on his way home from the war, tipping his wings while my grandmother stood on the roof waving a dish towel—to Williamsburg, where my mother and her mother before her had grown up, where Gaga shook her fist at the Hindenburg as it sailed through the graying sky on its way to Lakehurst, New Jersey. I wanted to end up in Manhattan, to have a Gray's Papaya dog on West Seventy-Second Street; and to show her the miraculous Bridge Kitchenware, where I had purchased my stash of carbon-steel French paring knives so long ago under the gaze of angry, snarling Fred Bridge. There was the street that Julie and I had lived on down in Chelsea, where, around the corner at a hole-in-the-wall luncheonette on Eighth Avenue, you could have the most spectacular Cubano this side of Havana. And then there was Arnaud, who I hadn't seen in weeks and who, when I finally showed up one afternoon, slyly wondered exactly *what it was* that had made me fall in love with Susan, so much so that I was never, ever at home in the city anymore.

"You're *supposed* to be French, Arnaud," I told him, blushing, one evening when I popped in when Susan was having an overnight with her mother. "Don't you people automatically understand *these things—*"

"I understand how to slice the perfect *bavette*, Elissa," he grunted, pushing his grease-speckled glasses up on his nose. "But you women, I do not understand." He smiled shyly and slipped a sample of pâté de campagne he'd just made over the counter toward me on the blade of his Opinel knife.

✛✛✛

I plotted it all out: Susan and I would drive down to Avenue J in Brooklyn and have an early lunch at Di Fara's pizza, with its charred, explosive bubbles of cheese and tomato. I hadn't been there in fifteen years and Susan had never been there, and although Pepe's famous New Haven pizza was known all over the world for its gorgeous salty greasiness and black-splotched, oven-blasted crust, it still couldn't come close to drippy, mouth-singeing Di Fara's. Then we would head into the city, park the car in the lot under my building on East Fifty-Seventh Street, walk everywhere, and later in the evening, we would splurge and have dinner at Le Bernardin, where hunky Eric Ripert performs glorious, extraterrestrial magic with every manner of sea creature.

A few days before my birthday, Susan picked up the kitchen phone to confirm the reservation we had incredibly managed to secure, for a table that probably would have wound up being in Siberia, or near the bathroom, or both; I stopped her.

"Cancel them, honey," I said, touching her arm, before she started dialing.

"What? *Why?*"

"Um, no money?"

Susan's work had quieted down for the summer, when every publisher traditionally settles in for a long seasonal nap before waking up again after Labor Day; I was still licking my dot-com wounds, collecting unemployment, and trying to figure out a way to make some sort of living in a tiny Connecticut town with exactly one stoplight and six liquor stores in a three-mile radius.

"But it's your *birthday*!" She looked distraught, and for a second I thought that perhaps she'd tucked other, incidental plans into the trip that couldn't be cancelled.

"It's *frivolous*." I winced. I couldn't get excited in the way that my father, as a ritual, could never get excited about his birthday, which always ended up being a dour, slightly sad occasion for him. One year, already in his sixties, feeling particularly gloomy, and in the midst of a trivial disagreement with his mother that prompted her to ignore him on his birthday, the two of us went out to the Four Seasons, where we shared Châteaubriand and a bottle of 1975 Figeac; we ate in a silence heavily cloaked with old sadness and queasy financial self-destruction, and when the check arrived, he didn't even look at it before slipping his American Express card over to the maître d'. My stomach gaped at the old, nauseating feeling I had driving through the Battery Tunnel with him when, despite maxed-out credit cards and a visceral inability to live within his means, he celebrated birthdays in the most self-destructive of ways—as though tomorrow would never come, with its bills and collection callers. Over the years, he had taught me to expect the fancy, tall foods and the reckless celebrations—the lobster fleur de lys and the foie gras—and the thick, syrupy vintage Stags Leap Cab, and the busload of my friends going to the Spaghetti Factoria just a year before his magazine company folded. The memory disoriented and rattled me, like the ground beneath my feet wasn't quite solid. I didn't want to go down that road, where delicious, overwrought meals were instantly followed by the bitter aftertaste of financial carelessness.

"So what do you want to do?" Susan asked flatly, and just a little bit exasperated.

I stood looking out into the garden and thought about it.

I thought of all the places that Susan had shown me in Connecticut; once we actually started leaving the house, there were hikes and trails and the museums in Hartford and New Britain. But we had met in the dead of winter, and had never gone to the Connecticut shore—to the beach—which had long been her family's destination of choice. Dotted with small, blue-collar towns littered with clam shacks and family-owned pizza places, penny arcades and miniature-golf concessions astride the old Yankee wealth of Saybrook, Lyme, and Fenwick—site of Katharine Hepburn's longtime home, rebuilt after the hurricane of 1939—the shore could be rural and rustic, laced with Americana, quiet and Hamptons-y, all at once.

"I would like to have the best lobster roll on the shore," I answered, turning around. "And to run my feet in the water." The noise of the city, the money we'd spend eating our way through Brooklyn and Manhattan, only to end up at Le Bernardin, was overwhelming.

"That's it? Really? Instead of New York?" Susan looked aghast.

"Really. But running my feet in the water"—as a Cancer and a water baby profoundly attracted to pools and oceans and lakes and bodies of water of all kinds, standing in sea water is a curative for me—"is non-negotiable."

We got up early on my birthday and drove east, past the cliff-like West Peak that hovers over Meriden, and on toward Route 1, and then, north, where, driving along the narrowing road with the ocean tucked at the end of private road after private road, tarmac and gravel gave way to ashy sand, and the air began to smell sweet.

At a small, slightly decrepit seafood shack jutting out over a small boat basin filled with broken-down tugs and rusting local fishing boats and old buoys, we placed our order with the red-faced, bleached-blonde woman in the kitchen who handed us a ticket with a number.

"Come up when I call it out," she barked, and when our lunch was ready and set down on a blue plastic tray, we carried it back to a wooden table overlooking the boat launch and the underside of I-95. We ate flaccid French fries with tiny wooden forks out of square, red-gingham cardboard platters, and virginal chunks of sweet, cold fresh lobster meat—unencumbered by mayonnaise and dizzyingly luscious—stuffed haphazardly into untoasted, New England–style rolls shaped like ordinary slices of white bread folded in half. The assumed sides of tartar sauce and coleslaw that we expected never arrived; all that accompanied the lobster rolls were two wedges of lemon, wrapped in gauze to catch the errant pits, and the bottles of frigid, golden Sam Adams Summer Ale that we drank to cut the richness of the shellfish and salty French fries.

Late that afternoon, we drove south, stopping at a crazy used bookstore decorated with Tibetan prayer flags and posters, and where I bought a first edition of John Cheever's *The Wapshot Chronicle* for twenty dollars and Susan unearthed a 1920 *Baedeker's Guide to Florence and Livorno*—we had just begun talking about finding a way, somehow, to get to Italy sometime soon—and then she decided that it was time to find me a beach.

We drove and drove along Route 1, where all of the access roads to the water were either private or blocked or manned by security guards.

"We can just head home—it's okay." I sighed, looking out the window, and sounding totally pathetic.

"Give me a chance—please?" she replied, looking over at me. "The water is right over *there*." She nodded her head to the left.

We drove past a trestle and an underpass, and Susan pulled off onto the gravelly shoulder, and made a U-turn. It looked familiar to her.

"Do you mind if we have a look?" she asked, pulling the car off the road.

A sign on the other side of the trestle said POINT O' WOODS—the cottage community that Susan had last visited as a child, forty years earlier, when all of her cousins on her father's side used to rent cottages for weeks at a time. An only child, she'd spend hours with her cousins—the nearest thing she had to siblings—in the warm, gentle waters of the Sound, until one day without warning, her parents just stopped going there. Her mother never wanted to stay overnight—her various fears and phobias made her terrified of fog and foghorns, both of which were prevalent along the shoreline—and her father thought a two-way drive from Farmington every day for a vacation was just too much. And just like that, Susan's love of the tiny Connecticut-shoreline cottage community became a hazy, fond memory and nothing more. How she managed to find it after so long was beyond me.

Hearing an abbreviated version of her story, the smiling, portly security guard let us in through the community gate, and allowed us to drive around this place that Susan had always loved so much, and in the end, had missed for years. We got out and Susan just stared at the water and the houses around us, trying to remember.

"I'd like to come back one day," she said, gazing wistfully out over the Sound, her hands in her pockets. "Maybe we can even rent a cottage—nothing fancy."

We will, I said, putting my arm around her waist. *I promise.*

We got into her car and she pulled down another unmarked private cottage community road until we got to the very end.

"Happy birthday, honey," she smiled, nodding her head toward the water.

No one was around, so I flung off my sandals, rolled up my jeans, and stood in the tepid, slow waves of the Sound, amid the endless possibility of water and memory, and a quiet birthday without foie gras, heedless extravagance, or magicians; the sweet chill of the succulent cold lobster meat was still on my tongue.

THE PERFECT LOBSTER ROLL

It's all about texture for me: I'm one of those (not-Yankee) people who wants the combination of a hot, buttered, and pan-toasted roll to be married to a chilled lobster, in this dish that is absolute summertime excess. Close your eyes and you can smell the salty sea air; you can hear the bells in the buoys off Mount Desert Island; you can imagine in your mind's eye coming home from a week of eating these babies, to an overdrawn notice from your bank. The fact is, lobster rolls are special, and it takes only one medium-size 'bug to make two well-packed rolls with this recipe. Serve it with a fork, to scoop up the excess sweet meat when it comes bursting out the sides, which it will.

Makes 2 rolls

One 1½-pound female lobster, boiled and cooled

½ small onion, diced

1 stalk celery, diced

½ cup mayonnaise

Juice of 1 lemon

¼ teaspoon cayenne pepper

½ teaspoon celery salt

1 tablespoon chopped fresh dill

1 tablespoon unsalted butter

2 New England–style hot dog buns

continued

1. Remove the lobster meat from the shell; pull off the claws where they attach to the body, and break the body in half, discarding the head portion. Drive a knife down the middle of the underside of the tail portion, remove the meat, and set it aside. Using shell crackers, a crab mallet, or a hammer, crack open the claws and remove all of the meat. Chop the claw meat and the tail meat into bite-size pieces, place in a bowl, cover, and refrigerate.

2. In a medium bowl, combine the onion, celery, mayonnaise, lemon juice, cayenne, celery salt, and dill; taste and correct the seasoning if necessary. Blend together the dressing and the lobster meat, cover, and refrigerate for at least 2 hours.

3. In a medium, well-seasoned cast-iron skillet set over medium-high heat, melt the butter. Place two rolls in the pan and "toast" until brown; repeat on the opposite side. Carefully remove the rolls from the heat and fill with the lobster.

4. Gorge yourself, immediately.

CHAPTER 28

Merging

My few days a week in Connecticut began to stretch to four, and then, to five, and little by little, my stuff started to migrate north with me every week on the train. It's an old punch line—what do two lesbians do on their first date? Rent a U-Haul—so dangerously inclined are we to nesting, often prematurely. It starts with the inevitable toothbrush and hair gel, then clothes, and CDs, and, in my case, my beloved Martin guitar that my father had given me as a twenty-first birthday present. Two months into our relationship, Susan came into the city for dinner, and, sitting on my apartment couch, pointed to the road-style, bumper-sticker-littered professional touring case sitting on the floor. She knew that I'd played the guitar very seriously since the age of four, and that music, like cooking and food, was a creative outlet for me. It was like breathing.

"Can you play 'I Will Follow Him,' by Little Peggy March?" she asked that evening, half joking, and I did. Susan was stunned and blurted out *I think I love you,* so I played that, too.

"No, *really*—" She laughed sheepishly, looking a little embarrassed.

So when she asked me to bring my guitar up to Connecticut that first summer, I did, and left it there, to play on the deck on warm evenings while we were having cocktails. There seemed no reason not to, since I was spending more time there than I was in the hot bustle of the city.

"It's really serious, isn't it?" Abigail sighed, standing in my apartment one Thursday afternoon while I was haphazardly pulling cookbooks out of my floor-to-ceiling bookcase and stacking them in piles to decide which to bring up, and which to leave in Manhattan.

"It *is*—" I agreed, putting some of my more complicated books—the Georges Blanc, the Jeremiah Tower—in the small stack meant to be hauled up to Connecticut that evening.

"So first it's the guitar, and now the books? When are you moving in permanently?"

"We haven't really talked about it," I lied, loading my favorite tomes into a fraying, canvas L.L. Bean bag. There was the Blanc and the Tower, but also Diana Kennedy's first book on Mexican cooking, splattered over the years with the tomatillo salsa it had taught me to make for drizzling on everything from eggs to gently poached white fish; there was Edna Lewis's *The Taste of Country Cooking*, which I'd bought as a paperback with my Dean & DeLuca discount after helping the author one day while she was shopping at the store back when I worked there in the late 1980s. After I'd read the book cover to cover, I smoked Julie out of our Chelsea apartment by attempting to make Miss Lewis's pan-fried chicken in a high-heat combination of lard, butter, and bacon fat without a stove hood.

But in fact, Susan and I *had* talked, cautiously and hesitantly, about my moving in full-time; still, there was a difference between spending some nights but not *all* of them together. Two days a week, we retreated to our own corners—to see our mothers, to cook for ourselves, to come up for the cold, practical slap of air that would remind us that there was a real, harsh world out there that plaited together the realities of relentless job-searching with the messiness of Susan's ex, Jennifer, who not only wouldn't stop calling us but was expecting financial support, and an apartment for which I was still paying a monthly maintenance—ostensibly citing the psychological and financial importance of not moving too quickly and impetuously. But on those two nights alone, with me puttering around in my apartment and Susan puttering around in her house, we spent hours on the phone talking while making ourselves dinners that we wished we were sharing together. Over the many months since we had first met, my solo, Manhattan apartment cooking had changed: it had gone from painstaking, extravagant, and tall to simple, inexpensive, and sometimes careless, like the very act of cooking for myself was now just a means to an end, like fueling a car before driving it. The days of my roasting a pancetta-wrapped poussin for myself were gone. One night, while spending a marathon two hours on the phone together, I tossed mounds of fresh spinach leaves with chopped ginger, hot red pepper, minced garlic, and a drizzle of toasted sesame oil in a copper soup pot that had grown dusty with disuse, watching the mess deflate to a tangle of fragrant greens while Susan, on the other end of the phone, crunched on a bowl of Grape-Nuts and milk. It was only after I decided to eat the spinach right out of the pot with the phone wedged between my chin and my shoulder that I realized I'd forgotten to remove its woody, fibrous, indigestible stems. Unless I was cooking for Susan—for the two of us—the act was accomplished quickly, mechanically, and suddenly, sometimes thoughtlessly.

By the early summer of our first year together, our books had become integrated and they fought for space on the tiny pine shelf above Susan's farmhouse sink, where all her important, most-often-used cookbooks lived. My *Mastering the Art of French Cooking* was in better condition than hers, so it stayed while hers was relegated to a box in the crawl space; her Maida Heatter's *New Book of Great Desserts* was there to remind her that, even though I have no sweet tooth, she loves to bake; Marion Cunningham's *The Breakfast Book*, despite the aggravatingly cooing inscription by Jennifer, stayed to remind us that feeding each other a hot Dutch baby—a rustic, puffy pancake baked in a cast-iron skillet until crispy brown and airy, and delicately coated with confectioners' sugar and lemon—is about as carnal as the best sex on a late Sunday morning in the freezing depths of winter.

Sitting in the middle of the kitchen shelf, there was one red, jacket-less volume that was cracked down the spine, its cover stained with overuse. Susan refused to remove it, not even to make room for Jacques Pépin's treatise, *La Technique,* which I wanted to have on hand in the event that I needed a quick visual reminder on how to bone a chicken with a paring knife, as Jacques does in sixty seconds.

"If I could have only *one* cookbook," she said, cradling the ancient red tome like it was a Gutenberg Bible, "this would be it."

Susan had picked up her splattered and stained 1975 *Doubleday Cookbook* at a used bookstore in Brooklyn, when she lived there in the early 1980s. The center of Susan's culinary universe, it was the book and its author, Jean Anderson, who she turned to before any other. On the nights when my train to Connecticut was stuck or I was delayed at work back before my dot-com had folded, I would finally walk into Susan's kitchen late in the evening and find the book propped open on the counter next to the stove, where she'd left it when she went to pick me up in Hartford. Out of it she made all manner of comfort food for us: creamed chipped beef on toast, meat loaf, Swedish meatballs, hue-vos rancheros. There were recipes for goose braised with onions, hangtown fry, taramasalata, guinea fowl, kedgeree, and a Christmas cookie called spitzbuben. I had proclaimed the book a towering mon-ument to American provincial cooking—the sort of folksy food that comes out of gingham-clad grandmothers' kitchens all over the Midwest—until one night when I showed up with a five-pound stand-ing rump roast from Arnaud that we were making for friends who were passing through Connecticut on their way to Boston. For years, I had prepared this quietly frugal, hard-to-find cut of meat for fancy dinner parties in Manhattan, when I couldn't afford its pricey coun-terpart, the standing rib roast; I'd force the oven up past five hundred degrees, blast the beef for about ten minutes, and then drop the tem-perature down to almost nothing, and the result was tasty, but some-how always a bit dry and a light, gunmetal gray. Nowhere could I find the precise cooking time in minutes per pound that would yield the gorgeous ruby beef and the crispy exterior I was desperate to achieve; I consulted every cookbook I had dragged up to Connecticut—chef cookbooks, restaurant cookbooks, even the Culinary Institute of America textbook—and came up with nothing: Standing rib? Yes. Standing rump? No. Relenting, I checked *The Doubleday Cookbook*: it said twenty-three minutes per pound for medium-rare. Exactly.

"*Now* maybe you'll stop making fun of it?" Susan said, laughing, as we sliced into the perfectly tender, rosy meat while we sat at the counter, our friends cooing in delight.

Days later, we were on the back deck perusing a stack of new television-chef cookbooks sent to me by a publisher friend; they turned out to be more color and pretty pictures than substance. We thumbed through them the way we read the headlines in the rag *The Star* while standing on line at Value Mart, mostly out of morbid curiosity.

"You going to bring up *all* of them?" Susan asked, leaning over to get a better glimpse of the unfortunate one I was looking at, written by a chef known for his fabulous hair, for hosing down hapless ingredients with liquid nitrogen, and for making trout Twinkies. His Manhattan restaurant was impossible to get into and utterly unaffordable.

"Only the ones that I think we can possibly cook from," I responded, tapping the page. "Like this great lobster bisque recipe—why don't we have it tonight? Looks pretty basic—" And it was, apart from the list of eighteen ingredients, which included two pounds of fresh lobster shells.

Soup, which is generally dirt cheap to make and can be stretched for days, had been showing up in Susan's kitchen a lot; we were both between freelance jobs—me as an editor, she as a designer—and the cupboard and bank account had all the stability of the San Andreas Fault.

"Lobster bisque—you're kidding me, right?"

"No." I shook my head, thoughtlessly. "Why?"

"You really think we should spend the money on four lobsters, just to get two pounds of shells?" Susan got up, went into the kitchen, and pulled *The Doubleday* off the shelf where it was propped horizontally, on top of one of my heavy professional cooking textbooks I'd demanded live there, just in case we someday ever needed to know how to make a galantine for twenty, or clean caul fat.

"Pea soup," she announced, opening the book to a page marked with an ancient yellow sticky and handing it to me. "It's the best I've ever tasted."

In the recesses of my brain, pea soup conjured up ancient images of the lunch line in my grade school cafeteria, where hair-netted middle-aged women in pale yellow polyester janitorial uniforms ladled viscous, army-drab gruel into flat Buffalo china bowls. Devoid of primary colors—a minced red bell pepper would have at least given it some visual contrast—and flavor, the soup was enhanced with sub-stantial amounts of iodized salt and diminutive slices of canned Vienna sausages, which bobbed near the surface like tiny German U-boats.

I made a sour *that's disgusting* face.

"Will you trust me?" Susan pleaded. "Please? This soup is amazing, and *so* cheap—"

"When you're on a tight budget, you also eat *veal* loaf," I chided, commenting on the thinly sliced, stocking-beige Polish cold cut I'd unearthed from the back of her fridge one night. It had all the culi-nary appeal of commercially made headcheese.

"Veal loaf *happens* to be delicious in the same way that liverwurst is delicious. It's just an acquired taste."

I rolled my eyes and threw in the towel. Much as I hated to admit it, she was right: I was twenty bucks away from my next freelance check, and buying lobsters just to use their shells for bisque that would last for two days was nearly impossible, not to mention moronic.

We drove off to Value Mart and, for five dollars, left with a pound bag of dried golden peas, a small hunk of ham, and a loaf of good, crusty peasant bread. An hour later, we were side by side at the counter, eating thick, creamy, meaty pea soup redolent of earthy rosemary and ham. Smoky and utterly, addictively delectable, it could have commanded four times what we paid for it had we'd eaten it served as an irritatingly precious *amuse-bouche* presented in crisscrossed white Asian ceramic soupspoons, at the aforementioned celebrity chef's lower Manhattan restaurant.

That night, after we finished doing the dishes and I filled Susan's old RevereWare soup pot with hot soapy water and let it rest in the sink, I pulled the cooking textbook off the shelf and slipped *The Doubleday*, permanently, in its place.

YELLOW SPLIT PEA SOUP WITH HAM

(Adapted from *The Doubleday Cookbook*)

Honey-glazed, hickory-smoked, or Black Forest—virtually any kind of ham works beautifully in this hearty soup. Ham ends—which can be had by cozying up to your local deli counter and smiling a lot—also work very well here; they tend to be more bone than meat, and impart tremendous flavor for virtually no money. Freeze this soup for up to six months, or refrigerate for up to four days.

Makes 8 servings

1½ tablespoons extra-virgin olive oil

2 cups coarsely cubed cooked ham

1½ cups coarsely chopped onion

2 garlic cloves, minced

2 sprigs fresh rosemary, minced

1 pound dried yellow split peas

6 cups water

6 cups vegetable stock

Salt and freshly ground black pepper

Crusty Italian bread, for accompaniment

1. In a large stockpot set over medium-high heat, heat the olive oil until it shimmers; add the ham and cook it until it's just heated through. Add the onion and the garlic, and stir well to combine until the vegetables are translucent and glassy, about 8 minutes.

2. Decrease the heat to medium-low and add the rosemary, peas, water, and vegetable stock; stir and cover. Simmer very slowly for 1 hour, stirring occasionally, then seasoning with salt and pepper.

3. Serve with crusty Italian bread.

CHAPTER 29

Italy

The year before we met, Susan spent two weeks working in Italy during the summer, shooting the photographs for an illustrated book about popular operatic tenor Andrea Bocelli. Having trained as a photographer at the School of Visual Arts in New York in the late 1970s, she, one night over a bottle of wine, confessed to me her undying, slightly geek-ish love for the art of film photography and all that it meant in its uncontrollable natural variables like space, light, and movement. One of the things about Susan that made me swoon was her care and mindfulness in everything she did. While I could be impetuous and hotheaded and often slapdash, she was the polar opposite, and it showed in the film transparencies that I begged her to share with me from her trip to Italy, that she kept in a labeled binder in the bowels of her studio closet. Hovering over her light box with an artist's loupe, I could see that the shots—the seconds and thirds and outtakes that weren't used for the more staid needs of the book—were thoughtful, considered, and laden with emotion without being saccharine. The colors were heavily saturated and warm with bursts of vibrant blue, orange, yellow, and red, and the images were shot with the kind of deep, meditative care and studiousness normally attributed to students of Zen. Long before the advent of digital photography and the instant, immediate keep-or-delete gratification it offers, Susan admitted to me that she came home from working in

Italy that summer dreaming, for the first time in years, about putting a darkroom somewhere in her house. Her vintage, pristine, fully manual Pentax Spotmatic F—a high school graduation gift from her parents dating back to 1971—was never far out of reach, even if it went mostly unused; it sat alongside the computer in her studio as an icon of the possibility of travel and art, surrounded like Stonehenge by towering lenses encased in tall, brown leather tubes scuffed with time.

Susan's work trip to shoot the Bocelli book—the job was a complete fluke that came through a friend who was writing it—confirmed two things: she loved the silent anonymity that being on the other side of the camera lens afforded her, and she was completely desperate to get back to Italy. It was a country that, in such a short time, she had come to adore in all its crazy eccentricities and the sort of social contradictions that could have Benito Mussolini's granddaughter and Gina Lollobrigida running against each other for the same national public office.

But Susan was besotted with everything about going back, so much so that books about Italian literature, culture, art, travel, and food sat piled in stacks all over her house. On the two nights during the week when I was back in the city, she enrolled in an extension Italian class at a local high school, just to be able to communicate when she returned.

"*Assuming* I return," she'd say. "What do you think it would take for us to get there together?"

"Money—" I'd answer, "like everything else."

And while we had managed to find each other like two needles in a haystack and against all odds—the vagaries of everything from family and habit to religion and geography and ex-girlfriends conspiring against us—money, the reality of it, the fact that we had virtually none as the summer wore on, worked to shackle us to the house, where we spent days on end making plans that we were sure would never fly. Everything we thought of was a hope and a dream, and nothing more.

Susan's design work came in with all the consistency of a roller coaster—it was there and then gone, and there and then gone—and although I had just begun writing a column for a local newspaper, mine was even more sporadic. Our evenings were devoted to emptying out the refrigerator, the pantry, and the freezer, and cloaking the budget dishes we invented and those we extracted from the wartime tales of Jacques Pépin, Madeline Kamman, and Elizabeth David in a blanket of romance, just to make them psychologically palatable. Like the concept of peasant chic, hunger and the need to eat when coupled with culinary ingenuity could be made far more than just simply bearable—it could be deliciously *quixotic*. So we feigned delight and gleefully reveled in the allure of poverty-stricken gastronomical creativity, even as we lay awake at night staring at the ceiling in sweaty worry. There was *fromage fort*, which melded together all the leftover bits and ends of various cheeses that emerged from the depths of the fridge. Pulverized in a food processor with garlic cloves and half a cup of precious white wine, we spread it on baguettes and crackers, dolloped it into the center of small, one-egg omelettes, and tossed it with cheap pasta bought in bulk at the local Job Lot. We stuffed halved and scooped-out garden tomatoes with leftover rice, herbs, and cheese, running them under the broiler for an elemental version of Mrs. David's beloved tomatoes à la Grecque. And then here was the pound of chicken livers—*foie de volaille*—that we found at Value Mart for two bucks, which we slow-braised with shallots and red wine and creeping carpet thyme clipped from the herb garden in the backyard, and that we ate over slices of grilled, spongy white bread. I plated the brown, luscious mass of aromatic, ferric goodness high and tall on the plate the way I had done for ages in New York, using the last of my timbale molds that I'd bought, years before, for the sole purpose of making vertical food.

We were doing fine, we assured each other, trying to stay positive; things could only get better.

But one day, when there was no money to put gas in the car so I could drive the twenty-five miles to Hartford and a meeting with my editor, we siphoned what we could out of the lawn mower, pouring it into the gas tank of the car through a metal canning funnel attached to a narrow rubber hose. I drove to the bottom of Susan's hill at the end of her street, pulled over, rested my head on the steering wheel, and wept.

+++

The mere idea of traveling together was little more than a wishful obsession, the next stage in our relationship. It was an azure-blue figment of our overactive imaginations vicariously fueled by the tattered 1920 *Baedeker's* that Susan had picked up on our trip to the shoreline, by Frances Mayes's *Under the Tuscan Sun,* and E. M. Forster's *A Room with a View*—all of which we read, pathetically, until they fell apart. We sat at the counter, side by side, with a pile of old *Saveur* magazines, and re-read the many articles about Florence and Tuscany back in the day when the magazine was edited by supreme Italophile Colman Andrews. Susan would finish a page and scribble notes about traditions and restaurants and dishes—creamy cognac- and citrus-infused tagliarini, and little toasts with smoked mozzarella and anchovies— and I'd read it while she was writing, making my own notes in the small black leather notebook that had been my father's when he was a child. I had carried it throughout high school and now used it as a dedicated food journal, stuffed with the ramblings, musings, and clippings of dishes I wanted to make for us someday, and places I longed for us to visit together. We daydreamed and read guidebooks and essays and searched the Internet, imagining ourselves in a villa, with its silvery rattle of olive trees and long rows of grapes. We dreamt of fig trees, and the Brunellos that we loved but could never afford, as thick and voluptuous as melted chocolate. There was Dario Cecchini, the crazy, Dante-spouting butcher from Panzano who, we imagined, would flirt like mad with us until we blushed a bright crimson and bought one of his perfect *bisteccas*, which we'd cook over an open fire of grape vines and olive-wood embers.

And somehow, with such a meager income, we saved. We saved pennies and nickels and every single shekel that crossed Susan's threshold, dropping handfuls of loose change at the end of every day into that ancient Roseville bowl that Susan's mother had found at the tag sale so many years before. Each evening, we'd empty our pockets like children saving up for a new bicycle; and after an entire summer of fantasizing about it, we were, miraculously, able to make it happen. In the early autumn, off-season when the tourists go home and the prices plummet, we corralled two other female couples—old friends of mine from the city, both wildly wealthier than we—and together, we found a last-minute, simple, three-bedroom villa for a week's rent in Rapolano Terme, a small town in a little-visited, mostly industrial part of eastern Tuscany. Six hundred dollars a couple, for the week.

Susan drove us south from Florence in a tiny rental Nissan Micra— the only thing we could afford, and just big enough to hold the two of us and one large suitcase. As we bumped along the unmarked, rocky dirt path to the villa, we had no idea what lay at the end of the road: a comfortable, if elemental, haven where we could spend a week driving around the countryside, and cooking, eating, and drinking inexpensive local wine? Or a crumbling, uninhabitable mess of a building rented out to six moronic American women in search of a romantic Tuscany that exists only in the minds of the delusional, followed by utter destitution? We gasped as we got to the top of the path, and the road opened out to a thick green grove of olive trees on one side of us and a tiny vineyard on the other. Ahead, up a small incline between a stand of tall cypress trees, sat the small, ubiquitously orange stucco villa, with its stone patios and immense pots of miniature lemon trees, and flowers and herbs sprouting out of planters everywhere. The towers of Cortona were visible ten miles away in the distant haze, standing like a sentinel.

"*Jesus*—" Susan gasped, as we got out of the car and looked around, trampling over young olive-wood branches and fallen, overripe baby figs that had splattered to the ground like soft-boiled eggs. The air nearly overtook me: it smelled musky and sexy and sweet, like earth.

Each night at the villa, Susan and I cooked for the group, who agreed to take lunches out. There was bucatini *all'amatriciana*, made with guanciale—thick, toothsome, hollow-cored spaghetti tossed with tomato, onion, and smoked pork jowl, and difficult to find in America at the time. Fluffy frittatas the next morning made with the pasta leftovers softened in olive oil, bathed in beaten local eggs with yolks as red as the sun, and browned under the broiler with a thick scraping of salty sheep's milk pecorino from nearby Pienza. There were immense *bisteccas* cooked on the outdoor, olive wood–fired grill, and drizzled with oil and lemon juice from the fruit growing on the patio. There were platters of fennel-laden salumi and aged, strong local cheese. Bowls of young, recently cured herb-y cracked olives. Bowls of braised, local bitter greens drenched in strong, peppery olive oil pressed in the next town. Enormous oval lengths of traditionally unsalted Tuscan bread. And wine—jug after jug of inexpensive, low-alcohol red produced by our own villa from the grapes that lined the driveway, and brought to us a few times that week by Giordano, the house's older, frail maintenance man, whose fingers and white mustache were stained yellow from half a century of smoking cheap cigarettes.

I awoke early one morning to find Susan gone from our bed. Pulling on a sweater against the morning chill, I went down the stairs and found her hunched over the villa's front stoop, her Pentax in hand.

"I heard something, so I came down. Look at what he left," she said, looking up at me and pointing at the cracked, stone landing.

Giordano had already been out in the woods behind the house, collecting wildflowers for this gift: a massive wine jug refilled with the villa's red, its thumb-hook woven with the last of the season's violets and bright garnet Italian poppies, and a handful of fresh figs presented on broad, emerald-green fig leaves, in an obvious nod to his manhood.

"Liiiikaaa *Daa*vid—" He laughed, throwing his head back to the sky and howling with happiness when we thanked him for the gift.

✢✢✢

They say that travel is the ultimate test of a new relationship; everything is different—surroundings, food, routine—and when the vagaries of *modern touring* take hold, with its cancelled flights and steerage-class, wafer-thin Alitalia seats, its fluctuations in the dollar and lost luggage and body searches, not everyone fares well. But Susan and I had proven compatible beyond measure: we walked through the food stalls near Santa Croce arm-in-arm—so naturally affectionate are the people of this country that no one gave us a second look—in gape-mouthed silence at the lushness of the fresh produce, stopping for a late breakfast of sauce-drenched *trippa alla Fiorentina* sandwiches and scuffed juice glasses filled with coarse, young red wine at Nerbone. We sat in quiet awe, near tears, in the tiny, thirteenth-century chapel at Monteriggioni, high above the Tuscan hills. Susan brought her Pentax along with us everywhere we went, and shot things I could just never see without her: the sharp angle of light on a church spire; the muddy muzzle of a black Labrador who had just been out truffle hunting; miles of ash-dusted Pecorino di Pienza Stagionato, lined up like dominoes, for sale at a *fromageria*. We traveled carefully and judiciously, and while our friends went on daytime shopping jaunts to Deruta and Siena, we stayed closer to the villa, shopping for dinner at local markets and vegetable stands manned by smiling, elderly vendors who we could just barely speak to, thanks to Susan's Italian classes.

When we left our villa at the end of the week, we brought our little Micra back to the car rental office in the outskirts of Florence, and took the train back to Rome—Susan's favorite, most beloved city in Italy, or anywhere—for our last three days. Sitting on our luggage between hot cars thick with cigarette smoke—an Italian regional soccer team had gruffly bounced all second-class passengers from their seats—I dozed on and off, dreaming parched-mouth dreams of the Spanish Steps and Audrey Hepburn's crazy Vespa ride in *Roman Holiday*. I could taste the creamy carbonara I would eat the minute we got to Antica Trattoria da Carlone in Trastevere. When we arrived early that evening, we took a taxi from the station to our tiny hotel, right off the Piazza San Maria Maggiore, and the front desk clerk, no older than twenty, glared at us.

"*Non abbiamo camere.*"

"What?" I asked, looking at Susan. "What did he say?"

"*Che cosa hai detto?*" she barked at him, glowering. I had never heard her speak full-sentence Italian, much less speak like this to anyone.

"*Non abbiamo camere,*" he repeated, shrugging. *No rooms left.*

"But we reserved," Susan pleaded, shoving our confirming email at him across the front desk.

"Ah, signora," he said, "you *must* have not received the email we sent you after you left the States."

Susan looked weak-kneed and like she was going to cry.

"Let's sit for a minute," I said, turning into a Fucking New Yorker. I grabbed the phone book that sat on a shelf next to a pile of brochures advertising tours of the Coliseum led by a costumed gladiator, walked over to the front desk, and slammed it down in front of the clerk.

"Start calling, NOW," I grumbled through my teeth. "I start at A on *this* phone"—I turned around and pointed to the white plastic house phone on the lobby coffee table—"and you start at Z on *your* phone."

The clerk, wearing a grimy Manchester United football jersey and small square metal glasses with slightly darkened lenses, understood, and picked up the phone.

Every tourist in the world had managed to find their way to Rome that weekend for a major church holiday, and there was not a single room left during the last days of an event that happens in the city every five hundred years; the room that we had reserved had been sold out from under us to a party of four, in classically Roman, no-star hotel style. I called the four-hundred-dollar-a-night Hassler, imagining my credit card would melt into a puddle on the spot if they did have room for us, which they didn't. I called a suburban Italian Holiday Inn. I called a convent.

An hour later, the clerk yelled, "*Si, si, si,*" over his phone, and I grabbed it out of his hand while Susan sat on the lobby couch with our luggage and whimpered.

"We have *one* room left," a woman said in heavily accented English. "You will meet the Sri Lankan boy in front of the apartment building in Trastevere and give him the money in cash"—the equivalent of three hundred and fifty dollars a night, for two nights—"and Signora," she added, "I apologize to you in advance."

She gave me the address, and hung up.

The utterly filthy, cave-like ground-floor studio apartment we had just rented for two nights and seven hundred dollars in cash that we had handed over to the Sri Lanken boy in exchange for a single, rusting skeleton key stood just a few blocks from the Trastevere side of the Ponte Garibaldi; lining the small, dark room were drainage holes drilled into the floor every three feet, to keep the room dry when and if the Tiber ever breached its banks. In the laundry-draped, bleak courtyard outside the one, porthole-like window at the end of the room, a pack of feral cats screeched loudly at their prey. The bed, a double futon mattress draped over a single metal bed frame, was decorated with a mildewed bed pillow covered with a silk-screened movie still of Elvis in *Viva Las Vegas*. Instead of the towels that weren't supplied, we dried our hands with single-ply toilet paper. With absolutely no natural light, we had no way of knowing if it was day or night.

It rained furiously—the kind of rain that comes down in spattering, angry sheets and actually stings when it hits your skin—the two days we were there, stuck indoors, unable to venture outside to even visit the Vatican, just a short walk away. To pass the time, we drank every bottle of Avignonesi 1995 Vino Nobile di Montepulciano that we were planning on bringing home, while the hungry, horny, matted cats lurked around outside. We hadn't bought any food for our stay—we assumed we'd be in the skanky little hotel room near the Centro Storico—and instead ate the bits of remaining cheese and crumbling, dried-out bread we had picked up as a snack at the Auto-Grille outside of Florence, where we stopped to fill the car with gas before dropping it off at Avis. There was no coffee, no tea, no cups, and, as the howling of the feral cats became louder and the rain pounding on the sidewalks outside more violent, there was nothing to do but go to bed, force ourselves to sleep, and wake up the next day. We hoped it would be warm and sunny and filled with possibility, or at least that the weather would be decent enough for us to be outside, even though we had just emptied our respective bank accounts in order to pay for the room.

We lay in bed that night, in our clothes, and wept in each other's arms, drinking wine directly out of the bottle like Janis Joplin. Susan, using the end of a ballpoint pen, managed to push the cork in instead of pulling it out since there was no corkscrew—and weeping all the more. Susan had been responsible for this leg of the trip, for making and confirming the reservation, and so I imperiously, irrationally blamed her, and announced coldly that I'd never again be able to trust her to choose wisely or to make safe travel arrangements for us. She cried quietly that she was seeing another side of me that she didn't like, after a year, and that it was completely obvious to her that, after a lovely week and now faced with trial, we were incompatible travelers. This, she proclaimed through tears, was an indication of bigger issues that we would likely, inevitably face, and it frightened her. The single, horrible experience had negated and overtaken the previous, glorious week, like it had never happened. Hungry, angry, and sad, we fell into a fitful sleep for hours, queasy with worry about the next lucid conversation we would have: exhausted, we would both go for the metaphysical jugular—I would complain about her mother's constantly showing up at the house unannounced, about Jennifer's relentless calling, about the fact that she lived in a place where there was absolutely no work. She would call me harsh, and hard, and not a fair fighter.

The sound of voices coming from one of the upstairs apartments echoed through the courtyard, and roused us. Not sure if it was morning or evening, we lay on the dusty futon, staring at the ceiling, confusing the sound of a sizzling sauté pan with what we were sure was the continued, relentless rain. There was the sudden waft of a familiar aroma—neither of us could place it—the kind that permeates walls and hallways, and we sat up, salivating, threw off the moth-eaten beige coverlet, and went to the porthole window at the end of the room.

"What is it, do you think?" Susan asked, her eyes red and tired.

"I'm not sure—" I craned my neck to see out of the window and up to the other apartments off the courtyard. I felt like a prisoner, trying to get a glimpse of light for the first time since being allowed out of solitary.

The fragrance was sweet and fruity and earthy; whatever it was that was cooking crackled and spat, and suddenly, we were famished—

not just a little bit hungry, but the kind of ravenous that drives you to place into your mouth anything edible that you can lay your hands on. My watch said two P.M.; we had slept through the night and into the next day. Our neighbor's Sunday lunch, taken after the family came home from church, was little more than frying sweet peppers and onions that had lured us upright and in search of food with the remaining lire we had. It amounted to less than twenty dollars, ten of which had to be used to get to the airport the next day.

Silently and without a word to each other, we closed the courtyard door behind us and fell into the first tiny trattoria we found open, right down the street; the fluorescent lighting was so bad that it turned everything it shone on a grayish blue. That late afternoon, our heads down, we drank short juice glasses of fruity, cheap red wine, and ate small plates of elemental *cacio e pepe*—spaghetti tossed with salty local Roman sheep's milk cheese, oil, and an abundance of eye-watering black pepper—wiping up the excess fat and spice with torn pieces of fresh bread. We ate in silence, and at the end of our meal, our server—a robust, gray-haired man who spoke no English—carried over a small tray, bent over formally at the waist, and put down between us four perfectly roasted, steaming, buttery hot chestnuts, and two tall, narrow glasses of syrupy cold limoncello. And then he walked away without saying a word.

Perhaps it was our desiccated pallor that made him take pity on us. Or maybe it was just the graciousness of an older, kind Italian man. We, the two of us as a unit, needed to be taken care of, and this man— this total stranger—did just that.

I looked up at Susan through grateful tears, trying not to cry, as the limoncello slipped down my throat like chilled velvet.

"I'm *so* sorry—" I whispered, the words catching in my throat. But I was. I loved her.

"I wanted Rome to be perfect for you," she answered softly, her eyes welling up. She reached across the table for me, and lightly touched the tiny scar beneath the middle finger of my right hand, the way she had nearly a year earlier during our very first meal at Christine's Polish Kitchen in Manhattan, over plates of kielbasa and boiled pierogi.

Weary and tired, we smiled at each other weakly for the first time in days, and we began to talk quietly and with only a drop of hesitance, of our next trip together, and of going home.

FRIED CUBANELLE PEPPERS

The quintessentially Roman mash-up of fried peppers and eggs causes apoplectic swoons whenever I ask any of my Italian friends how they make it: do they peel their peppers first? (Some do, some don't.) What kind of peppers do they use? (Mostly, Cubanelle.) Do they add a hot pepper just for excitement? (Most Italians don't need that kind of excitement.) Regardless of the answers they gave, nearly everyone I spoke to about my experience in Rome shook their heads in agreement; they would have known in an instant what was wafting down into our apartment. Why? It's de rigueur, post-Mass food, made by Italian grandmothers everywhere, with love. Note: The amount of oil used ensures that it will be the oily, rich mess that it is meant to be.

Serves 2

3 tablespoons extra-virgin olive oil

4 garlic cloves, minced

6 Cubanelle peppers, slit lengthwise, seeds and ribs removed, and cut into wide strips

Salt and freshly ground black pepper

Dash of white wine vinegar

1. In a large, straight-sided sauté pan over medium-low heat, heat the olive oil until it shimmers, and add the garlic. Cook slowly, until the garlic begins to take on golden color, about 6 minutes.

2. Add the Cubanelle peppers to the pan, increase the heat to medium, and season them with salt, pepper, and a dash of vinegar. Cook the peppers until they have completely wilted and cooked through, tossing and turning them frequently, about 30 minutes.

3. Serve hot, with scrambled eggs or on a roll, tossed with pasta, on polenta, or at room temperature.

CHAPTER 30

After the Storm

It began with rain and sleet, and eventually it left an inch of solid rime ice coating everything—the ground, the garden, the deck, the fence— like layers of thick paint on an old apartment wall. The car was frozen to the driveway, the latch on the front-yard gate near the driveway had to be chipped open with a hammer and a screwdriver, the skylight over the bed was covered so heavily that no light shone through at all, the roof leaked murky cold water into my sixteen-quart All-Clad stockpot. A sheet of ice had wrapped itself around Susan's house like Tyvek, attaching itself to the siding and the outer basement walls, and had frozen the exterior heating line like a clogged artery from the oil tank to the furnace; by three A.M., there was nothing left to burn, and the furnace groaned, old and human-sounding, and shivered to a halt. Susan and I lay in bed under four blankets and a down comforter, the dog trembling between us, waiting for an emergency oil-company crew to slither its way up the frozen hill to her tiny house that, after nearly a year together, had become our home.

It was the first week of November, and a few days before the freak storm, a jumble of enormous moving boxes sat in the den and the studio and the upstairs bathroom; we had dragged my double pine Danish dresser upstairs into our bedroom, and set up the ancient mahogany bed from my Chelsea apartment in the guest room. Ever since we'd returned from Italy a few weeks before, we'd spent every weekend together painting, reorganizing bookcases, emptying closets, sorting through kitchen drawers, creating a writing area for me near the kitchen, and making room for two lives living permanently in Susan's small space. The physical, individual dregs of our selves before we met—uncomfortable, lumpy chairs that Susan had inherited from long-dead relatives and felt she couldn't say no to; Jennifer's books and supplies that had been sitting in Susan's crawl space, that took up precious storage room that we needed to use for files and documents; shoe boxes of Julie's Jane Fonda videos and CDs that had somehow managed to find their way into the bowels of my apartment linen closet, where they had lived, long forgotten, for nearly a decade; my blue-lipped Mexican glass goblets from the late 1980s, my stacks of over-bleached aprons and copper molds and short wooden baking dowels from Dean & DeLuca that I hadn't looked at or touched in nearly a year—had been packed up and driven to Goodwill in nearby Torrington. We pulled up in Susan's car and then backed in, trunk-first, to the broad, barn-size door marked DONATIONS; an employee grabbed everything, piece by piece, and tossed it underhand into an enormous gray plastic Dumpster-size bin marked SORTING, like it was the place where the forgotten detritus of life goes to die. He gave me a receipt and we drove away in silence, my hand resting on Susan's as it shifted gears, the car empty.

That previous weekend had been my last in Manhattan; I'd gone back to my apartment to close it—my fluctuating freelance income forced me to put it on the market rather than continue to pay the small maintenance fee while it sat empty—and my mother met me in the lobby, dressed to the nines in the same short sable jacket she'd casually thrown over her shoulders the night that she and Craig Claiborne floated around Dean & DeLuca arm-in-arm during the opening party. Her eyes were swollen and red.

My stomach turned over; I wanted to do what I needed to do, to say goodbye to the space by myself, and to get on the road quickly, and without looking back. As a New Yorker, I loved my life there; I loved my apartments—the airy, loft walk-up in Chelsea that I'd shared with Julie; this small studio on a busy midtown street sandwiched between Central Park and Bloomingdale's. I loved the metaphysical contortions that New Yorkers have to put themselves through in order to live empirically normal lives, that everyone rolls their eyes at: getting up at six A.M. in order to move their cars from one side of the street to the other; waiting on line for two hours during the holiday season to buy half a pound of lox at Zabar's; training their dogs to not pee from anxiety while going before their building's co-op board, usually a group of humorless malcontents on a power trip. It suddenly all felt so quaint and a distinctively other, *former*, part of my life.

"I can't believe that you're *actually* doing this," my mother gasped, as I put my key in the lock, turned it, and pushed the door open. My small studio with no natural light, and a tiny-but-wonderful seven-foot-square kitchen out of which I—forever searching for the convivial and the food and the magic that comes with the act of feeding people—had once cooked formal dinner parties for twenty, echoed. I flipped the light on.

"But it's time though, Mom—*don't you think*?" I asked.

"No," she responded, shaking her head. "*I don't.*"

"You want me to stay here *forever*, then, alone," I said softly, my back to her as I walked over to the window and pushed it up. I leaned my head out and looked up to the thin strip of blue sky that hovered above the penthouse floor. My apartment was on the sixth floor, and the skyscraper directly across the way had made it impossible for me to see whether or not the sun was out. Instead, every morning for the nine years that I lived there, I had to stick my head out and crane my neck, the way I had in the small apartment Susan and I had found ourselves in, in Trastevere.

"No," she admitted, like a child. "But you belong in the city—"

"I *belong* with Susan," I responded sharply, pulling the window down and locking the latch. "We belong *together*—"

"But what about your life *here*?" she whined, following me around like a puppy, first into the kitchen, then into the bathroom and the dressing room. The kitchen was empty, the refrigerator turned off; the little oak table where I'd kept my more well-used cookbooks was now functioning as a desk near the kitchen in Susan's house—*our* house, with the vegetable garden and the roses and the farmhouse sink and the once-hearty asparagus patch that Susan had mistaken for over-grown dill and yanked out—three hours away in a tiny town in a rural pocket of northern Connecticut generally overlooked by rich New Yorkers searching for summer homes and country estates in nearby Litchfield.

"Won't you miss it?"

I smiled. I would miss the edgy attitude required to live in the city, and the ability to eat platters of kielbasa for breakfast, extraordinary dim sum for lunch, and steak tartare with caviar and a duck egg for dinner. I would miss Arnaud, who could speak about meat like it was pure poetry, and the knowledge that if I ever needed to bake some-thing involving candied violets, there would be no searching involved: I could find them at Dean & DeLuca, in a big glass jar on the candy shelf next to the artisanal chocolate nibs and the Swedish fish.

"I'm sure I'll miss it, Mom," I sighed. "I love you, and I love the city. But I'm already gone—"

And I was.

Days later, what started out as a gentle, late autumn rainstorm in the country became relentless, and violent: power lines collapsed, lights flickered and darkened, and the temperature plummeted, caus-ing one of the worst ice emergencies the region had seen in years. Our neighbor Laurie's brother, Mike, who had known Cherisse, and years earlier installed a generator under her front deck—we never knew it was there—ran over to our house, sick with a raging case of the flu, filled the generator with gasoline and started it so, despite the power outages, we could at least run the refrigerator, the electric stove, the well pump, and the hanging light in the kitchen.

Once the oil company's emergency crew made it up the hill at four in the morning, they wheeled an enormous hundred-gallon tank into the chill of the basement, filled it with heating oil, clipped off the frozen exterior line, and re-ran it directly into the tank. Within an hour, the temperature in the house had risen to sixty degrees. Susan and I crept downstairs at six to let the dog out.

"Breakfast?" she asked, her teeth chattering.

"Yes," I nodded.

I remembered back to the night before my father's accident: Susan was on her way back from a day in Hartford, and a summer storm had blown through and knocked out the electricity. I was alone in the house with MacGillicuddy, huddled on the sofa in the dusk, feeling suddenly, inexplicably terrified as the thunder boomed and trees snapped like dead twigs. The landline was out, so, with Susan's ninety-pound dog in my lap, I called my father on my cell, and got his answering machine.

It's just me, Dad. Having a terrible storm here. No electricity. Susan's in Hartford. Just called to say hi, and that I love you.

The next day, a few hours before running the errand that would ultimately kill him, he called us back and left a return message on our machine; we were out early, walking the dog, and then headed straight out into the vegetable garden to work.

Hiya Liss, I hope the storm is over and that you two are safe and sound. Wish I could be there to tell you I love you both in person. Until then, hug each other for me and have a good breakfast. All will be well. You've got each other. Love, Papa.

He signed it, like it was a letter. That was the last time I heard his voice; we picked up the message after he was already gone.

The morning after the ice storm was over, Susan made a small pot of tea for herself, boiled water to pour on top of the black grounds in my French press, and slipped four slices of soft white bread onto the oven broiling rack while I sat at the counter, rubbing my hands together. After a few minutes, she turned the bread slices over to brown both sides, plunged the coffee, and poured herself a cup of tea. We slathered our hot toast from edge to edge with sweet butter and the thick fig preserves that we had brought home from Italy the month before. We ate in silence, nothing fancy.

We came to the table to eat and to love, and to look for affection and the kindness in sharing, and we had found it. We had a sweet, simple breakfast, and, as my father had promised it would be, all was well.

ACKNOWLEDGMENTS

My sincerest, most humble thanks to two people who saw the potential in *Poor Man's Feast*, and pushed me—long and hard and with great intelligence and compassion—to be the kind of fearless storyteller I can only hope I've managed to become: my dream editor, Leigh Haber, who nurtured this simple tale of love and food with an abundance of skill and wisdom. And to my incredible agent, Michael Psaltis, who held my hand through the process and helped me to get out of my own way. My warmest and grateful thanks, too, to the extraordinary team at Chronicle Books—Lorena Jones, Sarah Billingsley, Vanessa Dina, Joseph De Leo, Tera Killip, Peter Perez, David Hawk, Jane Horn, Doug Ogan, and Claire Fletcher—who define the words *creative excellence*.

Thanks to my dear friends, Deborah Madison and Patrick McFarlin, Lisa Feuer and Alyssa Awe, Steve Ford at Butcher's Best, Tracey Ryder and Carole Topalian, Kate Manchester, Melissa Hamilton, Christopher Hirsheimer, Kurt Michael Friese, Molly Wizenberg, Monica Bhide, Bonnie Friedman, Jill Lightner, Mimi Jerome Krumholz, Laura Zimmerman and Joey Johns, Stevie and Porter Boggess, Mark Scarbrough and Bruce Weinstein, and all the readers of PoorMansFeast.com. Thanks to my incredibly supportive and loving family, the Gordons, Wulfsons, Schwartzes, Jaegers, Londons, Fiebers, Puchkoffs, Turners, Cassellas, Podolaks, Sindlands, Deans, Wardens, and Hopkins. Thanks to my neighbors the Turners, Latowickis, Brigantis, Watsons, Pennarolas, and Murphys, who kept me awash in deliveries of fresh eggs while I was chained to the computer. Thanks to James Oseland and his team at *Saveur*, Francis Lam and Ruth Reichl at Gilt Taste, Holly Hughes of *Best Food Writing*, the James Beard Foundation, and the fairy godmother of American food writers everywhere, Antonia Allegra.

RECIPE INDEX